UNZIPPING THE DIGITAL WORLD

HOW TO THRIVE AND SURVIVE

First published in Great Britain in 2012 by
TM Forum
240 Headquarters Plaza
East Tower, 10th Floor
Morristown, NJ 07960-6628
USA

www.tmforum.org

ISBN 978-0-9852058-6-7

Design and art direction by thePAGEDESIGN Consultancy Ltd
www.thepagedesign.co.uk

Illustrations by Clear as Mud
www.clear-as-mud.co.uk

Additional imagery by Shutterstock images

Printed and bound in Great Britain by Butler Tanner & Dennis

To my cousin David Quinton, who was never much of a technologist but would have thought the idea of watching a 3D holographic picture of West Ham playing live was pretty cool.

"There are big opportunities in the digital world for those who get it right, but big challenges too. This book offers valuable insight into the new global economy and a practical guide on how to get to where you want to be."

Liu Aili, EVP & Board Member
China Mobile Communications

"Two thumbs up! The future for operators will come from exploiting new sources of revenue in the digital world, which are so well set out and explored in this book."

Paul Berriman
Chief Technology Officer, PCCW Hong Kong

"Many companies are struggling to reinvent themselves in the spider's web of the digital world and this book provides some really valuable insights into how to manage this difficult transition."

Michael Lawrey
Executive Director, Defence Engagement, Telstra Enterprise and Government

"The two words that stay in my mind after reading this are 'leadership' and 'partnership', which are at the heart of this practical guide to thriving in the digital world."

Phil Dance
Former Chief Information Officer, BT

"This sets the stage for the digital world nicely. It teaches a lot about the journey of various players, and highlights essential partnership strategies. The intertwining of the key role of standards is brilliantly done – they have to be in the bloodstream for service providers to succeed by delivering value."

Alpna Doshi
Chief Information Officer, Reliance Communications India

"CxO-level executives in the communications industry need to be thinking hard about the issues and solutions outlined in this book right now. If they do not, they will be left with nothing but infrastructure – and there won't be room for many of them, because the secret of running a successful infrastructure business is scale."

Dr. Hossein Eslambolchi
Chairman and Chief Executive Officer, 2020 Venture Partners

"Super book… well done… far-reaching, visionary approach to the networked society…"

Jon Collins
Vice President, Ericsson

CONTENTS

FOREWORD

IT'S LIFE, JIM, BUT NOT AS WE KNOW IT...

Before the end of this decade, the world will be a very different place because of the foundations we have laid to create a vibrant new world based on a fully digital economy. By that time, anything that can be digital, will be[1] – that's to say, supplied online and not because it's cool technology but simply because it is economically more sensible to provide it that way.

We will see its effects everywhere in what we buy, how we do business, our education, our healthcare, our government, how we are entertained, how we interact with others, how we live, our homes and our offices, our environment and countless other ways. It has the power for enormous good and to provide huge economic and social benefits. It also has the power for evil in the wrong hands.

It will change businesses around the globe and will probably be the single most important step change in economic life the world has ever seen, with far bigger impacts than the father of economics Adam Smith or the GATT[2] ever envisaged. The phone companies, the computer firms, the power utilities, the Hollywood studios, the shopping malls won't exist as we know them today. Governments won't operate in the same way; dictators will either be flushed away – or will harness the digital world for their own ends.

It's going to be quite a ride!

It's taken me 15 years to get around to writing a sequel to *The Lean Communications Provider*[3]. I kept hoping that if I waited long enough, all would become crystal clear. Of course, it never does and anyway if I had waited until my predictions were perfected, this would be a history book rather than what I intend, which is to help someone out there take the bold steps needed to capitalize on the fantastic opportunities of the digital economy.

To avoid too much embarrassment from getting things badly wrong, I'm going to anchor this book in some of the wisdom of many friends in many countries and the ideas, tools and techniques that many people have used successfully in navigating rapid change.

The Lean Communications Provider was stimulated by the global wave of competition that was sweeping the communications industry at that time. It focused on the need for players to get lean and mean if they were going to survive. My co-author, Beth Adams, and I tried to describe the 'eternal triangle' of running with ultra-low operating costs while providing a great customer experience and being very agile in the delivery of innovative new services. It's conventional wisdom now of course, but it happened much more slowly than we predicted because the phenomenal growth of mobile and its massive new revenues allowed many operators to delay making the kind of changes they needed to run their businesses super effectively.

---

[1] Paraphrasing Benny Landa, the 'father of digital offset color printing' who said in 1993 "Everything that can go digital, will go digital."
[2] The General Agreement on Tariffs and Trade
[3] *The Lean Communications Provider*, Keith Willetts and Elizabeth Adams, McGraw-Hill 1996. ISBN 0-07-070306-x

Mobile extended the easy days of communications being almost a license to print money. It became increasingly frustrating to witness how much time, effort and stupendous amounts of money were wasted by operators each handcrafting their business operations and reinventing the wheel for every new service. That era of proprietary, inflexible processes, systems and software delivering poor results for both customers and shareholders motivated John Miller and me to found what became the TM Forum. We wanted to promote the use of replicable and repeatable processes using standardized commercial off-the-shelf software across the industry.

At the core of the Forum is collaboration on the things that reduce 'friction' in business terms and I talk about the importance of this in detail in Chapter 2. With the fat profits in communications finally over, that's become very important, but in the digital economy it will be vital. The Forum grew quickly from a small idea to around 1,000 member companies worldwide. More than 50,000 individuals are active in our Collaboration Communities, developing best practices and much, much more for the industry, by the industry.

Around the same time as *The Lean Communications Provider* came out, luminaries like Nicholas Negroponte, then at the Massachusetts Institute of Technology Media Lab, published his highly influential book *Being Digital*[4]; Bill Gates' best-seller *The Road Ahead* appeared and Clayton Christensen published an article called *Disruptive Technologies: Catching the Wave*. Since the mid-1990s, we've seen a massive financial boom and even bigger bust: the dot-com bubble and 3G spectrum bonanza of the early 20th century were followed by financial free-fall.

As I was writing this book, we were into the fifth year of a challenging financial climate globally, a huge driver towards making everything digital that can be. I struggled with what to call the online world and the services that we are seeing evolve around us so quickly. I decided on the terms *digital world* and *digital economy* first because they are self-explanatory but mainly in deference to Negroponte, who originally set the industry on this path.

Just as the Internet is not one network but a network of networks, the digital world is not a single, big, digital machine – it's an ecosystem comprising a vast number of 'moving parts', such as networks, devices, data stores, processing power and services operating together through a series of standards to form useful and usable capabilities.

There isn't a proper collective noun for all the types of service that make up this cloud-based, virtual, digital world, so I refer to all of them as *digital services,* covering everything from the underpinning communications services to storage services and computing services, plus application services and the brokerage or aggregation of them via app stores.

The digital world is still very young and, like any infant, will stumble occasionally.

[4]*Being Digital*, N. Negroponte. ISBN 0-679-43919-6

As Negroponte once said, *"This is just the beginning, the beginning of understanding that cyberspace has no limits, no boundaries."*

But what a beginning: the revolution in the way we communicate and how we create and access information has been making sure and steady progress. Back in the mid-1990s there were only around half a billion phones, mainly in privileged developed countries and mostly fixed-line. At the time of writing this book, nearly 6 billion of the 7 billion people on the planet have a mobile phone.

Africa has gone from a communications backwater to become the second largest mobile market on the planet. We've seen early winners and losers in the digital revolution – Apple coming back from the dead to be the world's most valuable company; giants of the music and entertainment business seeing their business models going up in smoke; Sony losing its apparently unassailable position in consumer electronics; and Nokia going from zero to hero and back again.

The global communications infrastructure was already the largest machine on the planet. Now we are seeing its next big evolutionary spurt: those billions of mobiles are quickly changing from offering simple voice and messaging to being web-connected and forming the platform for a global digital tsunami of applications, social networking, instant information, entertainment, commerce and education. The digital world is here and it's growing faster than anything mankind has seen.

While it might be difficult to remember life before instant messaging, Google, Facebook, eBay, Groupon, Amazon and Twitter, imagine just how dramatic the transformation of your world would be if you had gone in a few years from having access to a few secondhand books in a distant library to having almost the sum total of all human knowledge at your fingertips! Whatever I can do from my village in the U.K., a villager in India or the Sudan or Indonesia can do too – that's a truly liberating use of technology. We should all feel immensely proud of that progress, which will accelerate profound economic rebalancing and shifts of political power.

The digital transformation is happening a lot faster than many people realize and now that all of the key enablers of the digital world are in place – affordable, mass-market communications, computing, storage and consumer devices – the connected digital world is exploding.

Evolution doesn't take place in smooth linear steps. It goes in fits and starts. While all the key ingredients that enable the digital economy are now in place, there is usually a lag between a capability becoming available and the social and economic exploitation of it. We are seeing those changes happening: driven by individuals first, by companies second and last by governments – who are the least prepared to understand and deal with its implications.

The enablers of global, low-cost and reliable communications; low-cost devices; cloud-based storage, computing and applications will not only be relevant to people, the next big leap will be the so-called 'Internet of things' – connecting billions of devices that have an ounce of processing power in them, situated in cars, homes, energy utilities and healthcare. The digital economy will impact every business on the planet with new markets, new business models and new rules bringing unprecedented opportunities to those with the vision and innovation to grasp them.

Like every other discontinuity dating back to the Triassic period, it will also bring major threats for those that don't seize those opportunities because others – typically new, unforeseen competitors – will, leaving them the poorer.

I hesitate to use the term 'digital tsunami', yet it is descriptive of the power that it has to sweep all before it. So far the digital world has only swept over a relatively small number of industry sectors but still with devastating effect. Those 'digital foothills' have been the music, publishing and entertainment businesses, which have been changed beyond recognition with online music stores and the mushrooming of devices like smartphones, tablets and eReaders. Record stores and DVDs are on the endangered species list and soon books may be, too: the iPad now has more than 300 pixels per inch resolution, which is very close to being comparable with print. This will accelerate the demise of paper-based reading material – most of you are reading this on an eReader now.

For each of us, the social impacts will be profound and we've already seen some big changes: those of us who are connected have begun to take it for granted that almost all the knowledge ever created is available instantly with a few taps on a touch screen – but imagine the impact on societies that have only ever had limited access to a small number of books. We've seen that people can defeat dictators and their armies with nothing more substantial than Facebook and Twitter and we've also seen democratic governments beginning to understand that they must listen to people who can now express opinions directly rather than through elected representatives.

We're thinking about work and leisure in entirely different ways – commuting in and out of cities every day just to communicate with other people and gain access to information already seems ridiculous to many. In the U.K. alone, around 10 percent of people already work from home[5], with around 80 percent running their own business. We watch TV programs when *we* want to while chatting to our friends through Facebook. We listen to unlimited amounts of downloaded music. Our kids Google the answer to a question rather than ask Mum or Dad. We read books on our e-readers and always have a high-quality camera in our pockets. We shop in digital shopping malls and check-in for flights online, using a smartphone app as the boarding pass.

[5]UK National Office of Statistics, Times Newspapers.

This is just the beginning. Over the next decade we will see an even more rapid rise in ways of communicating and gaining access to information; a vast increase in intelligent and network-connected machines; undreamt of, novel applications that will change the way we work, the way we play and the way we live. Being connected has the potential to bring better education and eHealth services to millions, provide new jobs and reduce the cost of goods. It will help us address global warming through better control of energy use with smart, connected homes, smart transportation, smart grids and smart power generation.

Human beings have had social networks since they dwelt in caves, but being able to communicate instantly in a variety of formats with anyone or anything, anywhere, at any time is throwing up new and unseen opportunities. And it's no longer just people across the planet *talking* to each other, but people and machines interacting with information, entertainment, business and applications in every conceivable way.

The digital world won't just be our old 'analog' one recast into a digital format. Wholly new businesses opportunities will appear that would not have been possible before. New ideas will emerge to help save our environment from the damage we have done. New cultures and arts may emerge (look at British artist David Hockney's innovative use of the iPad[6] as a new medium) because people who would never otherwise have met can do so and spark new creativity.

The digital world will become a 'flatter' one, as countries once regarded as emerging economies grow while the developed world may slip backwards in relative terms. This may have truly far-reaching consequences: altering global balances of power, trade and even migrations of people. And it's not just digital information either: we are not far away from the day when machines will be able to remotely construct all sorts of items, using designs produced hundreds or thousands of miles away. 3D printing is in its infancy, but clearly it has massive potential.

There are so many 'moving parts' to the connected digital world that it's not surprising that it's scary: the human race has never before faced such a massive change in so many aspects of life, so fast.

The magic of communications

When I was a child, an information portal was a small hole cut in your front door for newspapers and letters to be delivered. A database was the local public library and telecommunication was a black Bakelite phone with a rotary dial and intricately plaited wires snaking away to a small box in your hallway. Telephones were a luxury item to be used sparingly and usually in case of emergencies.

[6]David Hockney's instant iPad art – www.bbc.co.uk/news/technology-11666162

So, to communicate with my friends who lived a few houses away, I decided to create my own system by running a couple of hundred meters of wire along the fence that ran at the back of our properties. Only being 10 years old meant very limited funds, so the wire came from unwinding an old transformer and using the shellac insulated copper wire connected to a small transistorized amplifier and loudspeaker given to me by an older cousin.

Using another loudspeaker at the other end as both microphone and receiver worked tolerably well, if somewhat noisily, as we had to use the ground as a return leg. Little did I know of asynchronous, metropolitan area networks at the time, but it did give me a lifelong interest in the magic of communications – being able to communicate without actually having to visit someone.

I've spent my whole career working in the communications and computer industries and I'm extremely proud of the benefits they have brought to everyone. The innovations in information and communications technology that make it possible for people to communicate anyhow, anywhere, any time, are staggering; the rate of change continues to accelerate, not only at the technology level, but in the services they support and the markets in which they are evolving.

The digital world is speeding up so fast because innovations build on top of each other at an exponential rate and in my career I've been lucky enough to be a part of one of the most exciting industries ever conceived.

This book is my personal view of where those changes might be leading over the next few years, including key moves players want to make to succeed and those they might need to consider to avoid being swept away by the digital tsunami. Basic economics will dictate that anything that can be traded digitally will be, transforming the way that we live, do business, shop, inform and entertain ourselves. Traditional businesses models will find it impossible to compete with digital enterprises that can trade with the entire planet, with very low barriers to entry and minimal transaction costs.

Since nothing like this has ever happened before it is difficult to predict the future with any certainty, but we can reasonably assume that the basic laws of economics are likely to remain sound.

It's also possible that much of this book will be out of date almost as soon as it is printed because, as Donald Rumsfeld[7] might have said, it's the unknown unknowns that really trip you up. Whichever course events take, it will change our planet for as long as human beings inhabit it.

I hope the digital world will be a benign one, bringing benefits to everyone, but there are dangers that it may not be entirely a force for good: a digital world makes war or repression

[7] Donald Rumsfeld, former U.S. Secretary of Defense, speaking at a Press Conference at NATO Headquarters, June 2002

much more affordable and a lower risk for aggressors, be they governments or terrorists. War is already being fought by unmanned drones controlled by a new breed of soldier sitting at screens in underground bunkers thousands of miles from the conflict.

Personal privacy is being eroded at terrific speed and we could see much worse things happen than identity theft. Without much better safeguards, anyone from insurance companies to totalitarian governments could use our personal information in unpleasant ways: to track what we look at on the web, with whom we communicate, our movements, our medical records, our DNA and so on.

Change always brings winners and losers and the digital world is the biggest economic opportunity the world has ever seen. Steve Jobs, Bill Gates and Carlos Slim created unbelievable wealth from the foothills of the digital economy and we can only imagine the wealth for all of our global society that could be created from a fully-fledged digital world.

To try and make sense of it all, I'm going to try to bring together the learnings of a lifetime in the communications and software world; add a dash or two of the business experience, some basic economics, quite a bit of research, plus 1,001 thoughts and ideas gleaned from friends and business colleagues over the past four decades, who I'll try to credit as we go along.

Writing this book has been very educational for me – you think you understand what's going on but it's only when you stop and take a very hard look that you see the whole picture. It's reinforced my belief that, while the communications industry has driven many of the key technology revolutions that have helped create the digital world, it is largely disconnected from how the digital world is moving and not fully exploiting the opportunities that it offers.

Alexander Graham Bell would be truly baffled by today's communications technology but he would instantly recognize its business models and core services: in other words, the industry has been proactive at inventing better mousetraps but poor at innovating and exploiting new business opportunities. You could see the communications industry as being like a diligent mother bird that builds a safe and warm nest and spends all day collecting worms to feed to its young, which turn out to be cuckoo fledglings. Moving from being a digital service enabler, creating untold wealth for others, to becoming a digital service innovator is easy to say but very hard to do. I hope this book will give someone, somewhere the motivation and the ideas to do it anyway.

The digital world offers fantastic and unprecedented opportunities – but they won't fall into your lap. Most established players have been slow to grasp them and even slower at understanding the threats inaction will bring. This is a very important point: the digital world isn't simply a case of exploiting new, incremental business on top of those already there. Rather the current way of doing business will disappear and morph into new business models and services. Standing still or playing 'wait and see' is a very dangerous strategy.

After a lifetime spent in this industry, I understand only too well how difficult it is to change the way we do things and why. Nevertheless we have to face reality and we need to embrace it, not shy away. The ultimate purpose of this book is to offer some insights and advice into what I think is needed and ways to achieve it. Of course, no one size fits all and much will depend both on where you're starting from and where you want to go, but perhaps one of the most worrying things I observe is that so many players don't seem to know where that is. My hope is that this book will trigger some thoughts and constructive action, even if it's only because you profoundly disagree with the views expressed.

I'm eternally grateful for the contributions, reviews and editing support of Annie Turner, Mary Whatman, Deb Osswald, my editor Claire Manuel and my publishers Katy Gambino and Beccy Henderson – and of course my long-suffering wife Kirianne. I guess that's proof positive that behind every successful man there is always an army of hard-working and very smart women!

In addition, the diligent reviews by Bill Ahlstrom and Phil Dance helped sharpen my logic, while the ideas of Matt Bross, Jon Collins, Hossein Eslambolchi, Kenny Frank, Michael Lawrey, Colin Orviss, Gene Reznik and Rob Rich have challenged and provoked me to make this book as good as I could. I hope it is worthy of all their time and that of many others who spent theirs talking to me.

1

CITIZENS OF CYBERSPACE

Never before in the history of humankind have we had such an opportunity to enhance the quality of life of so many people and so quickly. The coming years will see a massive shift towards exploiting a digital approach over conventional business models, but we are nowhere close to figuring out the implications yet. How did it happen, what's holding it all together, and can we sustain it? Where do we go from here? Not all companies will thrive and survive in the digital world.

This book is about how I think our society will continue to transform towards a fully inter-connected, digital world and the impact that will have on all of us. In particular, I want to focus on the impact of the rapidly moving digital world from the viewpoint of some of the key players that are powering it and are significantly affected by the opportunities and threats that it brings.

Evolution doesn't happen at a consistent pace: it tends to run in fits and starts. Human progress has been the same, with leaps based on people inventing new ideas that the rest of society then builds on. Everything we have and use in our world today is a result of the connected nature of ideas that build on each other and the more ideas that are shared, the faster the progress[8].

Harnessing fire, inventing the wheel and growing crops were world-changing ideas, but they took centuries to percolate through society because the means of communication at the time was so limited. So the three major innovations that boosted mankind's ability to *share* knowledge and ideas have had the most profound impact on the rate of all other innovations. First was the invention of writing in ancient Sumer around 3200 BC. Second came the invention of the printing press by Johannes Gutenberg in around 1440[9]. The third, however, wasn't a single event, but the sum of all the communications, computing and information innovations that stand on the shoulders of what has gone before. Their reach and impact continues to grow at an astonishing and exponential rate to create the digital world that allows anyone, anywhere to share yet more ideas.

How did we get here and where are we going?
This acceleration in sharing ideas and new innovations being created is taking place at a truly staggering pace that is catching many people, companies and governments unawares. Never before in the history of humankind have we had such an opportunity to change the quality of life of so many people so quickly through these innovations, although just how well we exploit them is a big issue. Timelines are compressing constantly as the digital world evolves and, with a bit of crystal-ball gazing, looks set to continue accelerating (see panel opposite).

Since the 1980s, the communications industry has been transformed from sleepy monopolistic utilities the world over, to mushroom into the fastest industry in history to reach $1 trillion[10] – with mobile communications moving from prototype to global mass market adoption in fewer than 30 years. The Internet and related technologies such as the web have also evolved at stunning speed, from a very limited world of academics and early adopters in the early 1990s to provide unprecedented access to information that we now take for granted in a few milliseconds of searching on Google.

None of those technologies would be any use without the fantastic advances in processing, storage and touch-screen devices. These technology streams have demonstrated the remarkable

[8]This connected nature of progress was articulated in James Burke's splendid book *Connections*. Little Brown & Co. ISBN-10: 0316116726
[9]Although printing was invented some 400 years earlier in China, it didn't proliferate because of the complexity of ideograms rather than the alphabet
[10]Source: Wireless Intelligence

How the rate of change is speeding up in the digital world

Invention of writing – around 3200 BC
Invention of printing in Europe – around 1440 (some 400 years earlier in China)
Understanding of electricity and magnetism – 19th century
Telegraphy, in Bavaria, Germany in 1809 – commercialized in the U.S. in the 1840s
Invention of the telephone – 1870s
Strowger electromechanical telephone switching system patented – 1891
First transatlantic radio communication – 1901
Invention of digital computer – 1940s
Invention of optical fiber – 1970s
Launch of cellular phones – 1970s
Evolution of the Internet – 1970s
First communications markets liberalized – 1984
Availability of DSL broadband – 1990s
Invention of the World Wide Web – 1991
Development of IPv6 by IETF to allow almost limitless connectivity – 1998
Introduction of the iPhone – 2007
First government toppled by social media – 2011
Majority of people on the planet have a mobile phone – 2012
Widespread availability of cloud computing, storage and applications – 2013
Widespread availability of 100Megabit 4G mobile technology – 2014
Web-based health monitoring becomes commonplace – 2016
Widespread adoption of cyber security and personal information standards – 2017
Launch of 1Gigabit 5G mobile technology – 2017
Smart energy and smart home technology commonplace – 2018
Government though mass online interaction becomes a reality – 2019
50 billion active wireless devices – 2020
Practical, commercial quantum computers appear – 2020

benefits of competition and economies of scale that have dramatically reduced prices, enabling ever more people to afford them.

While the second decade of the 21st century seems to have been beset by seemingly unending economic difficulties, it's extremely fortunate that the digital world continues to accelerate because it can be the way out of economic trouble. By bringing so many additional people into productive economic activity, the global economic 'pie' expands, helping to stimulate growth. That in itself is a major win, but the digital world can deliver numerous other benefits, such as bringing decent education, better healthcare, a better environment, better quality government (due to greater accountability) and economic success to huge numbers of people who otherwise would be condemned to a life of poverty. In turn, the digital economy has the power to shift economic and government power from the few to the many, but how well this pans out remains to be seen.

My time horizon on page 17 took a snapshot up to the year 2020, which at the time I'm writing this is only eight years away – not very long in the scheme of things. To appreciate how rapidly the digital world is changing, just look back over the *past* eight years. For me, writing in 2012, my eight-year horizon is 2004. Back then, there were fewer than 2 billion mobile phones in use[11] and nearly all of them could only be used to talk and send short messages: the most popular phones available are now museum pieces like the Nokia 2600 and the Motorola RAZR V3. The Arab Spring was just a commentary on the weather; fewer than 17 percent of the world's population had access to the Internet; Apple was ranked number 301 in the Fortune 500 list – way behind Sony, Nokia and Motorola (#82, #83 and #131 respectively).

Today, mobile communications and mobile broadband now dominate the communications landscape, the rise of net-based applications like Facebook and Google have become global phenomena. Apple is the world's most valuable brand and the once amazing PC is giving way to smartphones, tablets, ultrabooks, smart TVs and cloud-based applications that are rapidly becoming affordable by just about everyone as large economies of scale are unlocked. Ericsson expects virtually all phones to be some type of smartphone by 2014 and the rise of the HTML5 standard for structuring and presenting content will add many web-based smart features to budget-end feature phones. As tablets plunge in price, the global market for mobile broadband will continue to explode.

Consumers and businesses have an ever-increasing appetite for information, entertainment, shopping and keeping in touch with their friends and family using online services. All manner of industries are also becoming increasingly digitized, using a wide variety of new services that allow them to do business faster, better and cheaper. We are seeing what Matt Bross[12] calls the "cyberfication" of our society as we live our lives increasingly online.

If we have come this far technologically over the past eight years, what can we expect from the next eight? Today's smart devices look cool now, but just like the RAZR they will look slow and clunky by 2020. With today's smartphone driving 24 times the data of a typical cellphone and a tablet generating a huge 122 times[13], it's clear their global adoption will vastly expand mobile data traffic and that the network engineering underneath it will need to evolve extremely rapidly. In the U.S. alone, AT&T expects a rise in data traffic of between eight and 10 times between 2011 and 2015.

These are mainly technological milestones, but great technology often fails to get past the prototype stage: in reality, markets make things happen. When I started my career in communications, every country had a single, monopoly, sclerotic phone service – there wasn't a *market* at all and even the supply side for the underlying technology was built by protected, 'national champion' suppliers.

[11]Source – ITU Communications and IT statistics database
[12]Former group CTO at British Telecom and now in a similar role with Huawei: www.lightreading.com/blog.asp?blog_sectionid=384&doc_id=199088
[13]Source – LightSquared

Although market liberalization started in the U.S. and U.K. back in 1984, even as late as 1996 when I wrote my first book, the pace of liberalization was glacially slow and ensured that there were only around 500 million phones globally – and most of them were fixed-line in developed countries[14]. Liberalization and global standards have created a vibrant, competitive market for communications services and technology suppliers, which have increased by at least 10 times over that period and now are close to being used by nearly everyone on the planet.

Just read some of the back issues of the proceedings of the International Telecommunication Union[15] to see the jaw-dropping speed of how we have gone from an almost total absence of communications in underdeveloped and remote parts of the world to having an incalculable and positive effect on the lives of billions of people. Communications costs have tumbled as the triple effects of competition, standardization and economies of scale have come into play. The growth of data services initially followed and now exceeds Moore's law[16], rapidly increasing in speed and falling prices.

This is only the beginning – talking on the phone is great, but being able to access all the information in the world is even better: it is truly liberating to be able to access information, buy, sell, entertain, inform, learn, diagnose, help, govern and so much more when and where *you* want. Again, the will to do this is all that will hold us back.

What's holding it all together?

All the basic enablers of the digital world exist: ubiquitous, reliable and high-speed communications are here now and networks touch almost everybody on the Earth, though they are not yet as reliable or as high-speed as the digital economy requires. This will change because the demand is there and markets will provide them, provided that regulation doesn't get in the way.

Not so long ago, networks were supply-led, with network designers trying to think up uses for the increasing bandwidth they could deliver. The advent of smartphones and applications has reversed this situation: now the market is demand-led with networks struggling to provide sufficient capacity to cope with the exponential growth of high-bandwidth traffic such as video. Technologically this isn't a huge problem, it's more an economic issue, often linked to outmoded forms of regulation, which dis-incentivize operators from investing at the right pace (see Chapter 5).

Second, consider the mass availability of simple and cheap end-user technologies such as smartphones, tablets, book readers, Internet-based TVs and network-connected devices such as smart meters. The digital economy can't work without being able to interact with the data it generates, and so the massive growth of next generation, instant-on, affordable tools is essential to support more uses for digital services.

[14]Source – ITU
[15]International Telecommunication Union (www.itu.int)
[16]Moore, Gordon E. *Cramming more components onto integrated circuits*

The third ingredient of the digital economy is the evolution of cloud-based, virtualized computing and storage. As with the others, the concept is not new. One begets the other and, as we saw when application service providers failed to take off a decade ago, without ubiquitous high-speed communications, cloud-based services can't deliver a good user experience.

Cloud is evolving rapidly. The huge economies of scale offered by vastly concentrated computing and storage – which exploits spare capacity, wherever it exists at any time – is revolutionizing our approach to designing, managing and hosting software applications.

The final ingredient is more amorphous – techniques and technologies to master 'big data'. Data is being produced in previously unimaginable quantities, every nanosecond of every day. It is increasing in both volume and detail, captured by enterprises, multimedia, social media and machine-to-machine communications (M2M). The impact of big data on networks processing and storage is obvious but, in addition, a fourth 'pillar' of the digital economy is managing all that data and turning it into usable information. I'll talk more about the growing need for technologies such as data analytics and policy-based management later in Chapter 8 but, for now, it's worth appreciating the scale of the problem.

Big data has three chief characteristics:
Volume – Big data comes in one size: gigantic. Enterprises are awash with data, amassing petabytes of information.
Velocity – Often time-sensitive, big data must be used quickly to maximize its value.
Variety – Big data extends beyond structured data, including unstructured data of all varieties: text, audio, video, click streams, log files and more.

A variety of techniques and technologies have been developed and adapted to aggregate, manipulate, analyze and visualize big data, which draw on several fields including statistics, computer science, applied mathematics and economics. Some were developed by academics and others by companies, especially those with online business models predicated on analyzing big data.

A report by McKinsey and Company[17] found that different sectors will benefit by different amounts from mastering the big data challenge but that the computer, electronic products and information sectors, as well as finance, insurance and government are poised to gain substantially from its use. However, McKinsey also reported that there will be a big shortage of talent necessary for organizations to take advantage of big data and by 2018, it reckons that the U.S. alone could face a shortage of 140,000 to 190,000 people with deep analytical skills, as well as a lack of 1.5 million managers and analysts with the know-how to use the analysis of big data to make effective decisions.

[17]McKinsey Global Institute – *Big Data: The next frontier for innovation, competition, and productivity*, June 2011

All of those changes in society are driving an enormous growth in information flowing around the world, which will continue for the foreseeable future – just like traffic on roads, traffic on networks follows a version of Parkinson's Law[18] – it expands to fill the space available and in the digital world, it grows at logarithmic rates.

Big data is being fueled and enabled by the same underpinning technologies as the overall digital world: inexpensive virtualized storage, increasingly fast connectivity and cloud-based processing. Machine-to-machine sensor and data capture technologies are generating more data while innovative software and analytics tools are essential to turn raw data into useful information. Another big factor in growth is the economics of the digital economy – the cost of generating information is falling and at the same time investment in the digital world is rising.

Figure 1 – The digital world growth paradox: falling cost and rising investment

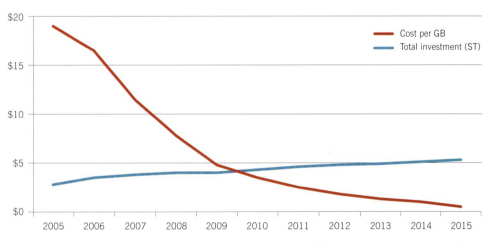

Source: IDC Digital Universe Study, sponsored by EMC, June 2011

Big data is not separate from the digital world – it's more like a cross section through it and includes transactional data, warehoused data, metadata and other data residing in massive files and generated by individuals and enterprises. Examples of such services include YouTube, Facebook, Foursquare and Twitter, as well as downloaded media, entertainment, healthcare and video surveillance. It isn't just the original data content that's being stored, big data includes the growing amount of data that is generated around information consumption. I'll talk a lot more about this later, since 'usage' of information is the basis of many new business models where this information can be monetized, such as those used by Google or Facebook. So the key here is not to see big data as a burden, but rather to work out how to turn meaningless data into valuable information.

[18]http://en.wikipedia.org/wiki/Parkinson's_law

IDC emphasizes this economic aspect in its definition: "Big data technologies describe a new generation of technologies and architectures, designed to economically extract value from very large volumes of a wide variety of data, by enabling high-velocity capture, discovery and/or analysis."[19]

The scale and scope of big data

The scope of big data is breathtaking: various sources indicate a long-term growth trend in annual Internet data traffic of around 50 to 60 percent annually[20] – in other words, a 100-fold increase every decade.

At the start of 2012, an estimated 44 million servers in the world created and replicated over 1.8 zettabytes[21] of data held in 500 quadrillion[22] files – nine-fold growth in five years. If I have my zeros in the right place, that's over 50 million years of DVD-quality data and a similar number of bits as there are stars in the entire universe! At the network level, AT&T has been seeing mobile data traffic rates grow in the region of 8,000 percent a year.

Today, data circles the earth on over 1 million kilometers of subsea fiber optic cable, connecting servers that can be located anywhere in the cloud and used anywhere. At least 2 percent of those servers belong to Google, which processes more than 80 percent of the world's Internet searches – each of which travels an average of 2,400 kilometers, with an average response time of 0.18 seconds.

According to IDC[23], by 2020, the number of servers will have grown by a factor of 10; the amount of information by a factor of 50, while the number of files in datacenters will grow by a factor of 75 – yet the number of IT professionals will grow by less than a factor of 1.5.

By 2015, at least 20 percent of all data will be impacted in some way by cloud-based services (that is somewhere in a byte's journey from originator to disposal it will have been processed or stored in a cloud somewhere) – and by then cloud-based traffic is expected to grow 12-fold[24] to reach a total of 1.6 zettabytes annually – a 66 percent compound annual growth rate (CAGR).

According to Cisco's Global Cloud Index (2010- 2015), cloud is the fastest growing component of data center traffic, which itself will grow four-fold at a 33 percent CAGR during this period.

[20]European Commission Experts Group: www.future-internet.eu/fileadmin/documents/reports/FI_Panel_Report_v3.1_Final.pdf
[21]1 petabyte = 1,024 terabytes; 1 exabyte = 1,024 petabytes (or 1 million trillion bytes); 1 zettabyte = 1,024 exabytes and can be estimated as 1,000,000,000,000,000,000,000 bytes.
[22]1 Quadrillion = 1×10^{15}
[23]IDC Digital Universe Study, sponsored by EMC, June 2011.
[24]Source: Cisco

[19]IDC White Paper, sponsored by AMD, *Big Data: What It Is and Why You Should Care*, June 2011

The word *enabler* has come up a lot in this chapter and will play a big part in this book. On their own these technologies do nothing: they are merely tools that allow something to happen and that something is the creativity of people all over the world inventing, refining and using them. Phone companies *enable* people to talk and send messages but they don't do the talking.

Similarly, these enabling technologies and services are not the digital economy itself – that only happens when you add things that *use* these enablers: applications, information, entertainment, people, machines and, of course, commerce and money. I make this point because the various roles often get very intertwined and confused, so when we are discussing evolution and transformation to the digital economy, it's important to understand the role people are playing.

It is also worth clarifying what I mean by 'transformation', which I use many times because it's become a somewhat devalued term of late with almost any change in an organization being labeled as a 'transformation'. I use it in its original business sense to mean the process of profound and radical change that steers an organization in a new direction to exploit new markets, business models or products, and to take it to an entirely different level of effectiveness. Unlike evolutionary change, which is incremental progress on the same business or operating model, transformation implies a basic change of character and little or no resemblance with the past configuration or structure. I discuss the use of transformational and evolutionary approaches in more detail in Chapter 11.

Can we sustain and expand the digital world?

There are hundreds of niches in the digital economy and being clear about your positioning in it is vital to success. Understanding the shape and nature of the market; understanding where the 'sweet spots' are; understanding your core competencies, strengths and weaknesses to succeed in your chosen market; and understanding how to get there are vital first steps before embarking on huge investment programs. Many massive investments will fail, for reasons I'll explore throughout this book.

The theory is that the more people are connected and in scope for the digital economy, the faster investment flows into digital services and applications, creating a positive feedback loop, where markets feed on themselves. As the number of people who can consume digital services starts to saturate, data-hungry devices will add rocket boosters to that growth and as the cost of equipping today's dumb devices with 'smart' connected technology will fall with volume, virtually anything that *can* conceivably be connected *will* be – the cost of doing it will not be a barrier.

This will continue to create a sort of digital tsunami – smarter, better and easier to use devices drive more consumption of content and information. That drives demand for communications and computing, which make the services available on the devices richer and more consumable and so on.

Figure 2 – Drivers of the digital tsunami

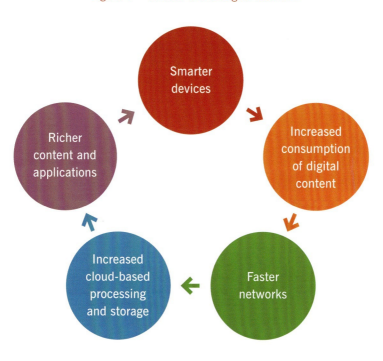

Over the coming years, the massive rise in demand for moving, storing and processing truly vast quantities of information will test technologies to their limits. Radical new innovations, architectures and technologies will be needed. As Dr. Hossein Eslambolchi puts it, radio spectrum is the "real estate of the sky" – and just like 'real' real estate, it is a finite resource. So we're already beginning to see 'spectrum wars' being played out by different interests in some countries and you can be sure that this will get much more ferocious as demand continues to outstrip supply. Advanced new concepts will need to evolve, such as multi-access wireless architectures; widespread deployments of pico and nano cells; advanced wireless radio technologies; and concepts such as cognitive radio[25].

Cognitive radio is in its early stages, but is based on the idea of exploiting radio frequencies that are temporarily not in use: in the U.S. the FCC thinks that, in some locations or at some times of day, 70 percent of the allocated radio spectrum may be sitting idle. Cognitive radios negotiate with other devices in their vicinity and while the designated owner of the spectrum gets priority, other devices can share unused spectrum.

Down at the chip technology end of the problem, the basic ingredient of digital technology – microprocessors – will push hard against the laws of physics to keep delivering ever-faster

[25]www.technologyreview.com/read_article.aspx?ch=specialsections&sc=emergingtech&id=16471

speeds. Although processors have always been able to be designed smaller, faster and more cheaply every year, as we approach 2020, crafting silicon into ever thinner slices starts to approach splitting the atom – and we all know where that led!

If the inexorable rise in information is not to be stuck in a bottleneck, different materials such as graphene could replace silicon. Also, the basic architecture of computing will shift dramatically as quantum computing starts to become a practical and commercial reality over the next decade.

The potential of quantum computers is that they can quickly and easily perform calculations that are incredibly time-consuming on conventional computers but are hard to get your head around. This is how the BBC's Science and Environment correspondent describes quantum computing: "Rather than the ones and zeroes of digital computing, quantum computers deal in what are known as superpositions – states of matter that can be thought of as both one and zero at once.

"In a sense, quantum computing's one trick is to perform calculations on all superposition states at once. With one quantum bit, or qubit, the difference [between quantum and conventional computing] is not great, but the effect scales rapidly as the number of qubits rises."

Getting that scaling right is the challenge and today quantum computing devices are still unstable and rather impractical. However, continual advances are being made and the best estimates of commercially viable machines are expected to appear in the 2020s.

Technological challenges like managing the limitations of radio spectrum or processor designs are at least 'known unknowns', and are probably the least challenging issues ahead of us. Given the size of the opportunity in the digital economy and its potential revenues, companies will always invest in R&D to overcome these problems. A greater 'unknown unknown' is the outcome of the workings of the market, which is far from being predictable.

Where are we going?

As Joseph Licklider,[26] one of the original visionaries behind the Internet, famously said: "People tend to overestimate what can be done in one year and to underestimate what can be done in five or 10 years," and I think most people are underestimating massively both the scale and the impact of the digital world in the next few years.

Companies the world over can transform their businesses to leverage the digital world – those that don't will get left behind and those that do so early will reap a rich reward. For example, Procter & Gamble CEO Robert McDonald[27] recently said: "With digital technology, it's now

[26]Joseph Licklider, *Libraries of the Future*, MIT Press, 1965. Reference http://en.wikipedia.org/wiki/Joseph_Licklider
[27]McKinsey Quarterly, November 2011

possible to have a one-on-one relationship with every consumer in the world." Imagine the impact of that thinking played out in myriad different ways in every company and organization around the globe, where new ways of working, producing goods and managing relationships with customers can bring a better result, at lower cost and using fewer resources.

In a few short years we will have a fully-fledged digital economy: the *anything, anywhere, anytime* world where just about every activity we can devise has some aspect of it impacted by advanced, digital services. Licklider notwithstanding, the implications for the economy, for society and for individuals are profound: the digital world isn't just about the convenience of shopping online rather than going to a store, or searching the Internet rather than visiting a library – for billions of people around the globe, it's almost the only way that they can access education, information, trade and healthcare.

Bringing those capabilities to large numbers of people creates huge new markets (perhaps three times larger than North America and Western Europe combined) hungry to have a comfortable lifestyle, good jobs, good education and good healthcare – and much of this could be made possible through the consumption of state of the art technologies and services as they become available – with availability being the big issue.

With the world's population continuing to grow at about 1.3 percent[28] every year and all of those people expecting a good quality of life, the pressures on food production, energy production, water resources and climate change will become even more intense. Nearly 8 billion people will be part of the connected global digital economy by 2020[29] and in that time, an additional 3 billion people will become comparatively wealthy in fast-developing economies. At least an extra 1 billion people, who are today living below subsistence levels, will become economically active.

The evolving geographic shifts in economic power are also profound: in 2000, the U.S., Europe and Japan accounted for 72 percent of global GDP[30] but by 2030, they are likely to only account for just 29 percent, meaning that the rest of the world will grow by a staggering 154 percent. Emerging economic powerhouses like China, India, Brazil and Indonesia won't be playing catch-up technologically: they will embed the digital economy deep into the way they evolve, adding to the positive feedback loop of growth – if only supply can keep up with the soaring demand.

A 2012 report by Booz & Co[31] showed a way of assessing the impact of the digital world on societies using various measures. It examined 150 economies around the world and grouped them into categories based on the evolution of the digital economy in each, using a scale of 0 to 100, with

[28]United Nations estimate
[29]http://www.un.org/esa/population/publications/sixbillion/sixbilpart1.pdf
[30]International Monetary Fund
[31]The Global Information Technology Report 2012: *Maximizing the Impact of Digitization*

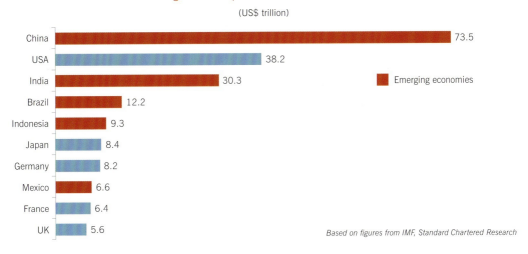

Figure 3 – Top 10 economies in 2030

(US$ trillion)

China	73.5
USA	38.2
India	30.3
Brazil	12.2
Indonesia	9.3
Japan	8.4
Germany	8.2
Mexico	6.6
France	6.4
UK	5.6

■ Emerging economies

Based on figures from IMF, Standard Chartered Research

100 being the highest level of 'digitization'. From this the report assessed impacts on the economy, society and governance of every country for every 10 points' improvement on the scale.

The results are most interesting, showing an average of 0.6 percent increase in GDP for every 10 points on the scale; big improvements to quality of life and access to basic services and education; and a 6.2 percent increase in innovation, and telling reductions in unemployment and corruption.

These improved living conditions, combined with better healthcare would mean that the world's population will continue to age and with median life expectancy having doubled in a century, the costs of caring for people – already in 2012 between 8 percent and 11 percent of GDP in the developed world – are becoming unsustainable and will rapidly drive advances in digitally based healthcare. With people living longer, the effects on natural resources – particularly food, water and energy ought to drive advances in 'smart' approaches to energy and resource management, if there is the political will and necessary investment to do so.

Current predictions are that most of those people will live in cities in the future. As I said in the Foreword, I'm not convinced about this since the digital world has the potential to allow us to live and work from almost anywhere provided you have good connectivity. But even if they do, the digital world will enable a shift from the old industrial-age city model to new approaches to everything from government to education, public safety, the environment, clean water and air, transportation and energy.

For many in those cities today, poor government and corruption is a daily curse. The digital world has the power to let citizens see and contribute their ideas to the way decisions are made on their behalf and help drive the more efficient and transparent operation of government services. Information and corruption are harder to hide in an open society, providing a platform for citizens to self-organize and create a better quality of life, but let's not kid ourselves here, already certain governments are using the digital world's capabilities for their own ends, to increase control of their populations, rather than help those they govern benefit.

So the digital world could have a big effect on democracy and the way that governments operate. It's much harder for totalitarian regimes to survive when people have access to information and can tell the world what is happening in their country. The ability of large numbers of the population to vote on issues instantaneously calls into question the whole basis of government through representation. We shall see how much effect e-petitions and the like will have on governments and legislation – they are usually are pretty good at preserving themselves!

Even in democracies, the digital world won't all be positive– social media can be used to whip up rioting and civil disobedience for bad reasons as well as good and, in any case, as many people can't be bothered to vote, it could well turn out that e-petitions and e-government get used primarily by activists and extremists.

Industrial-scale laryngitis: losing your voice

In a theme I will return to over again in this book: the digital world will create many winners, but also many losers. For example, the communications industry will undergo huge changes. We are very likely to see this sector in a very different form over the next few years and the traditional 'telco' as we have known them for decades will no longer exist. While the incredible rise in data traffic is a racing certainty, declines in traditional voice and messaging services seem inevitable, while increases in broadband speed and data volumes are unlikely to command higher prices. All of which means margins have to be driven by innovation of new services supported by ever more efficient technologies and operations.

The computer industry showed over a generation ago that it is possible for every new model to exploit faster processors with more storage while prices remain almost constant – more for less is a fact of life in the technology business. While communications service providers might push through premium pricing for differentiated packages with better quality of service and higher throughput, the best we can really hope for is that people will continue to pay the same, in real terms, for network access as they pay today.

The digital economy will have a big problem if the communications industry can't evolve a business model where revenues sustain the capital costs of expanding network technology (for example, new fiber and radio access technologies like long-term evolution) along with spectrum acquisition and operating costs, while returning a reasonable margin to investors.

In an unconstrained world, market economics would normally look after this, so we'll almost certainly see a big contraction from the 1,000 or so operators around the world now to far fewer in future, enabling much larger providers who can exploit economies of scale. In reality, this is an area fraught with difficulties, as legislators and regulators tinker, disrupting normal economics and I'll talk about this more in Chapter 5. It would help greatly if regulators update their approach from encouraging multiple, competing infrastructures to facilitating the most efficient and effective infrastructure possible, commensurate with open and equal access.

Like an anxious parent, there comes a time when the child is grown and needs to be left to get on with its life. Regulators have achieved spectacular success in breaking down monopolies and setting in train a digital revolution in information, trade, services and entertainment without borders and without limits. As I'll conclude in Chapter 5, I think it's time for market economics to do the job from now on, otherwise the digital economy is going to be throttled by fixed and mobile access bandwidth and that will hurt everybody.

Securing a fair rate of return on infrastructure isn't the only problem on the horizon for communications companies. Today they dominate the customer relationship for fixed and/or mobile phone service and have strong, recognizable brands. Competition has previously come from other communications companies, either with their own network infrastructure or sometimes operating on a virtual network basis (that is, layering their service over someone else's network). But the rise of strong and respected brands is tightly related to digital stores like Apple's iTunes and Google Play[32], which is showing just how much this relationship can be disrupted – customers are starting to see the device manufacturers and *their* brand as the company they have a relationship with. We look at this issue in some detail in Chapter 2.

Historically a network and a service were much the same thing, with each service requiring a separate network. All of that has changed with the advent of Internet protocol (IP) technologies and the underlying broadband service is a common enabler for all types of service. IP-based voice and messaging were of limited impact prior to the emergence of the smartphone because they were largely available only via a PC and therefore inconvenient. Even with that limitation, IP voice market leader Skype has built its way to become the world's largest international voice carrier[33], carrying more than a billion minutes of traffic daily, according to Microsoft. As every phone becomes a smartphone and therefore able to run apps, including easy to use IP-voice and messaging services from a variety of suppliers, traditional voice and messaging services will be under great pressure.

We've seen Apple quietly introduce iMessage, which disrupts the SMS revenue flow by routing a message for free via IP-based messaging and only passes over the SMS network as a second choice. Other messaging apps like WhatsApp also offer a richer and free alternative to SMS, which

[32]Formerly Android Market
[33]Source: TeleGeography

has been the most profitable communications service in history. It is now declining in the face of a combination of IP-based messaging alternatives and other forms of communication via social networks such as Twitter and Facebook. Microsoft is reported to be bundling Skype with Windows Mobile 8 – not as a loosely coupled app but embedded deep in the operating system. How sharp the decline is and how fast it is accelerating was outlined by Ovum in a report[34] published in February 2012, which estimated that consumers' increasing use of IP-based messaging services on their smartphones cost telecom operators $8.7 billion in lost SMS revenues in 2010, and $13.9 billion in 2011, representing nearly 9 percent of total messaging revenue in 2011.

All of these moves present traditional communications products with a very real headache, probably causing a rapid and sharp decline in revenues, but that might not be the worst-case scenario – their whole consumer retail business may be in peril. Phone companies have little to differentiate their products today other than price and network coverage, so are not very 'sticky' in marketing terms. Being brutally honest, many of them have failed to either fully understand or invest in driving customer loyalty through providing a great customer experience, even clinging stubbornly to the term *subscriber* rather than *customer.* Compare that with the loyalty that Apple and Amazon generate in their customer base: when did you last see people queuing all night for the release of a new tariff from a phone operator?

Historically people have contracted with their phone company for mobile phone service but increasingly have a growing commercial relationship with their device and digital store provider for applications, music and video. While the device was primarily a voice and messaging phone with a few extras, the primary contract for service remains between the user and the communications company but, as more and more of the service mix is bundled with the device and digital store, the logic (and brand loyalty) may well switch round the other way.

To complete the scenario where the phone company is well and truly pushed out of a consumer retail position altogether is if the device providers supply a 'one stop shop' package that includes the mobile broadband airtime services bundled in with the device contract on a mobile virtual network operator (MVNO) basis. This 'batteries included' type of business model is already being offered by Amazon through its Whispernet service bundled with the Kindle tablet range. This final step in what might be called a cuckoo strategy[35] threatens to reduce the role of the communications provider to a bulk wholesale supplier, deep down in the ecosystem.

As digital store retailers like Apple, Google and Amazon capture ever larger shares of end customers' attention and revenue, their purchasing power for sourcing bulk bandwidth and airtime deals with network operators obviously rises and ensures that they get the very best wholesale prices from operators. They don't need to invest countless billions of capital in building and running their own access networks and the idea that they will do so that grabs a

---

[34]http://ovum.com/press_releases/ovum-estimates-that-operators-lost-13-9bn-in-2011-due-to-social-messaging/
[35]Whereby an alien chick is introduced into the nest, without the parents realizing, so they nurture the intruder

headline every few months is ludicrous – why would they, when they can buy it as they need it from communications companies who will only be too willing to give them a great price?

So the 'phone' operator suffers the multiple blows of falling revenues from its core services, losing their relationship with the end customer and becoming a commodity supplier of the enabling bandwidth. This is not just about future revenues that the communications company is seeing taken by the over-the-top providers, it's their *current* revenues that are seriously threatened.

Another confirmation that operators are 'losing their voice' comes in a report predicting that, for the first time, U.S. data revenues will overtake those from voice as early as 2013 and by 2015, with twice as much being spent on the data component than on the voice component.[36] More positively, the report also predicted that while the growing appetite for mobile data will push up U.S. mobile operators' average revenue per user (which has been shrinking since 2005), it will rise by nearly 10 percent from 2012 to 2015 to $51 per month. Although this will generate an additional $144.2 billion for the U.S. mobile industry, taking inflation into account it's hardly going to get the champagne corks popping!

Obviously, this trend is not restricted to the U.S., but is being seen the world over – communications service providers need to figure out ways of using spectrum and transporting data more cheaply and efficiently. It's no coincidence that there is increasing emphasis on femto, micro and pico cells as options for doing that. They have been talked about for a long time, but now as the demise of voice is in sight, action finally looks imminent. The Small Cell Forum predicts small cells will account for 88 percent of all base stations by 2016.

Nobody's immune system is perfect
Even though they have a symbiotic relationship, it won't stop aggressive moves as players in the digital ecosystem jockey to maximize their share of the overall revenue. Device and digital store providers are very likely to continue to want to push infrastructure providers of both computing and communications 'down' the chain. Regulation around the world may slow this evolution (see Chapter 5), but anyone who has the customer's heart and mind is in a powerful position.

Of course the communications providers can do the same in reverse, that is to say provide an attractive package of application services in addition to their services. However, retailing is all about economies of scope: that is to say you need an attractive range of goods on offer, and so far at least, few if any communications players have been able to attract significant numbers of applications to their proprietary digital stores. The two big disadvantages that communications companies have in the consumer applications market is that they don't control the devices and have a structural flaw in being highly fragmented, with hundreds of companies covering the globe collectively.

[36]Arthur Gruen, economist and principal author of the U.S. Telecommunications Industry Association report, March 2012

Outside a small number of large global communications provider groups, it means that they cannot offer the originators of those applications, games or entertainment any real economies of scale for distribution. Even in these groups, each country-level operating company is very likely to have different branding, contractual terms and conditions, revenue-sharing approaches and technical interfaces. These all add to the cost and complexity for an application or games developer wanting to get to the end customer on razor thin margins.

While each operator may have many millions of those customers, the economics of the digital world works on a customer base of billions. If your go-to-market partner can't deliver that breadth of distribution and is hard to work with for good measure, then rather like water, which always takes the easiest course, application providers will naturally use those few distributors with a big global footprint who can provide a 'one-stop, easy shop'.

In response, a consortium of communications companies have established the Wholesale Applications Community (WAC)[37], an organization that is creating a unified and open platform to allow mobile software developers to more easily write applications usable on a variety of devices, operating systems and networks. Time will tell if the WAC is able to move quickly enough and provide communications companies with a sufficiently attractive applications portfolio for them to compete successfully with digital stores and device combinations. So far it has not proven a winning approach because with many dozens of shareholders, getting consensus on the way forward is always a slow process.

I'll return to this theme in the next chapter, but an alternative way of avoiding the slow-down that a joint consortium often imposes and allowing each player to move at their own speed and make their own decisions could be through a federated approach. This would mean involving a minimum number of standards, which are the 'glue' that binds the grouping together. Such standards need to be open and not controlled by any one party to form an open digital economy.

It's not just communications companies that are facing problems with their current business models in the digital world: almost any company whose business model was honed in the pre-digital world is vulnerable. Not that long ago, Microsoft had 90 percent market share of the operating system market for Internet-connected devices, but with the rise of smartphones and tablets, that's falling fast and some commentators predict that it could be as low as 30 percent before long. Even Google can't escape, the number of indexed searches has actually started to decline as people use more and more apps to get to the information they need.

Decline isn't inevitable – if you want proof, just look at the remarkable renaissance of Apple or remember that Nokia once changed from losing hundreds of millions of dollars as a forestry and rubber company. Players under pressure in their existing markets and business models can and must exploit alternative strategies and never more so than in the digital world, particularly

[37]www.wacapps.net

by broadening their portfolio of services beyond their traditional comfort zone and especially leveraging enterprise services and the M2M market. I'll talk about this in later chapters but the growth potential is enormous.

Even the fastest growth players like Facebook and Twitter have their challenges because many business models now rely on the exchange of personal information rather than money in return for using the service. That depends on people's willingness to continue to give up an element of their privacy. Scott McNealy[38] once said, "Privacy is dead, get over it", but it wasn't and we didn't, but we continue to see a steady and irreversible erosion of personal privacy. While interested parties like Mark Zuckerberg[39] tell us that people don't care about privacy that much, I wonder how easily such a deeply rooted cultural aspect can be overturned? I think privacy concerns could yet have a backlash that will damage or even destroy some of these information-based business models we see as a fundamental part of the digital world – we explore this further in Chapter 3.

As I've said, nobody is immune from the digital world: it's the nature of evolution. For example, systems integrators have made a great living for a long time from gluing together the various complex technologies that companies need in their back office to make their companies work. But will those Titans still be the companies who dominate a world of mashed digital services that provide the same functions? Alongside that, the world clearly will consume vast amounts of processing, storage and software, but as the shift occurs from horsepower on your desktop and in your server room to being in vast data centers in the cloud, will the current suppliers continue to dominate?

Maybe, maybe not: it all depends on how they perceive and react to the digital tsunami that's heading their way. React too soon and you may lose your current markets before the new one has really developed. React too late and you may have literally missed the boat. So, as I examine in more detail in Chapter 4, the age-old question, "What do you want to be when you grow up?" is a really important one to answer: what role *do* you want to play in the digital ecosystem?

Answering this question is one of the main themes of this book, which then goes on to explore three further questions. What are your goals, do you have the right competencies to achieve them and how should you go about the journey? This book tries to lay out pathways to profit from the digital economy. The problem with a lot of thinking, articles and presentations on this issue is that they tend to assume a 'one size fits all' approach. In fact, what you need is guidance to implement a plan unique to your individual company because of many differing needs, even if that plan is based on a generic framework and best practices.

[38]Former CEO of Sun Microsystems
[39]CEO of Facebook http://en-gb.facebook.com/zuck?sk=wiki

Whatever you want to be, remember that economics will ultimately drive the digital world, not technology, because in many instances, it's likely to be the most efficient way of doing business rather than through the 'physical economy' we have known for hundreds of years. It's cheaper to have an online store than a physical store, providing customers with a better choice and, if it's done right, a better experience. It costs less to transport goods electronically than in ships and trucks, and they arrive more or less instantaneously. It's cheaper to read utility meters digitally than send someone out with a flashlight. It costs less for a doctor to examine vital medical data remotely than getting the patient to the doctor's consulting room and so on. Put simply, if a thing can be done at lower cost and with the same or better customer experience in a digital fashion, then it will displace the physical approach.

This means that an ever-increasing number of industries and professions will become part of and reliant upon the digital economy. This creates major opportunities for new entrants to disrupt markets and grab their share of markets previously closed to them – and the digital economy greatly lowers the barriers to entry. In the early stages of the digital world we saw banking, insurance and other financial industries take the lead. So Apple can move from being a second tier computer manufacturer to being the world's premier distributor of music. Google can displace advertising revenue from TV, radio and print industries.

Just like your own immune system, when you're not feeling so good you're much more prone to attack by a virus, the digital world is like that virus, weakening traditional business models and creating opportunities in almost every industry. We're just scratching the surface of the digital economy – it's perhaps a decade or so old and just a juvenile – there are enormous opportunities for new players to creep in and oust companies that haven't moved fast enough.

To win, you have to be in the game. Unless you are positioned in the right place at the right time, with a bit of luck thrown in, you'll just be an observer watching somebody else taking that prize. Sometime later you'll scratch your head and say "How did that happen?"

(2)

THE DIGITAL ECOSYSTEM AND ITS STRUCTURE

As the wagons roll to grab turf in the digital ecosystem, it's not yet clear who will end up where but it is possible to spot who has the right wheels on their cart and who is good at driving horses. Many contestants are already out of the race but don't know it yet, and many more have yet to reach the starting line.

I said in Chapter 1 that the enabling technologies and industries that underpin the digital world are well established: telecommunications dates back around 150 years; the computer industry back to World War II and hosted applications (the Godfather of cloud services) date back to the 1960s. Some of the sectors that are now being impacted by the digital world, such as publishing, go back centuries.

While these industries may be well established, history shows us that the big players of one era tend to be diminished or even eliminated during periods of radical market change and the digital world is likely to be the most radical thing to ever happen to many companies in many industry sectors. This doesn't mean that market incumbents can't thrive, but they have to learn the new rules of the game, and fast, if they are not to be outpaced by the new kids on the block.

There probably isn't going to be a sector that *doesn't* adopt some aspects of the digital economy in the way they do business. This creates chances for well-placed, fleet of foot players to disaggregate some aspects of what may previously have been closed markets through focused, enterprise-class, digital services.

The trouble is, what's good for the goose is good for the gander[40] – the digital economy opens doors for everyone, including those who want to attack the markets of companies that are enabling the digital economy in the first place. As I said, some players are vulnerable; the digital world is mostly about new vision and business models – technological innovation is just an enabler.

Oil on the gears of the world's economy

To understand the basic shape of the ecosystem, it's worth taking a look at a far-sighted *Harvard Business Review* paper, written at the dawn of the digital era by John Hagel and Marc Singer[41]. They looked, in detail, at the impacts the digital world would have on corporate structures. Their focus was on the crucial role that interaction costs play in shaping industries and companies. They defined these costs as the time and money incurred whenever people and companies exchange goods, services or ideas and can occur within a company, between companies, or between a company and a customer. The interactions might include sales calls, reports, memos, transportation, storage, management costs, conferences, phone conversations and so on. So interaction costs are the 'friction' points of doing business.

The authors' main point is that the digital economy allows companies to trade and exchange information far more quickly and cheaply than ever before, dramatically reducing interaction costs and enabling a rethink about how businesses should be organized. The digital economy is progressively taking over from a physical economy because there is a lot less friction on its gears: put another way, the digital world is like oil on the economy's gears.

---

[40]English proverb; gander is a male goose, so what applies to one party equally applies to the other
[41]John Hagel and Marc Singer, *Net Worth: Shaping Markets When Customers Make the Rules,* Havard Business School Press, 1999. ISBN: 0-87584-889-3

This has some interesting effects. Hagel and Singer accurately predicted that activities companies have believed were central to their businesses would be increasingly handed over to new, specialized providers that can carry out those activities better, faster and more efficiently. Executives would be forced to ask the most basic and uncomfortable questions about which key roles their companies should play as the world moves towards an economy that suffers less friction.

They pointed out that beneath the surface of nearly every company there are three kinds of businesses: a customer relationship business (which looks after customers and sells things); a product or service innovation business (which develops things people want); and an infrastructure business (the underpinning means of producing those products, such as a factory or a network). Although organizationally intertwined, these businesses differ a great deal in their objectives, structure and needs, and are often in conflict. For example:

- The customer relationship business role is to find customers and build relationships with them. Although people may belong to different organizational units, they have a common goal: to attract and hold on to as many customers as possible.
- The product or service innovation business role is to conceive of attractive new products and services and figure out how best to bring them to market: constantly searching for interesting new products and effective ways of presenting them to customers.
- The infrastructure business role is different again: to deliver products and services at the best possible customer experience and the lowest possible operating cost by building and operating facilities for high-volume, repetitive and often complex operational tasks.

Almost a century of conventional management wisdom says that these three functions should be combined within a single 'big is beautiful' company to minimize the interaction costs. However, as Hagel and Singer point out, the three core processes are often in conflict and bundling them into a single corporation inevitably forces a compromise in the performance of each.

This is because the customer relationship business needs as broad a *scope* as possible – such as a broad portfolio of products to attract customers – while maximum speed drives product and service innovation businesses. The infrastructure business needs as much scale as possible because it is highly capital-intensive – as unit costs fall as scale increases, it becomes essential for profitability to minimize the scope of services offered. This results in a one-size-fits-all culture that steers towards a minimum number of products and away from innovating niche products and services.

A great example of this conundrum is the challenges that large communications service providers have. Their thinking is often dominated by their infrastructure business at the expense of their service innovation and customer-facing activities. This often leads to their product innovation business being hampered in developing wholly new, exciting services and a poor customer experience.

On the other hand, the infrastructure business is also constrained; it can't go full out to provide wholesale capacity and services to other providers for fear of hurting its own retail business. This 'dog chasing its own tail' problem, created by inbuilt conflicts of interest within a service provider, limits the growth and profitability of all three core businesses. They are not alone – many companies across lots of sectors suffer from similar problems. The great news is that the digital economy can liberate them from these constraints by allowing them to split into separate businesses, with each generating new growth opportunities.

The publishing business provides a good example: during the 1990s and early 2000s, the three core processes were tightly integrated within most newspapers and magazines. A publisher took full responsibility for attracting customers (readers and advertisers); developing most of its editorial content – and at the same time managed an extensive printing and distribution infrastructure, printing only its own editions on its own presses and distributing them with its own fleet of trucks.

Companies like News Corporation pioneered a different approach: much of a typical newspaper's product is now outsourced to niche providers such as syndicated columnists, publishers of specialty inserts and wire services. Specialist printers produce the newspaper with tight contracts for quality, delivery and price and increasingly newspapers are exploiting digital delivery because they are no longer caught up in conflicts like worrying about damaging their printing business, because it's someone else's problem.

By unbundling these three core functions, printers can exploit economies of scale by printing publications for lots of publishers who in turn can offer a broader range of innovative content, created by specialist freelancers that the newspaper could have never afforded to have permanently on its staff. The customer-facing part of the company is free to focus on understanding customers' needs and tailoring content to different market sectors or regions.

In other words, everyone gains because the traditional interaction costs that caused a newspaper to be vertically integrated have been substantially reduced by elements of the digital economy.

The same approach is being taken by many industries, including pharmaceuticals, manufacturing and financial services. Investment by major drug companies in product development has greatly reduced in favor of either taking equity stakes in or acquiring niche drug research companies – in effect outsourcing product innovation. Others have begun to outsource the planning and execution of large-scale pharmaceutical trials to contract research organizations and turned to big distribution specialists who warehouse and deliver most drugs.

The Matryoshka doll
So turning this concept back onto the enablers of the digital economy itself, this explosion

into focused segments will impact what is sometimes called the Telecommunications, Media and Technology sector (TMT)[42] just as much as any other company operating in the digital economy. To give you an idea of these niches, these three principle business segments are shown in Figure 4. Here I've tried to show how the digital economy might evolve with the digital enabler layer being all of the infrastructure services based on hardware, software, computing, communications and storage that any type of higher order digital service may need, plus a range of supporting services such as security, authentication, revenue management and so on.

The digital services themselves are any type of application, information, entertainment or other type of service innovation and the digital retailer layer is the customer relationship role described above. All three go together to provide the consumer with business services shown at the top of the diagram.

Figure 4 – Simplified view of the digital ecosystem

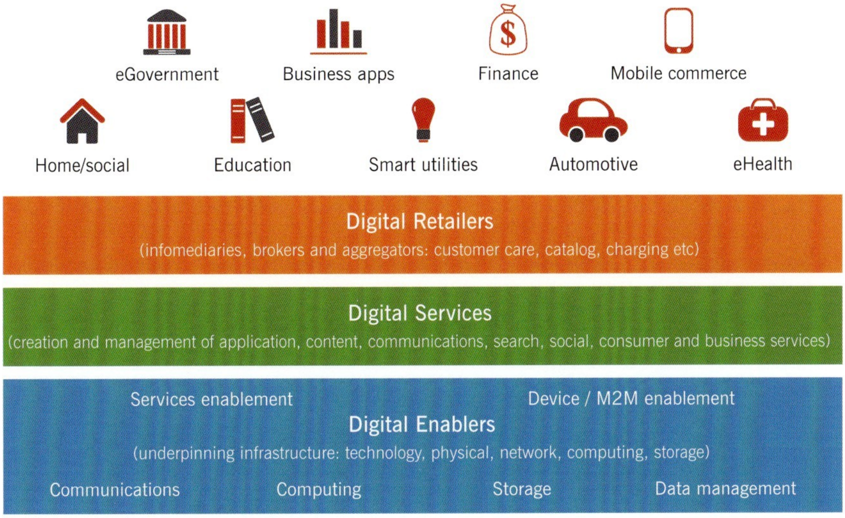

| eGovernment | Business apps | Finance | Mobile commerce |
| Home/social | Education | Smart utilities | Automotive | eHealth |

Digital Retailers
(infomediaries, brokers and aggregators: customer care, catalog, charging etc)

Digital Services
(creation and management of application, content, communications, search, social, consumer and business services)

Services enablement   Device / M2M enablement
Digital Enablers
(underpinning infrastructure: technology, physical, network, computing, storage)

Communications   Computing   Storage   Data management

Source: Parhelion Global Communications Advisors

The layers are not very relevant to the consumer – all they see is a service which they want to work first time, every time. This is rather like a Matryoshka (or Russian) doll, in that what you see on the outside contains many others dolls. So it is with the digital ecosystem – each layer of service comprises other services and the number and complexity of the layers will almost certainly rise as more, different players exploit the digital economy. It looks complicated and is becoming more so. Some companies will play in more than one segment, some will break into smaller, more specialist units, and new entrants will abound, especially in areas with low barriers to entry.

[42]Comprises a wide spectrum of segments, including fixed-line telephony, mobile communications, communications equipment, broadcasting, e-commerce retailers, software, computer hardware and semi-conductors

Figure 5 – The digital ecosystem

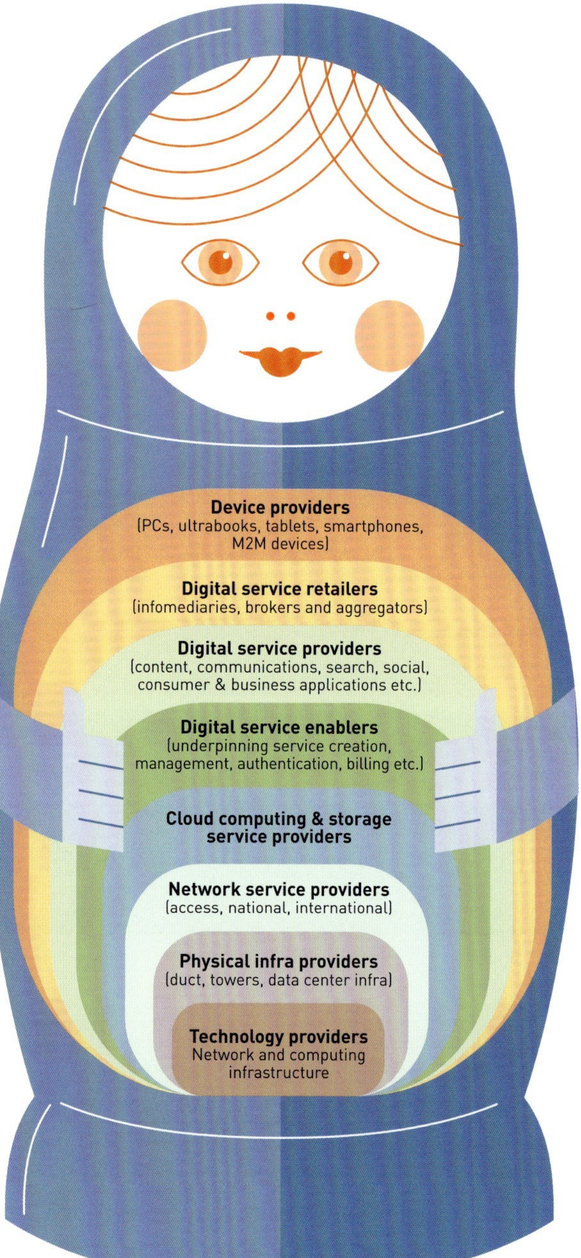

Device providers
(PCs, ultrabooks, tablets, smartphones, M2M devices)

Digital service retailers
(infomediaries, brokers and aggregators)

Digital service providers
(content, communications, search, social, consumer & business applications etc.)

Digital service enablers
(underpinning service creation, management, authentication, billing etc.)

Cloud computing & storage service providers

Network service providers
(access, national, international)

Physical infra providers
(duct, towers, data center infra)

Technology providers
Network and computing infrastructure

I've tried to show some of the principal 'dolls' in Figure 5, although each layer itself could be expanded into more strata – for example, the inner layer of technology providers could be extended to include suppliers of semiconductors, power supply providers, backplane makers and so on. I decided that the number of layers in Figure 5 was broken down sufficiently for me to illustrate my main points regarding the digital economy and the rest of this chapter is dedicated to an examination of each of the 'dolls'.

Technology providers – network and computing infrastructure

The very heart of the whole digital economy is technology as the key enabler and it will continue to evolve and become ever more sophisticated to handle the explosive growth of information and transactions. The providers of the underlying hardware and software are an essential part of the ecosystem – without them, nothing works.

These technologies include optical transport, mobile radio access, IP switching, chip fabrication, processing and storage, along with associated management systems and other supporting technologies. This segment has been consolidating for some time, initially in the computing and storage technology markets, but more recently among communications technology suppliers. This trend is likely to continue with further mergers and acquisitions.

Examples are companies like Intel, AMD, Ericsson, Huawei, Alcatel-Lucent, Cisco Systems, Oracle, Amdocs, HP and IBM.

Physical infrastructure providers

This layer didn't exist as a separate business a few years ago because communications companies invariably owned their infrastructure. Typically this was because their operating license granted certain licenses or wayleaves[43] to put ducts and manholes in the ground or erect cell towers. Change has been driven by economics, pressure from civic planners to force multiple operators to share cell sites and by some regulators demanding that underground ducts are made available to competitors.

At the same time, communications technology has become cheaper but concrete, steel and labor has become relatively more expensive, so that the capital cost of the civil engineering aspects of a network now usually exceeds the technology costs. This has opened the door to niche providers who can exploit their specialist expertise and economies of scale. Companies like Crown Castle and American Tower are typical examples of companies that have competencies in civil engineering plus planning and regulatory permissions, land acquisition, capital financing and so on. Even when an operator continues to own this infrastructure, civil engineering work is outsourced to specialist firms.

Data center infrastructure providers also belong in this group. As with networks, economies

[43]Access to property granted by a landowner for payment, for example to allow cables to pass over or under land or the erection of a cell-tower

of scale are important; vast data centers are being constructed on a pre-built, modular basis, which often use shipping containers packed with 1,000 or more servers each. When repairs or upgrades are needed, whole containers are replaced rather than repairing individual servers.

These are 'lights-out' data centers, which only need direct access by personnel in extraordinary circumstances, so they don't need lighting, which is a big cost and energy saving. The devices are accessed and managed by remote systems, with automation programs used to perform unattended operations. In addition to lower staffing costs, centers can be located away from population centers, which reduces the likelihood of malicious attacks and, if located intelligently next to major power sources, they can enjoy cheap energy.

Energy is a major cost issue in the operation of data centers as their power draw can be tens of megawatts for large facilities. Even better if the site is highly secure and can help reduce cooling costs – Norway's Green Mountain Data Center is a good example. This 9,000 square meter facility, located at a former NATO ammunition depot (the largest in northern Europe), is cooled by the steady flow of water from an adjacent fjord and built to the highest military security standards. It is secured against electromagnetic pulses, sabotage and direct attack from the sea.

The U.S. Environmental Protection Agency estimates that servers and data centers are responsible for up to 1.5 percent of total U.S. electricity consumption. Indeed, the entire information and communication technology base of the digital world is not very green and estimated to be responsible for roughly 2 percent of the total global carbon emissions footprint. Both the computing and communications industries have recognized they need to address this as energy consumption soars. They are pursuing the redesign of systems and power-saving techniques with vigor. Examples of companies in this sector include Telehouse, Rackspace and Vantage.

Network service providers

Network providers offer network infrastructure and related services to other players in the ecosystem, differentiating themselves through four key capabilities:

- cost-efficiency in the operation of their infrastructure through large economies of scale;
- scalability in replicating their technology platforms and operating models;
- reliability in terms of network and IT availability and quality; and
- highly efficient operations through automated, standardized processes and integrated IT.

Most wholesale network services were initially the product of regulation where governments sought to force incumbent providers to deliver equal access to competitors. Not surprisingly, and following Hagel and Singer's ideas on internal business conflicts, wholesale communications services were (and often still are) regarded with disdain by many incumbents (who see it as helping their retail competitors) and with suspicion by their competitors.

However, looked at as a business in its own right, providing wholesale 'cloud' network capacity (either stand-alone or bundled with other enabling services, such as cloud-based computing and storage capabilities) to other digital service providers who then add value, is likely to be a huge area of growth over the next decade, as the consumer base grows and the big data problems multiply.

Growth will come from two sources. The first is the inherent growth in the capacity needed by the digital economy and the second is from an increasing number of service providers to decide to exit the infrastructure business because of pressures on capital and other reasons. India's Bharti Airtel was one of the first players in mobile to have its entire network and IT infrastructure provided by third parties as managed services (that is on an outsourced basis – I explore this theme in detail in Chapter 7).

This consolidation means that in the next few years there will likely be a relatively small number of very large network providers who will succeed by exploiting huge economies of scale and enjoying relative protection from new competitors because of the high barriers to entry.

Far from being the much feared *dumb pipe* provider, these focused network providers will be well positioned to broaden their capabilities to the entire suite of enabling infrastructure services, including cloud-based processing or storage capabilities. In their own right, or through partners, they could offer an entire range of capabilities to digital service providers as a 'one-stop-shop', including security services, authentication, quality of service management and also many routine back-office functions. These could range from billing to settlements, fraud management and so on. In this way they can also move up the value chain to become a digital service enabler or what Kenny Frank, EVP at Alcatel-Lucent, calls the "enabled utility".

A number of operators are already providing some of these capabilities, mainly through joint ventures which merge and share infrastructure and so reduce costs. For example, T-Mobile and Orange in the U.K. joined forces to create Everything Everywhere, allowing their 28 combined million U.K. mobile customers to move easily between their mobile networks, while T-Mobile and Orange remain separate brands.

Olaf Swantee, CEO of Everything Everywhere, reported some impressive savings in his annual report in February 2012: "We have now achieved an annual run rate of $445 million in annual gross OpEx savings, more than 60 percent of the $712 million annual run rate goal by 2014, and are on track for over $5.6 billion in synergy savings by 2014." KPN has undertaken a similar network approach for its European brands Base and E-Plus.

Governments in Australia, Korea and Singapore are taking a different route, building out national broadband networks designed to provide open access to all operators and Internet service providers. They will be highly reliable, operationally efficient and built so that platforms and services can scale to meet the many partners' needs. More governments are taking action to bring broadband communications to everyone, even those in the most remote communities, as politicians wake up to the fact that the provision of broadband creates jobs, increases commerce, enhances social cohesion and boosts the local, regional and national economy.

Even a country as wealthy as the U.S. has begun to recognize this: when introducing proposals to ensure that broadband reaches everyone in the U.S., Julius Genachowski, Chairman of the U.S. regulator, the Federal Communications Commission, said: "Broadband has gone from being a luxury to a necessity in the 21st century. Times have changed and [broadband] is now essential for finding a job, for example, as job postings have moved online and for landing a job, as companies increasingly require basic digital skills."

I'm skeptical of governments making too much happen in this area – they often promise much but deliver less. It would be better to make regulators responsible for encouraging the right investment in the right parts of the digital economy rather than concentrating on constraining service providers, which is a hangover from the days when regulators needed to break up the old monopolies. That time is long gone.

Despite the infrastructure and value-added services being an obvious market for some of the larger communications providers, most growth in this sector has come from network equipment companies undertaking outsourced network operations. In 2012, roughly 20 percent of the world's mobile subscribers rely on managed network services from the four big network technology vendors.

Since the infrastructure business is highly capital intensive, it needs to be extremely efficient and leverage large economies of scale to be profitable, so volume is king. The more network operators that outsource their infrastructure operations to their suppliers, the more difficult their own potential entry into this sector because they are diluting their economies of scale by handing over responsibility for, or ownership of, assets to their outsourcing providers.

However, even when operators outsource, they are usually smart enough to hang on to the 'crown jewels' – their most valuable assets, including radio spectrum and operating licenses – so keeping control of the situation. Nevertheless, it may well be that in future operators don't buy technology from equipment suppliers, rather they buy a network capability, in other words, a managed service.

This is an obvious area for joint ventures or other cooperation between the managed services arms of the equipment providers and those network operators who want to pursue the enabling infrastructure market, as we explore in detail in Chapter 7.

Access networks

Access provision is a specific niche of the network provider layer: fixed access networks have always been seen as an integral part of overall network design but, recognizing that the 'last mile' is a heavy cost and commercial bottleneck, specialist access network providers are emerging either through regulatory action (such as in Australia, Singapore and the U.K.) or through joint ventures which own access network infrastructure. This is then made available to the joint owners and to others.

Mobile networks are by their nature access networks, since they only provide wireless connectivity from the mobile base station to the handset and then back-haul that traffic into the backbone network via fiber, DSL or microwave technologies. The costs of 3G rollout started the trend to access network sharing and joint ventures and the costs of 4G and future bandwidth technologies will accelerate this trend considerably. In fixed networking, the shift from copper access networks to fiber will also make the access sector very interesting.

Access is a major problem area for the development of the digital economy because network economics are geared to scale – the more concentrated the network, the cheaper the unit costs get. The inverse is also true and access networks, feeding service to an individual house or a small number of handsets, have a very high cost, especially in rural areas where population density is low. Thus access networks, especially outside urban areas, struggle to attract investment at the best of times. If they also have to contend with regulatory constraints on access pricing, often at marginal costs, the business case evaporates.

Not surprisingly, many countries are experiencing a serious 'digital divide' where concentrated urban areas are becoming well served with fast broadband wireless and fiber, while less populated areas suffer poor, slow service. Various schemes are being tried by governments to try to address this, including the formation of regulated monopolies like the National Broadband Company in Australia, or Nucleus Connect in Singapore, while others are providing grants or other incentives to incumbent operators to encourage more investment in very fast broadband. Still the pace of rollout is slow in many places: for example, my house is less than five kilometers from a major town in the U.K., yet I get less than 0.5Mbps via fixed broadband and a weak 2G wireless connection.

The first fiber-to-the home trials took place in the 1980s and the technology is very well proven, but the installed base is tiny compared to decades-old copper. The insatiable data demands of the digital economy will need substantial and sustained investment in access fiber and related 4G and 5G wireless technologies. So far, few governments have tackled the problem of how to make the access sector an attractive business proposition. Solving this problem will ultimately be more about politics and a realization that a vibrant digital economy is a major driver of the overall economic health of a country, so countries as well as companies will compete for a major slice of it. Those places that wake up first and move their regulatory actions to focus on encouraging inward investment rather than preventing progress will reap a rich harvest.

Cloud computing and storage service providers

Cloud computing is the delivery of processing capability as a virtualized service rather than a physical product like a server. It shares resources to exploit economies of scale, offering attractive pricing models. Consumers typically pay for what you use, (in the same way we pay for electricity) and hence it is sometimes referred to as utility computing. This market is at the apex of the Gartner hype curve[44] as interest in the sector reaches fever pitch.

It's not just computing that can be delivered using a cloud-based model. The term 'cloud' can refer to a wide range of application services and storage capabilities as well as raw computing horsepower delivered as a web-based, virtual service rather than as physical hardware and software. While the underlying concept goes back decades, the practical reality of cloud services is relatively recent, made possible by the availability of low-cost broadband networks, processing and storage devices combined with advanced software techniques such as virtualization[45], service-oriented architectures and autonomic[46] computing.

The term *cloud* comes from the cloud symbol often used to represent a network. Until the 1990s communications providers generally supplied dedicated point-to-point data circuits but moved to offering Virtual Private Network services with comparable quality of service at a much lower cost. This was because they could balance utilization as they saw fit and were able to exploit their overall network bandwidth more effectively. The cloud symbol was used to mark the point between the provider's responsibility and the user.

Cloud services extend this concept – it's a 'black box' type of service where you neither know nor care what's inside it, all you care about is what it gives you. Cloud services are typically sold on demand, usually by the minute, by the hour or by the transaction. The service is dynamic and scalable (or 'elastic' as in Amazon's descriptive product name) – a user can have as much or as little of a service as they want at any given time. The service is fully managed by the cloud service provider.

Amazon played a key role in the development of cloud computing by optimizing its data centers, which, like most computer networks, were designed for peak demands but in general only ran at a fraction of their capacity (as low as 10 percent). As new cloud architecture resulted in big efficiency improvements, Amazon initiated a product development effort to provide cloud computing to external customers and launched Amazon Web Service (AWS) on a utility computing basis back in 2006.

The company was soon followed by many others, including a number of European Commission-funded projects, and the cloud concept was given a big boost by Gartner and other commentators. Cloud is now a rapidly growing reality across a range of services on a public,

---

[44]www.gartner.com/technology/research/methodologies/hype-cycle.jsp
[45]Virtualization hides the physical characteristics of a computing platform from users, instead showing another abstract computing platform
[46]Autonomic computing refers to the self-managing characteristics of distributed computing resources, adapting to unpredictable changes while hiding intrinsic complexity to operators and users

private and hybrid basis. Public clouds are available to anyone with a valid credit card while a private cloud is a proprietary facility that supplies services to a closed user group, typically within a company. A hybrid is the virtual private cloud where a service provider uses partitioned public cloud resources to create or augment their private cloud.

Cloud services can be broadly divided into three categories:

- Infrastructure-as-a-Service (IaaS) refers to cloud computing, storage and networking that replaces the physical versions of the same thing.
- Platform-as-a-Service (PaaS) is usually a set of software and product development tools hosted on the service provider's infrastructure (such as GoogleApps or Force.com) where developers can create applications remotely on the service provider's platform. Today, these tools and indeed much of the cloud market is proprietary in nature with few standards for interoperability or data portability. Some providers will not allow software created by their customers to be moved off the provider's platform. This issue is being tackled by groups such as TM Forum's Enterprise Cloud Leadership Council, the Distributed Management Task Force and the U.S. National Institute of Standards and Technology (better known as NIST). The market will almost certainly need to come to consensus on standards soon, otherwise growth and competition will be limited.
- Software-as-a-Service (SaaS) is the most potent area for rapid growth in the digital world because the barriers to entry for innovators are low through leveraging IaaS services to avoid large capital set-up costs. SaaS service providers provide application functions again as a 'black box', that is they shield the end user from having to worry about any underlying hardware and software. The user can interact with the service through a browser on any type of device from anywhere. SaaS is a broad market already and will become vast as the digital world expands.

Digital service enablers
The industry doesn't yet have universally accepted terminology to describe the cloud world and the types of provider and segments within it. As I indicated in Figure 5, I use 'digital service enabler' as a generic name applying to providers of all of the underpinning technology, software, network and computing infrastructure that a digital service needs – in other words the IaaS and PaaS layers described above. It's an imprecise term but I mean the enabling capabilities that the SaaS provider might provide for themselves, but more likely would want to buy from a provider that can provide it at scale, more economically.

In addition to the underlying infrastructure services of computing, networking and storage, a digital service provider will likely also need common services such as security and authentication; catalog management; revenue management services such as charging, settlements and fraud management; monitoring services, such as quality of service metrics, problem and service level agreement management, and customer relationship management;

as well as services which allow digital service providers to directly interact and control the underlying infrastructure, such as the network.

These are value-added services that can be provided in addition to infrastructure services. They are an attractive proposition for network, cloud computing and storage service providers. The provision of such capabilities is appealing as it helps them differentiate their services and generates additional revenue while helping to avoid a purely utility positioning that could be marginalized on price.

Many infrastructure providers already operate these types of capability for their own internal use and have a high level of competency in them, so it would be a natural fit to provide a broad range of enabling services externally to digital service providers on a 'white label' basis (that is, that the digital service providers can rebrand as their own). Such services will be an important factor as enterprise-class digital services (aimed at various industry sectors and used for strategically important purposes) become more prevalent.

As examples, both Verizon and AT&T are already offering a range of enabling services. As they build this enabling service portfolio, they are also creating the opportunity to aggregate their various platforms into packages to be sold to different vertical sectors.

The communications sector is learning fast from early forays that enable third parties to leverage their infrastructure: initial attempts were often hard to use, delivered too little or the provider tried to charge too much. The second generation of enabling platforms is now becoming more successful, such as Telefónica' s BlueVia business, a global program that helps developers take their apps, web services and ideas to market.

The program enables other operators to bill their users for apps and then share the revenues with the app's developers. Portugal's PT Sapo is also providing some interesting capabilities and helping drive some of its ideas into international standards. In Asia, Hong Kong's PCCW and CSL are also very active in these 'enabling' markets.

Paul Berriman at PCCW views interactive services enablement for media content, applications and transactional services as vital: "In PCCW, we've modeled our company around these principles and view that continuous adaptation and innovation of compelling offerings is the only way to remain relevant."

Developing tailored capabilities that enable useful service offerings in specific verticals is a smart strategy – it leverages the existing competencies of the infrastructure-based players and taps into the creativity of specific sectors that understand their own business, like financial services, healthcare, automotive and retail, among many others. I'll develop this idea in more detail later on, but leveraging what you know how to do to exploit new opportunities is much less risky that making huge leaps into unfamiliar markets and areas. Key to success here are competencies, such as:

- managing large-scale infrastructure to provide highly reliable, quality services that others trust to run their business on;
- the ability to broker and manage relationships with many different partners, offering tailored services to each customer segment;
- the flexibility to cater for the needs of different partners with different business models; and
- the capacity to aggregate platforms and services into attractive packages for business partners.

Despite notable exceptions, many large infrastructure players are not good at managing partnerships, often because they have been such a dominant player in their market – as we'll see later, and particularly in Chapter 7, building a successful and sustaining ecosystem of partners and treating them equably is an essential skill.

Digital service providers

Digital service providers create and deliver services that provide applications for the end user from an individual consumer (for example Ancestry.com) or to an enterprise (such as Salesforce.com). There is a very broad range of services in this segment – content, communications, medical, application, messaging, gaming, social networking services and so on. Online digital services have big economic and operational advantages over their physical counterparts: for instance, much reduced support and maintenance requirements as well as less need to maintain variants of the software for different end-user hardware. Providers also get big economies of scale as their user base grows.

These services are cloud-based and can be used on multiple devices (smartphones, tablets, ultrabooks, smart TVs and so on) through browsers or very thin client applications. They are often demand-based (that is, pay-as-you-go or subscription-based) and are highly scalable, making them attractive to the changing needs of both consumers and enterprises.
Until recently, the term 'service provider' was synonymous with a communications service provider, but with the massive growth of many types of digital service provider, we will need to qualify the term because there will be thousands of niches for new service providers to occupy, such as application service provider, content service provider and so on.

Communications services fall into this category and increasingly existing circuit-switched voice and SMS services will be replaced by digital applications but, as I said in Chapter 1, these may not come from today's communications service providers. Few have yet succeeded in launching digital services outside their established portfolio, although there are notable exceptions, such as PCCW in Hong Kong.

Paul Berriman says: "We've been transforming to meet the demanding, tech-aware, customer base in this part of the world with customer-controlled media such as on-demand streaming media, music, home shopping, home management, machine-to-machine and eHealth programs. We have incorporated a fully personalized experience into how offerings are viewed, managed and visualized, extended to remote locations through smartphone virtualization and these initiatives have enabled us to create a high degree of customer satisfaction, enhancing our revenues and customer loyalty along with retention of our traditional access products."

Machine-to-machine services – the growth of the 'Internet of things'

Digital services are not just aimed at people: the biggest area of growth will be the emerging machine-to-machine (M2M) sector. Rather like cloud, M2M services are the subject of huge hype, but aren't new: a range of specialized telemetry applications has been around for a long time – even the humble fax machine was an M2M service. Mobile M2M services have been around for at least a decade with services like OnStar's in-vehicle security, communications and diagnostics system.

The economics of M2M services are changing fast and approaching a mass-market tipping point. Early on they typically relied on expensive, specialized networks, hardware and software but today the growth in M2M is driven by the same mechanisms as the overall digital world: ubiquitous, standardized, low-cost wireless communications and high functionality mass-market applications. Estimates of the market size vary widely: the GSMA[47] estimates that the market will be almost as big as the whole of the communications sector today by 2020, at $1.2 trillion, with over 12 billion connected mobile devices. Dave Evans, Cisco's Chief Futurist, puts the estimate higher at 50 billion[48] with the adoption of IPv6[49] supporting almost limitless connectivity by that time. No wonder it has caught the imagination of the entire communications business.

Already more 'things' are connected to the Internet than people – and according to Evans, the big growth is likely to be in sensor networks, using low-power sensors that collect, transmit, analyze and distribute data on a massive scale. Such sensors, based on standards like Zigbee[50] are being embedded in everything from smart appliances and smart meters to shoes, asthma inhalers and medical exploratory surgery devices.

To exploit this, more and more mobile providers are forming joint ventures with companies like Qualcomm, Honeywell and many others. In the U.S., in addition to Verizon's tie-up with Qualcomm, AT&T has an agreement with Jasper Wireless to support the creation of M2M devices and exploit the growing connectivity between consumer electronics and M2M wireless networks. They have been joined by KPN, Rogers Communications and Telcel/America Movil, to work together on the creation of an M2M site, which will serve as a hub for developers of M2M

[47]Formerly known as GSM Association
[48]Cisco IBSG
[49]IPv6 (Internet Protocol version 6) is the latest version designed to overcome limits on the number of IP connected devices and has virtually limitless capacity: 2^{128}
[50]www.zigbee.org/Home.aspx

communication electronics. Sprint and Axeda Corporation have announced an M2M alliance and recently Aeris Communications announced it is providing M2M telematics services for Hyundai Motor Corporation.

In Europe, Telenor Connexion in Sweden has launched services across segments as diverse as logistics, fleet management, car safety, healthcare and smart metering of electricity consumption. Vodafone, Verizon Wireless and nPhase (the joint venture set up by Verizon Wireless and Qualcomm in 2009, fully owned by Verizon since January 2012) announced a strategic alliance to provide global M2M solutions that would offer their customers an easy way to roll out M2M solutions across Europe and the U.S. Germany's E-Plus estimates that by 2013 over 5 million connections on their network will be M2M-related with the main growth areas being tracking and tracing applications (growing at around 30 percent a year) and connected consumer electronics (growing at nearly 50 percent a year).

The possibilities for M2M in the digital world are endless and are usually driven by economic or environmental factors. Both come into play in the energy and utilities sectors where early adopters include 'smart' utility companies, using M2M in both energy production – such as oil and gas – as well as energy distribution through smart meters and more dynamic load management. For example, remote sensors can monitor an oil production site with details such as pressure, flow rates and temperatures or even fuel levels in on-site equipment. In return, remote management systems can automatically adjust on-site equipment to maximize efficiency.

Smart electricity grids make widespread use of M2M services and devices such as Automated Metering Infrastructure, which makes use of two-way connectivity between the meter and the central management systems. They can be extended into smart devices such as smart air conditioning, hot water, heating and so on, to manage consumption intelligently. Smart appliances are at the heart of what is known as demand response capabilities, where customers are incentivized to allow power companies to proactively manage the timing and quantity of power supplied to individual appliances.

This combination of automated metering, intelligent appliances and demand response is often referred to as Home Area Networks or home grids and present other opportunities, such as home security.

Vehicle and traffic telematics is another major growth area for M2M. With more than a billion vehicles around the world today[51] and the potential of 80 million new cars and light commercial vehicles being sold each year by 2020 (half of which may be in China), this sector is driven by a combination of economic and environmental issues, plus differentiation between manufacturers. For example, sensors can monitor variables such as traffic volume and speed while centralized management software controls maximize traffic flow by dynamically altering traffic-control signals and variable informational signs.

[51]Wards Auto Research http://wardsauto.com/ar/world_vehicle_population_110815/

Vehicle monitoring supports functions such as engine and system diagnostics; automatic crash notifications to the police; stolen vehicle monitoring; vehicle fleet tracking and tracing; real-time traffic and navigation capabilities, weather and parking information; state of charge monitoring and so on for electric vehicles. A number of communications companies are very active in this sector – for example, Vodafone has partnerships with Hyundai, Kia and Ford. AT&T is set to provide BMW Assist services while Verizon and Telenor Connexion have numerous vehicle and telematics partnerships and applications.

The 'smart home' applications of M2M are also growing, offering everything from remote video surveillance, residential security and home energy management, entertainment and even the much vaunted 'smart fridge'. Global annual expenditure on surveillance equipment and services alone is forecast to grow to $18 billion by 2015[52] with China as the largest single market.

Home video surveillance as a service (VSaaS) is emerging and again some communication players are at the forefront. Verizon Wireless offers its Home Monitoring and Control service, which allows users to bundle together different services like phone, Internet, cable, home automation and security features like motion detectors, remote access control and surveillance cameras. AT&T has acquired Xanboo, a provider of smart building solutions for residential and small business customers.

Healthcare is yet another great candidate for M2M. It is an enormous business representing about 10 percent of GDP in mature markets and as high as 17 percent of GDP in the U.S. at about $2.5 trillion. As the world's population ages and medicine advances, healthcare costs are spiraling out of control, while many parts of the world still lack the resources to provide basic medical care. Chronic disease accounts for 75 percent of heath costs[53] in developed countries like the U.S.

So, economic and social pressures are spurring innovation in the healthcare sector and the use of M2M and other digital technologies is growing rapidly. M2M is an ideal solution for helping improve patient outcomes and reducing costs when monitoring and managing conditions such as diabetes, cardiac or respiratory problems and the growing issues of caring for elderly people. It's predicted that by 2015 there could be around 500 million 'eHealth' users globally[54] with the market for the technology aspects of such services worth more than $11 billion.

Services can vary from simple dosage monitors and reminders for patients on routine medicine through to heart patients who wear sensors that monitor their heart functions and relay the data back to a central medical function. In serious cases, this can also involve corrective action, such as triggering an implanted device that shocks the heart back into a correct rhythm. With 17 million deaths from heart attacks worldwide in 2010, according to the World Health Organization, this alone represents a major social and economic benefit as speedy treatment is critical in dealing with heart problems.

[52] Frost & Sullivan estimates
[53] US Center for Disease Control & Prevention
[54] BizReport and BCC Research estimates

For diabetes, a problem that is increasing as populations get richer and people get heavier, companies like AT&T in the U.S. and Rogers Communications in Canada have partnered with nPhase and Positive ID to provide an integrated solution for online blood-glucose monitoring and insulin management.

In the U.K., the world's largest trial of eHealth concluded in late 2011 and, as a result, its National Health Service plans to install M2M monitoring technology in 3 million homes over the next five years. The trial of 6,000 patients with conditions including heart disease, lung problems and diabetes showed that eHealth cut deaths by 45 percent and emergency hospital admissions by 21 percent. Some 120 lives were saved as a result of the technology, while local health providers spent 8 percent less on each patient.

Systems electronically monitor signs such as pulse, breathing, blood sugar and oxygen levels and automatically upload results to nurses who can contact patients at the first sign of trouble, with advice such as changing their medication or other measures. By spotting problems early, eHealth reduces the time they need to spend with their doctor, or in hospital.

The full rollout is expected to cost around $1.2 billion but is expected to *save* around $2 billion over the next five years in costs of care. U.K. Government Health Minister Paul Burstow said: "Without change, the rise in costs of caring for long-term conditions could overwhelm the National Health Service – eHealth is about changing the relationship between patients and clinicians so that people can be more in control of their life."

eHealth is a good example of the ecosystem at work and shows that M2M services aren't just about dreaming up a service and launching it on an unsuspecting world – these services are specialized and all require strong partnerships between companies with market specific expertise and digital services companies. Figure 6 (on page 54) shows some of this complexity and again highlights the need to be good at partnering to succeed – a theme I'll return to often and in detail in Chapter 7 – and also significant innovation both at the technology end as well as the specific application area (see Chapter 9).

Examples like these show that M2M will form a vitally important aspect of our digital lifestyle and of the digital world. It will change our physical world and the way that we live in many ways – some foreseeable, others less so. The fundamentals of the digital world are that it has the potential to deliver better services at lower costs and make possible things that were previously prohibitively expensive. Every day, designers, businesses, engineers, scientists, doctors and countless others are exploring new ways to utilize increasingly cost-effective M2M networks for new sources of revenue or new ways of improving people's lives and their environment.

Figure 6: The eHealth ecosystem involves many players

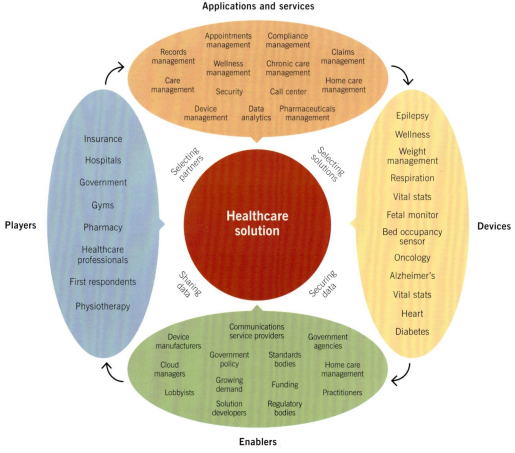

The impacts on our society – our health, well-being, environment, social interaction, government and education will be profound. By the end of this decade, we will look back and wonder how society could ever exist without the digital world. This is a major opportunity and one which undoubtedly will grow massively, giving a big advantage to those who take an early lead and establish the right competencies, partnerships and reputation.

Digital services retailers: stores, infomediaries and service aggregators

This is the sector where digital services meet the marketplace and may take several forms and business models. Today, many enterprise and many consumer services are delivered directly to the user. This approach is usually called 'over-the-top' – that is, riding over the network with the infrastructure provider not being involved beyond providing the transport. The increasing number and diversity of applications and services drives the need for digital stores where people can conveniently browse, compare and select the services they need, just like in a physical store. The first instance of this has been the App Store but the concept will grow rapidly and will expand to cover enterprises' needs.

Companies in this very important position in the ecosystem can gain control and influence over customers' purchases and customers' information, and intercept and influence revenue – Google, eBay, Amazon and Apple as well as comparison sites like Travelocity.com or Pricegrabber.com are prime examples of this. They have a powerful position that lets them intercept revenue from other industries that they could not tap into before and monetize it either directly (such as Apple and Amazon directly displacing record stores and book stores) or indirectly (like Google and Kelkoo) influencing purchasing in return for payments from sellers.

I referenced the work of John Hagel and Marc Singer earlier in this chapter, where they foresaw much of the shape of the digital world that is happening now. They coined the term 'infomediary' to describe companies whose rich store of customer information permits them to control the flow of business in the digital ecosystem and how they can analyze and monetize that store of information on the massive scale that is the key to success. Google first showed how such raw data could be transformed into valuable information, which could then be monetized by using advanced analytics in near real-time.

Facebook, Twitter and many others have followed, but surprisingly communications service providers haven't – this is strange considering that they arguably know a lot more about their customers. They often leave the information buried in vast quantities of unused raw data, instead of analyzing it to produce useful information they could monetize either through improving their own marketing or selling it to third parties.

The rise of infomediaries is causing companies who used to sell directly to customers to rethink their role. They may have to give up their customer relationship functions entirely and concentrate on either developing products or running the infrastructure which supports them while a digital infomediary takes over the role of acquiring and managing customer relationships. Infomediaries develop a deep understanding of each customer and play a critical central role in determining what a customer buys, eventually coming to fulfill virtually all of a customer's purchasing needs.

The digital economy will see more and more retailers surrendering the customer relationship role to infomediaries – they are likely to be few, but with enormous (and worrisome) market power. Some may specialize in particular industry sectors, which represent a big opportunity for early movers. As I said earlier, the retail arms of communications service providers could also see their entire business melt away in a relatively short time. I expand on the opportunities and threats and the consequences for disrupting business models in Chapter 3.

There are several types of digital infomediary.

Consumer digital stores: These are the most visible of the direct type of infomediary and an increasing number of consumer digital services are being retailed to customers via digital stores (such as Apple iTunes, Google Play or Amazon) where digital services from a range of providers are available for purchase. The concept equates to a bricks and mortar store where the retailer stocks goods from many suppliers and provides an enjoyable shopping experience for the end user with a huge choice. Like in a physical store, the digital retailer typically takes a percentage of the revenue (around 30 percent) in return for providing the supplier with a route to a very large market; for the payment and settlement process; and, most importantly, for leveraging the retailers' brand and market image. This part of the ecosystem is shown in Figure 7.

Figure 7 – Digital service retail value chain

Successful digital retailers are the ones who have created empathy with their customers, a level of user experience that sets it apart from competitors and the best possible combination of targeted applications and content. Apple and Amazon excel at this and in doing so gain deep insights into relevant customer segments, their needs and preferences. They stimulate buying through a lot of innovative tools that suggest additional purchases based on that understanding of their customer and customers with similar tastes.

The digital consumer market is extremely dynamic and competition is extremely fast moving. It is difficult for new entrants to compete as established digital stores have the brand, the customer base and the supplier base. A new entrant would need the following to begin to compete:

• the tools and techniques for analyzing and building an excellent understanding of the customers' needs and wants;

- dedication to creating the best customer experience possible, including the development of world-class user interfaces, strong customer management and great customer service; and
- developing innovative ways of interacting with customers and helping them buy things they didn't know they wanted or didn't know existed – Amazon's recommendation engine is perhaps the best-known example.

Despite what I have said about the communications sector being slow off the mark, the 'grand-daddy' of this type of digital retailing is actually a communications company: NTT DoCoMo of Japan, whose i-Mode mobile Internet service was launched in Japan back in February 1999. It offered downloadable content and apps before digital stores like iTunes, which launched in January 2001. It continues to offer a huge variety of innovative services, including an e-wallet, an advanced personalized information app combining data from a variety of sources, access to music, video clips and games. DoCoMo has also broadened its offerings into the enterprise sector, offering innovative services to industries as diverse as industrial equipment, automobiles, information appliances and broadcasting.

As with Apple, DoCoMo's strategy is to have complete and end-to-end control of the ecosystem and this helped it achieve top ranking in its market for customer satisfaction, a major contributor to the rapid growth of its customer base. However, while this end-to-end control allowed DoCoMo to achieve strong quality management and a great customer experience in its home market, i-Mode didn't travel well and was not successfully exported.

Most communications companies have attempted to either recreate DoCoMo's model or compete with Apple and others. None has been particularly successful; Vodafone Live! and Vodafone 360, for example, didn't flourish. All the communication providers' attempts are hampered by the same core factors: they lack a critical mass of app suppliers because they can't offer big enough markets compared to Apple and Google. In the past at least, this was often combined with a fatal arrogance regarding revenue sharing and other onerous terms and conditions.

The communications industry recognizes the problem, but has yet to find a solution. As I said in Chapter 1, the Wholesale Applications Community was set up to provide a uniform infrastructure and basket of application services to app developers on a common platform, to help mobile operators to compete with the likes of Apple. Progress is inevitably slow because all partners want to have a say in how it evolves and in such a fast-moving market this is a big impediment: time is rapidly running out if it is to succeed.

Enterprise digital service aggregators. Despite their success in high-growth consumer markets, the consumer digital store players have not yet made an impact on providing an equivalent range of digital services to enterprises. Enterprise markets have been slower to adopt digital services over the established approach of having their own software resident on their own servers, but Software-as-a-Service (SaaS) is now becoming more mainstream and sales are accelerating quickly. Global spending on SaaS is predicted to rise by nearly 18 percent in 2012 and expected to hit $22.1 billion by 2015, according to Gartner.

SaaS providers focus on business applications such as Salesforce.com for sales management capability or Netsuite and Officebooks for general accounting. Software suppliers like Oracle and SAP have both been investing strongly in the SaaS market with Oracle buying cloud-based talent management and employee recruitment software vendor Taleo for roughly $1.9 billion and SAP's move to acquire SuccessFactors, a close competitor of Taleo, for $3.4 billion.

Enterprises will need a variety of these business services and so larger companies are forming multi-service suites (for example, Oracle's Fusion brand) but a new type of infomediary is also forming, called the digital service aggregator – a cross between a digital store and a digital services integrator. These players aggregate a spectrum of SaaS services into sector-specific or even customer-specific packages. Their role is analogous to systems integrators, who combine software and hardware into solutions to meet a client's needs.

This kind of aggregated offering is attractive to small and medium-sized enterprises which, unlike larger enterprises, lack the in-house resources and expertise to manage the increasingly complex IT and communications infrastructure their businesses rely on. There will also be a growing market demand for such services from large enterprises. Meeting their needs will require even more specific skills and knowledge of targeted sectors such as healthcare, transport, government, education, retail and financial services.

Digitally savvy consumers and companies are increasingly expecting access to applications, digital content and services while on the road, literally. For example, many company's workers need real-time access to corporate applications while en route to the next job or more efficient use of travel time to log information about completed work.

In either case, the company wins by enabling 'on the road' employees to be more productive. The employee gets home sooner instead of sitting in the office doing paperwork, which then probably needs to be entered into the corporate systems by another employee. There is great scope to increase employees' productivity and improve morale. In most cases, there is also a huge potential to cut costs at both the micro (company-specific) and macro (industry and community) levels when these solutions are deployed across industry sectors.

Take a small plumbing firm: it needs computers, phones, job estimation and sales quotation software; order processing; parts inventory management; customer billing; accounts receivable; general ledger and payroll processing; plus workforce and fleet management among other things. In the past, the cost and complexity of this usually means that the firm makes do with whatever it can stitch together, putting it at a disadvantage compared with larger rivals, and would typically be unable to meet the costs of hardware, software licenses and specialist support – the firm's employees are not likely to know much about how to configure, manage and maintain it.

Today, a service aggregator could offer the plumbing firm a 'one-stop shop', a single package of cloud-based services providing all these capabilities and related support, including cloud-based computing capacity and connectivity. The plumbing firm can buy the lot in one, integrated service contract, complete with a single customer support point on the basis of pay-for-what-you-use, typically priced on the number of users who are authorized to access the application(s).

In this aggregated digital services model, small firms can now have access to advanced applications and supporting IT capabilities (such as remote storage, backup and retrieval of files) that previously would have been available to larger companies. They can 'pay as they grow' and are spared the expense of in-house IT staff and the cost and difficulties associated with managing increasingly complex computing and communications infrastructure and business applications. Best of all, more and more of these SaaS applications can be made available to users on any number of end user devices, such as smartphones, tablets or PCs, so they can be used anywhere, giving the firm much greater business flexibility.

Cloud-based services also offer compelling cost and productivity advantages to those on the supply side of the equation. The aggregator does not necessarily have to create or own each application service, it could package a diverse assortment of cloud-based applications and related support capabilities procured from any number of ecosystem partners such as application and content providers, communications wholesalers and so on. These services needn't be purely cloud-based either – they could take on some human element as well.

In the plumbing firm, for example, the service aggregator could offer a service to the plumbers to handle their customer enquiries, billing and collections tailored to its specific needs. Add to that all of the integration between the individual applications and services to provide a completely integrated solution bundle, either directly to the plumbing firm itself or in partnership with a service enabler(s).

The broker/aggregator role provides a lot of added value to the underlying services packaged together because it would be aimed at and tuned to specific industries or sectors' business needs. Such bundles tend to be very 'sticky' (that is customers tend to stay with the provider) because switching to another supplier may be too disruptive for the business. The market is estimated to grow at a CAGR approaching 30 percent and be worth something in the region of $75 billion by 2015[55].

[55]Estimates: IDC

To capture a share of this market, with its dynamic and sophisticated delivery model, aspiring aggregators must invest properly in time and energy as well as capital to establish a highly automated, efficient and secure cloud services delivery and management environment, with cost-effective, complementary supporting operations.

Some aspiring cloud service providers are opting to start small and learn by their mistakes, but this can damage the reputation for this type of service in the marketplace. Others are jumping in with both feet, often with the help of one or more large IT partners, in an attempt to capture market share in the early stages and ride the growth curve.

Typically it is smaller companies or those without an established software applications business that are making the early running – as we've discussed, it's nearly always difficult for established and successful businesses to switch business models for fear of hurting revenue streams.

The cloud-based aggregator model ought to be extremely attractive to today's communications service providers. They have large customer bases of enterprises, strong brand recognition, major service delivery and support experience and capabilities, and a host of key assets – such as their billing and operational systems – that should be ideal to support this aggregated service delivery paradigm. Just as it is attractive for them to broaden their base of infrastructure services from networking to providing a whole suite of enabling IaaS services, they could also extend out from communications services to a much richer set of revenue-generating services, almost certainly working with application partners. Some of the larger IT and cloud service players see communications companies as a desirable, go-to-market partner.

When she was with IBM, Deb Osswald[56] developed the strategy for and championed the concept of the 'Cloud Service Provider Platform', a combination of hardware, software and services designed to provide communications companies around the world with the comprehensive service-enabling infrastructure they need to enter and thrive in this new market cost-effectively.

IBM's approach took as its base the concept of the 'Service Grid', another idea developed by John Hagel[57] (his name came up time and time again in my research for this book), which describes the business and technical basis for the kind of service aggregation I have outlined above. Hagel describes a layer of functionality that's required to solve key problems surrounding security, reliability, transaction integrity, billing and orchestration of functions that are core competencies of communications service providers.

Other companies like Microsoft have refocused their organization to put more emphasis on developing communications companies as 'sell through' partners and many of the communications players are recognizing the opportunity, even if many are not yet sure what to do about it.

[56]Now with industry analyst IDC
[57]John Hagel: *Out of the Box: Strategies for Achieving Profits Today and Growth Tomorrow Through Web Services* – Harvard Business Press Books, 2005. ISBN 9781591397595

This combination of 'push and pull' is certainly having an effect. According to Informa Telecoms & Media's Telecom Cloud Monitor[58], headed by Camille Mendler, the number of communications companies offering cloud services had doubled in the 18 months to the end of 2011, to around 120, and around $13.5 billion was being invested annually in building up data center assets.

Although $13.5 billion sounds like and is a lot of money, it is small compared to the hundreds of billions invested each year in networks. The types of cloud services on offer are roughly evenly split between enabling IaaS and aggregated business services generally provided in partnership with third parties. Figure 8 shows the current breakdown and service mix of the cloud portfolios of communications companies.

Figure 8: Communication players' cloud portfolio 2011

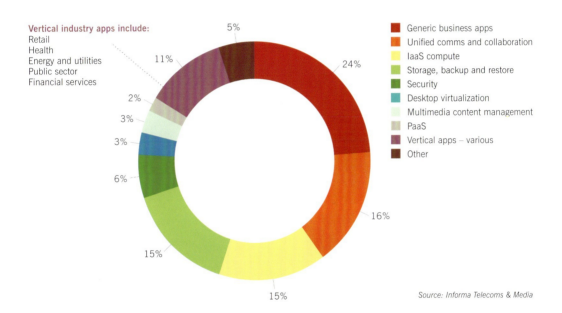

Vertical industry apps include:
Retail
Health
Energy and utilities
Public sector
Financial services

Generic business apps
Unified comms and collaboration
IaaS compute
Storage, backup and restore
Security
Desktop virtualization
Multimedia content management
PaaS
Vertical apps – various
Other

Source: Informa Telecoms & Media

Perhaps reflecting the chilly economic winds blowing through Europe, providers there lag a long way behind North America and Asia in making the largest and most strategic investments: the most visible early runners being Korea Telecom, Softbank, NTT and Telstra in Asia, and AT&T, CenturyLink, Verizon and Windstream in the U.S.

One of the continuing issues that dogs the idea of aggregation is the lack of any appropriate cloud standards that will help this kind of ecosystem to flourish. Everyone is 'doing their own thing', designing their own technical interfaces (called application programming interfaces or

[58]www.informatandm.com/cloud-monitor/

APIs) which are multiplying exponentially as different digital and cloud service providers, stores and communications service providers enter the market. At the end of March 2012 when I was writing this chapter, there were over 5,500[59] such APIs, only some six months since passing the 4,000 mark.

Figure 9: API growth over time

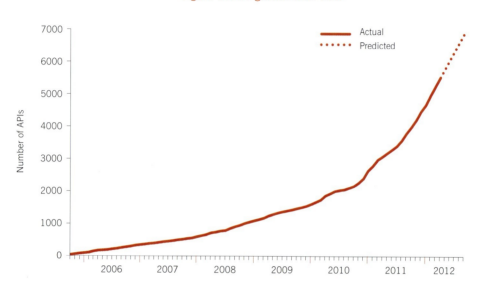

Source: *ProgrammableWeb.com*

In the phone business – where common standards allow you to tap 10 digits into any phone in the world to speak to anybody else on the planet – the end user doesn't see what happens behind the scenes to make sure everyone gets billed and paid. Standards allow all communications service providers to form one gigantic federated service delivery platform. This isn't true for the wider base of digital services and in fact, the problem gets worse every day as each of these players tries to differentiate itself through a different approach.

The costs of managing the seamless delivery of digital services to customers from many diverse and incompatible sources are likely to render them economically unviable unless standards appear to enable their straightforward integration. Although standards are in place to interconnect IP networks, standards for managing service level agreements, order management, catalog management, billing and so on have yet to be agreed in the digital services world. This is not for want of trying by standards bodies, it's more that the players involved have not yet fully understood how the market works – though they have millions of customers individually, digital service providers need access to billions of customers to make sustainable profits.

[59]www.informatandm.com/cloud-monitor/

Device providers

Devices are the vital technology layer that allows us to interact with the digital world and make it useable. Originally this was the PC and that early iteration of the digital world was something you peered into from your desk. This has changed dramatically through smartphones, tablets, ultrabooks, eReaders, smart TVs and soon it will be your car or fridge. As I described in Chapter 1, as the volume production of devices rises, their prices will fall, further accelerating the usability and variety of applications, making devices more appealing. This cycle is resulting in and will continue to cause the digital tsunami.

Technology evolution means that these devices will get smaller, lighter, more powerful and cheaper in rapid waves, making the PC as obsolete as the mini computer and mainframe before it. Unlike PCs, which offered only a singular, static portal into the digital world, the explosion in the number of connected mobile devices means users want to move seamlessly from device to device and get the same information and experience every time. This is increasingly met by cloud-based approaches, which push more and more capabilities, particularly storage, outside the device itself. This in turn means that the devices themselves can be lighter, faster and cheaper.

The advent of the Xerox-designed windows and mouse environment was a step-change in how people interacted with information, causing the legendary spat between Bill Gates and Steve Jobs. Some 20 years later, the development of touch-screen devices has been the next huge leap, enabling us to interact in a much more human way: touch-screen devices are instant-on, low weight, have no wires or moving parts, have few holes for dust to get into and are not constrained by the need for a keyboard.

Through all these attributes, they open up the digital world into many situations where a PC, even a laptop, would be impractical, allowing a whole new range of business applications. They change the way applications work, letting users zoom in and control with their fingertips, while GPS and accelerometers give applications an 'understanding' where they are and which way up they are. Already tablets and specialized apps are finding uses in a range of jobs, from archeology to surgeons, from engineers to chat-show hosts.

The tablet and PC market has big implications for established players. Most obvious is the impact on Microsoft, which unless Windows Mobile can turn the tide has seen its market share of interconnected devices become ever more rapidly diluted by the boom in smartphones, tablets and eReaders.

Another big potential loser is Google, as users turn to using apps as their way of reaching the information they need rather than indexed searches, which are falling as a percentage of ways people find what they need on the web. There are three main reasons for this – apps provide an instant way of getting the information you need in a format that is optimized to the device you are using. Indexed searches take longer and lead you first into an increasingly cluttered web and when you find what you want, the experience may not be ideal for your device. Third, apps are increasingly favored by businesses over search because they can carry their logo and be used in advertisements and other promotions via a Quick Response[60] (QR) code.

I look at Google's situation in more detail in the next chapter, *Life and death in the digital world,* as an example of the fact there is no guarantee that even the trailblazers in the digital world will prevail. Nor are their business models invincible, because there's always someone after your turf and you don't control all external factors, such as regulators, public confidence and users' changing preferences.

The strengthening bond between devices (or at least device operating systems) and digital retailing is important: this link was, of course, innovated by Apple and successfully followed the other way round by Google through their entry into devices with Android (Google Play) and Amazon's move through the Kindle. As all have shown, the combination of a well-featured device and a well-stocked digital store all wrapped in a great customer experience is an important combination in expanding the connected device market. The more services and applications are available, the more attractive the device and the more features are supported by the device (processor speed, memory, screen capabilities and so on), the better digital services work.

The key to success is a close coupling between the device provider and the digital services and app providers, enabling them to reach a large market, combined with an easy, well-supported developer environment. This highly controlled 'closed loop' of devices, operating system and store, was originally pioneered by DoCoMo but taken to far greater heights by Apple.

The Android and Microsoft's Windows Mobile are operating systems supported on a variety of hardware platforms so the environment offered to application providers is not so tightly controlled as Apple's. Nokia's attempt at a store tie-in through its operating system Symbian and its Ovi store brand failed to create this symbiotic relationship and is now being merged under the Windows brand as part of the cooperation with Microsoft and Samsung has replaced Nokia as the world's largest phone maker.

Time will tell if more open models work, but without the necessary, well-defined, open standards, the chances are slim. This could lead to an unappealing series of closed 'parallel universes' where each supplier controls its own ecosystem and users have to choose which one they want to be in. With Apple reputedly making more margin from the iPad than rivals can command as retail sales prices, you can see that the closed model is hugely attractive for the combined device and store provider. Arguably it is less so for everyone else!

---

[60]QR codes can store addresses and URLs and may appear in magazines, on signs, business cards etc

M2M connected devices. M2M connected devices are, by their nature, a much broader spectrum of device types than devices used by humans, like smartphones and tablets. The predicted 50 billion or so M2M devices being installed over the next few years will come in a huge variety of types. Many won't accommodate any kind of human interaction – they will be embedded in sensors under the hood of your car or under your stairs.

As the average monthly revenue from M2M devices will be a small fraction of those from devices like smartphones (probably around $3 per device) so to maintain margins similar to those from phones, operating costs need to be held in the $1.4 to $1.6 range through highly cost-effective provisioning, management and diagnostics. With such low incomes per device, management of them will need to be totally automated and highly standardized, requiring common management standards across the many devices used for so many different M2M applications.

Unlike phones, M2M devices will have their SIM[61] installed during the manufacturing process. Even a single customer, like an electricity company or auto-manufacturer, will need to provision many thousands of devices, which may be deployed on many different networks around the world, making the provisioning, authentication and ongoing management processes much more complex than for handsets.

Early market leaders like N-Phase and Jasper Wireless have introduced their own M2M management platforms to provide operational capabilities, such as:

• automated, bulk provisioning;
• wireless connectivity optimization;
• maintenance, troubleshooting and remote restoration; and
• service authentication, continuity and security.

These operational needs have a great impact on the costs of ownership and lifecycle costs for whoever is operating the M2M services the devices are connected to. If different devices have varied operational characteristics, then the operating costs will become substantial across multiple service providers – a classical many-to-many management problem. As we have seen in mobile networking, operators are rapidly moving to operational standardization and automation to cut costs in the face of shrinking profit margins.

When faced with many billions or possibly trillions of devices to manage, these needs will multiply and any early market advantages of differentiation at the operational level will melt away in the face of economies of scale. Standardization bodies such as TM Forum, which specializes in operational management issues (see Chapter 14), should become proactive in the underlying device management issues for M2M, drawing on the expertise of pioneering market entrants and existing, proven management techniques and architectures.

[61]Subscriber identity module

3

LIFE AND DEATH IN THE DIGITAL WORLD

"We believe that if we focus on the users, the money will come... if you're successful, you'll be working at something that's so necessary that people will pay for it" – Marissa Mayer, Google

"We knew we'd be successful when we were no longer cool – when we were such an integral part of people's lives that they took us for granted" – Mark Zuckerberg, Facebook

1889 Oklahoma Land Rush

So far we've looked at what the digital ecosystem is and the principal niches within it. Much of the rest of the book is about getting to where you want to be with as much success as possible. So in this chapter, I want to look at how some companies have succeeded and how some have failed and see what we can learn from both. Many of the secrets of success of the digital world are the same ones that business schools have taught for years – despite the hype, technology doesn't change the laws of economics and fundamentals of good management.

In Chapter 2, I talked about the digital economy having the capacity to reduce interaction costs (or friction) and this was allowing companies to disaggregate. In turn, disaggregation drives new business models – multi-sided structures where everyone is simultaneously a buyer and a seller, and models where the user and the customer are two different things. Sometimes, you just have to experiment to see what works. The early digital economy players have had a lot of room for experimentation with large amounts of venture capital investment flowing in the good years. Most of the big digital players today have evolved their business models through progressive experimentation and repositioning.

When the pioneers were taking part in the Oklahoma Land Rush in the U.S. back in the 1880s, they didn't survey the territory carefully or employ consultants to advise them. They didn't do an exhaustive cost-benefit analysis and develop a five-year strategic plan – they just set out to grab as much land as possible before their rivals got there. They didn't work out the percentages of nitrogen or phosphate in the soil that would be idea to grow their chosen crops – they just took what land they could and then worked out what to grow on it.

The early days of the digital world have been rather like that land grab – staking a claim to as many users as possible, as fast as possible and then working out how to monetize them. Some of the territory that the Oklahoma pioneers won turned out to be highly valuable arable land, while some had only poor quality grazing, but at least they had a stake and something to build on. So too will the land grab in the digital world continue – in fact, it's accelerating: Facebook took nearly six years to reach a base of 10 million users, Twitter did it in three years and Pinterest did it in less than one year – the fastest-growing independent website so far. Instagram took less than two years to reach 30 million users and a $1 billion valuation when it was acquired by Facebook.

Not everyone succeeds of course – some business models may just not work but at least they have a stake and a shot at success: those who sit on the sidelines analyzing and grumbling definitely don't. History shows us that many who idly reminisce about the good old days are the very players that *should* have won: they were generally top dogs in a market but failed to change fast enough when a major discontinuity came along and went into decline. The digital world is arguably the biggest discontinuity the global economy has ever seen – and I would think it's reasonable to assume that the casualties will be in record numbers.

In Chapter 9, I'll describe in more detail the barriers to innovation, the importance of avoiding over-planning and the need to be flexible enough to learn a little, adapt a little and keep doing that until success is assured. That's my point about the land grab – get hold of some turf before someone else and then work out what to plant on it, not the other way round. In markets that are moving this fast, months or years of hesitation mean you end up with nothing: look at how the mobile operators talked for years about the huge value of location-based services, only to watch in horror as the handset guys built in GPS technology and got there first.

As they say in the comedy business: timing is everything, and the successful new entrants to the digital world have gone for speed and concentrated on growth of users at the expense of growth of revenue, relying on investors to cover the gap. Digital services, whether it's 'fair' or not, leverage somebody else's megabucks infrastructure, have fairly low barriers to entry and can scale with user growth rather than having to support massive initial investment. This process of grabbing territory first and then monetizing it clearly works – as Messrs. Bezos, Brin, Omidyar, Page, Stone, Zuckerberg, Zennström and many others prove. Whether this model turns out to be a paradigm shift or another bubble, only time will tell but, for now at least, it's too powerful to ignore.

Starting with the basics, the underlying success criteria for any company are straightforward: pick a market where you are addressing a real customer need (that's to say, deliver things people want, even if they didn't realize it to begin with); deliver a service that provides good value for money to whoever is ultimately paying the bill (the customer or the user – they're not the same thing); provide a great customer experience (because your customers can very easily switch to someone else); constantly innovate as the market evolves; and operate your business as efficiently and effectively as possible to ensure that you can still make good returns for your shareholders while pricing appropriately in the marketplace.

In the digital world, we also need to add some additional success factors: it's likely that excellence in software and innovation will also be key factors. Look at the winners that have emerged in the early stages of the digital economy – Google, Facebook, PayPal, Amazon, Skype, Twitter, eBay, Apple – all of them have been highly creative and software-centric.

Many were so creative that they invented things that we didn't know we needed until we saw them and then found that we couldn't live without them. Others have improved on ways of delivering services we need, but through innovation and software engineering have made the customer experience so rich and the price so attractive that we switch.

Compare this with some of the 'also-rans' in the early stages of the digital economy, such as MySpace, Bebo and Friends Reunited in the social networking sector, or the long list of bygone players such as Netscape, Excite, Infoseek, Lycos, Inktomi, Northern Light, AltaVista and, maybe soon, Yahoo! and AOL[62]. They all have their own stories to tell and I'm sure there were a great many factors in play. The bottom line is that they didn't shift the needle far enough by innovating something new and 'must have' or move radically enough from the old world.

Mostly they were just out-innovated by others: Google didn't win because of a bigger marketing budget, it achieved better results with an innovation called PageRank that prioritizes web pages based on the number and ranking of other websites and pages that link there, on the premise that good or desirable pages are linked more than others. Google also maintained a fast loading, minimalist interface to its search engine while many of its competitors embedded search in a complex web portal.

However, Google's big innovation wasn't just being a better 'mousetrap' than Netscape – it made search into a *business* in its own right by monetizing your search preferences to advertisers and defying the previous conventional wisdom that search was there to help draw traffic to your portal. Every time you search on Google, you enrich the knowledge that Google has that can be monetized – the cost of providing you with ultra-fast searches for information is returned at up to 10 times by providing information to the real Google customers: advertisers and businesses.

[62]Within days of each other in April 2012, Yahoo! announced the layoff of 2,000 employees, or 14 percent of its workforce, and AOL announced a deal to sell 800 patents to Microsoft for $1.056 billion

Nothing is actually free – there is an implicit bargain between the user and the provider, namely that the provider can monetize the user's information to a third party.

This 'trade off' between user and provider by which services are provided in exchange for the right to use your data is a fundamental step which supports later players, particularly Facebook, Twitter, LinkedIn, Skype, Pinterest and countless other 'free' services and apps. Whether this unwritten contract between provider and user will be sustained is an open question: will the 'land grab first, then monetize' model last or will users become increasingly concerned about privacy and break the model?

For one, Mark Zuckerberg[63] believes that society *has* shifted irrevocably in the direction of demanding less privacy: "People have really gotten comfortable not only sharing more information and different kinds, but more openly and with more people. That social norm is just something that has evolved over time." Perhaps, but when a $100 billion company's fortunes hang by this notion being true and staying true over time, it's worth asking the question.

At the risk of committing conventional wisdom heresy, I'm not sure the 'free' paradigm *will* sustain over time because that bargain is so easily damaged. The concept of privacy has been around a lot longer than Zuckerberg has been a squillionaire and I'm not yet convinced that large slices of the population have ceased to care about it – I think it just hasn't hurt them badly enough yet.

As Matt Bross said to me recently, "If one relatively small volcano in Iceland[64] can bring much of the civilized world to its knees for weeks – it is entirely possible that at some point in the future an event will cause a massive loss of confidence amongst large numbers of users when providing unrestricted data to people over whom they have no control."

There have already been a number of minor privacy scares that have caused people to think twice (like Facebook and LinkedIn quietly changing privacy settings or finding out that iPhone apps have been quietly raiding our contact lists). However, before long, a major event may occur that will be the catalyst for a rethink. Perhaps an authoritarian state will round up 'dissidents' identified from their Twitter, Facebook or Google usage. Or maybe clumsy data management will enable large amounts of personal data to reach the hands of someone with sinister motives. Such an event could trigger a worldwide rethink as people find themselves less willing to be so open about personal information.

Certainly, privacy will be a major issue in eHealth because of the possibility of mining healthcare records, illnesses and possible genetic 'predispositions' to certain diseases, diagnosis of conditions and so on, which would have big implications for who is charged what or given

[63]Founder and CEO of Facebook
[64]2010 eruptions of Eyjafjallajökull were volcanic events in Iceland which, although relatively small for volcanic eruptions, caused enormous disruption to air travel across western and northern Europe in April 2010. Additional localized disruption continued into May 2010

access to which treatments. Given the likely explosion in eHealth services over the next decade, as discussed in Chapter 2, I think this could catapult privacy issues onto center stage more than anything else.

There seems to be a growing awareness and unease about the implications of privacy and Google's business model. Richard Falkenrath[65], a man not averse to electronic surveillance, wrote in the *Financial Times* in February 2012, "Google, by gaining the consent of its users in the form of a quick tick, has secured the power to build an electronic surveillance apparatus that far exceeds anything the Bush administration tried to do."

He added, "A right to be forgotten would make the counterterrorism mission harder. My support for it, however, comes from my recent experience as a parent. Last year my children's school shifted to a system called Google Apps for Education. It works brilliantly and costs the school little or nothing. But as Google's policy makes clear, Google intends to integrate data derived from students' school activities with data from any of its other digital services – and use this to make money. Forever. The potential is vast."

Then there are regulators and legislators (see Chapter 5 for more on this subject), who have been making noises off and on, on both sides of the Atlantic and elsewhere about privacy concerns. In March 2012, European data protection authorities asked Google to respond to worries about its new privacy policy. France's data protection agency, CNIL, the lead agency representing regulators in Europe, wrote to Google's CEO Larry Page asking the company not to proceed with its new privacy regime because it had "legitimate concerns about the protection of the personal data of European citizens".

CNIL is worried that by merging the privacy policies of its different services, Google is making it impossible to work out which access rights, personal data and purposes apply to which service. It cited the example of Google being able to display ads on YouTube relating to the user's activity on an Android phone, guided by its location data. CNIL also pointed out that Google has more than 80 percent of the European search engine market and about 30 percent of its smartphone market, as well as 40 percent of the global online video market and more than 40 percent of the global online ad market.

Interestingly, Amazon's privacy policy or possible abuse of personal information seems to have gone unchallenged, although the company clearly has one of the most sophisticated means of gathering and using personal data of any in the digital economy.

So, in addition to the concerns about privacy, there are also hints that more anti-trust investigations could follow what so far have been little more than skirmishes. There have been

[65]Previously Deputy Commissioner of Counter-Terrorism of the New York City Police Department; Director for Proliferation Strategy on the U.S. National Security Council staff; Special Assistant to the President; and Senior Director for Policy and Plans within the Office of Homeland Security. Principal author of the National Strategy for U.S. Homeland Security; Senior Fellow at The Brookings Institution in Washington, D.C.

many studies about the effects on IBM and Microsoft, mostly in the 1990s, of fighting anti-trust actions against the U.S. Department of Justice and the European authorities in terms of cost and the huge resources required, as well as sapping the attention of top management. It's telling that Bill Gates openly admitted that Microsoft almost missed the rise of the Internet in the 1990s and, some would argue, never quite caught up.

Should a rival to Google's search, with or without a different business model, appear at just the right time when confidence has been undermined and there is a public outcry, the newcomer could be a runaway success and harm the digital advertising giant badly. Apple is already on the case with its voice recognition app Siri, which, among other things, allows you to search the web by voice command. And it isn't short on either resources or intent, with about $100 billion in its war chest at the time of writing.

There is also evidence to suggest that people are increasingly turning to their social networks and the online recommendations of family and friends for help with purchasing decisions rather than searching the web, perhaps not least because the introduction of personalized search at the end of 2009 automatically tailors – perhaps limits is a better word – the results. Also, people are rightly becoming suspicious of how search can be manipulated in other ways, such as by search engine optimization.

It's an interesting thought that while Twitter and Facebook have been instrumental in bringing down governments, they could also be used against each other: one of my friends recently told me that his teenage children don't use Facebook much any more because it's passé and they prefer to tweet. It is easy to imagine fashions driving the type of social network that people want to use, however, Facebook may be so far ahead of the pack that it could simply buy up any rival that it perceived threatened its dominance.

For now at least, most users of Google, Facebook et al aren't deserting in droves because of privacy concerns and most don't really worry about it. Both sides of the equation have an almost Faustian pact[66]: users get free benefits and the providers are winning the Oklahoma Land Grab.

We've seen what happens to the global financial system when confidence is lost – if there is no trust, nothing works and the same is true in the digital world: maintaining confidence through good practices and improving security levels is critical to its evolution. It is something that everyone aiming to enable the digital world needs to take very seriously indeed.

As I outlined in Chapter 1, the growth of data generated every moment of every day is staggering and the amount of it that needs to be secured is growing faster than our ability to safeguard it. Confidence is built on how information is used, shared, archived and managed.

[66]A deal struck with little thought for the consequences. In Christopher Marlowe's (1564-1593) play, Dr. Faustus traded his soul with the Devil in exchange for immediate powers

That relates to the origin of the information and the integrity of the processes and the systems that generate, capture and manage the information, as well as the credentials and identities of the individuals and business entities that touch or have access to the information.

The digital world is enabling ever more invasive data mining and analytics and makes it possible to profile individuals to a highly intrusive degree. As people expand their digital footprint through mobile devices we may soon reach a tipping point in confidence. IDC[67] has put together a useful model of the types of information privacy and security in the digital world, classified into five categories, each requiring successively higher levels:

Privacy only	– such as an email address on a YouTube upload.
Compliance driven	– such as emails that might be discoverable in litigation or subject to retention rules.
Custodial	– account information, a breach of which could lead to or aid in identity theft.
Confidential	– information the originator wants to protect, such as trade secrets, customer lists, confidential memos and so on.
Lockdown	– information requiring the highest security, such as financial transactions, personnel files, medical records, military intelligence and so on.

IDC estimates that up to 30 percent of information in the digital world requires some level of security but also notes that it may not have it today. If that's true, and a growing part of the business models within the digital economy rely on confidence in the ecosystem, then it can't be ignored. Facebook isn't in the social media business any more than Google is in the search business: both are in the data analytics and information-marketing businesses.

Facebook has been tough to compete against because its business model has been so self-sustaining – you join Facebook because all your friends and relatives use it. Because everyone on the planet is connected by only six degrees of separation[68] and as Facebook now has over 1 billion users, anyone who wants to use social media will almost certainly choose use Facebook – until something newer and much more engaging comes along and/or unless the model falls apart because confidence is lost.

As Steve Jobs said on his return to Apple in the 1990s, he quit competing against Microsoft because it had already won. For the moment at least, if you can't beat Facebook, then the only way is to join it, by building applications on top of it.

That Kodak moment – a case of digital death
Companies like Google, Facebook and Amazon didn't need to go on a transformation journey – they didn't exist before the digital economy was born and so their journey was growing and

[67]IDC Digital Universe Study, sponsored by EMC, June 2011
[68]The idea that everyone is on average just six steps away, by way of introduction, from any other person on Earth

navigating in uncharted waters. They may have been truly inspired, downright lucky or a combination of the two, but they have emerged into very powerful positions that are difficult to challenge head on, unless of course, there is a big change in circumstances they cannot control.

One of the characteristics of the digital economy is that it has a self-inducing 'herd mentality'. If all your friends are on Facebook, why would you go anywhere else? If the biggest choice of goods is on Amazon, why bother spending time looking elsewhere? If more buyers use eBay, why bother to advertise in some backwater?

But the world doesn't stand still for long. Innovative start-ups rapidly become big corporations, then they start to inherit all of the overhead and problems that come with being big – and especially those that go with being successful. Boards of directors and particularly inspired founders find it very hard to change course from a strategy that has served them well. That inability to change direction has been the root cause of failure of many successful corporations, which were once at the top of their game, but failed to adapt to market changes.

The computer industry is a great one to study for a compressed view of this zero-to-hero-to-zero cycle. IBM failed to see the growth of the mini-computer, clung on to its mainframe view for too long and nearly came unstuck. Meanwhile, the then new darling of minicomputers, DEC, failed to spot the rise of the PC and ultimately disappeared. IBM gave birth to the PC but didn't spot that it was the software market that held the value and begot Microsoft, simultaneously writing its own obituary as a hardware supplier.

Microsoft so far has failed to capitalize on smartphones and tablets. Over in telecom-land, Motorola – the big winner in the first wave of the mobile market – failed to capitalize on the digital GSM era, losing out to Nokia. Nokia, in turn, failed to capitalize on the rise of the smartphone and at the time of writing was suffering horribly from the huge success of Apple and Samsung. What goes around certainly comes around.

America Online was the king of the dial-up Internet – so big it could buy out Time Warner and Netscape – but it didn't anticipate or capitalize on the growth of broadband. In the U.K., BT convinced itself that the mobile market would saturate at around 30 percent and that there would only ever be room for two mobile suppliers in any market. Its minnow rival, Racal, bought up operating licenses cheaply around the world and turned into the mobile giant Vodafone, while BT had to sell off its remaining mobile assets to Telefónica: as I write, Vodafone's market capitalization is four times larger than BT's.

Sony was once king of the personal music player, transitioning from cassettes to CDs under the apparently unstoppable Walkman brand. Yet it stumbled badly on the transition to solid-state storage, yielding the market to Apple's iPod.

Perhaps the most poignant case is the bankruptcy of Kodak. As Simon Waldman[69] noted in an article in the *Guardian* newspaper: "Kodak filing for Chapter 11 is rather like hearing about the death of a much-loved elderly relative: you've known for ages it was going to happen, but it's still a shock when it finally does."

Kodak is a classic case of the 'digital death' that is sweeping not just across companies but whole industries. We've seen the disappearance of music stores and bookshops as symptoms but we can probably soon kiss goodbye to small digital cameras, sat-navs, hand-held gaming devices and countless other technologies that are being made redundant by digital products and services.

Kodak was brilliantly successful for decades. It almost single-handedly invented the mass market for photography and kept innovating the way forward to ever greater dominance – and in the process got very big and bureaucratic. When it needed to move quickly, it was too slow; when it needed to be radical, it was too conservative. Despite being a pioneer of digital photography and having a viable digital camera by the early 1990s, the technology was too easily dismissed by executives who had spent their entire career in the world of film, chemicals and paper and were too worried about their rock solid business being cannibalized by digital.

So, when Fuji launched a price war in the late 1990s, Kodak's margins came under increasing pressure. While its film business remained profitable, the increasing popularity of digital photography shifted from consumers to professionals and finally to diehards. Its success had come from the continuous execution and optimization of a single business model and when that was made irrelevant, the business that had previously been a byword for generating cash, declined and finally died.

A salutary lesson for any other spectacularly successful business that relies on continuously improving a single business model and fails to spot the world has changed until it's too late. The mighty can and do fall, and often very soon after they reached their peak: IBM fell from grace as a computer manufacturer shortly after its best-ever results and the music industry was knocked sideways by digital downloads shortly after the biggest sales ever of CDs.

Google is currently at the top of its game and is fabulously profitable, but the well-known investor Roger McNamee foresees trouble: "Before the iPhone, Google accounted for roughly three-fourths of index search, which accounted for about 90 percent of web search. In the app model, customers use apps to search, not Google and index search happens with the following frequency by platform: desktop web 100 percent, iPad 10 percent, and iPhone 1 percent. Given that transactions are moving rapidly to mobile, it seems unlikely that index search will provide Google with the control point it has grown accustomed to. Margins must fall. Google has yet to produce any profits from smartphones. Even though Google's web business continues to grow, the company has lost half its addressable market."

[69]Author of *Creative Disruption: How to Shake Up Your Business in the Digital Age*

That Google's margins are falling was borne out by its quarterly results to the end of March 2012. That quarter saw its average cost per click – what an advertiser pays Google every time someone clicks on its ad – fall by 12 percent from a year ago, down 7 percent from the preceding quarter.

There are countless examples like this in every industry segment and while there are many reasons why companies fall from grace, the failure to adapt to new market conditions, new business models, new technologies and new customer needs is a clear and present danger. As more and more sectors come to grips with the new market realities of the digital economy there will be many more who failed to make the right moves at the right times to capitalize on the opportunities.

How can it be that top executives the world over and in countless industries fail to adapt to change? It's hardly unknown: after all, countless numbers of management books cite examples – from Neanderthals failing to spot that fire might be a good idea through to executives at Lehman Bros believing in their own invincibility.

The critical importance of leadership

It's too easy to characterize these CEOs as stupid and blind – you simply don't get to the top of major corporations without being very smart. In fact, some of the smartest people I ever worked with were at BT and look what happened to it. I don't think it's a failure to spot that change is happening, I think it's usually a failure to take the risk of *acting* on that change. Most corporations run on their results and although there are warning signs around the future, it's all too easy to say "look at our figures, we're doing OK."

The problem is that the time taken to restructure an organization to react to change is generally longer than the time taken for the market to change around you. Media companies have seen this very clearly in the last decade – shifts of advertising revenue from TV, radio and newspapers to the Internet has happened faster than most of those companies could change course. The whole value chain of music distribution has been blown away by online music retailing and publishing is following in its path.

By the time the change is apparent it's often too late and chief executives reach for heroic solutions. News Corporation's half billion dollar purchase of MySpace, only to see it fade into oblivion against Facebook, is a good example. eBay's $2.6 billion purchase of Skype only to sell it two years later is another and I wait to see whether Microsoft's $8.5 billion crack at Skype turns out to be an inspiration or doomed folly, along with Google's $12.5 billion foray into the foreign territory of being a handset manufacturer by acquiring Motorola Mobility.

Even when the leadership team 'get it', turning a large corporation into a new direction is immensely difficult. As the CEO of a large public company once said to me, "A decision by the board becomes a mandate on the CEO; an interesting discussion among senior management; an interminable debate among middle management while the field force just put their heads down and wait for the latest fad to pass."

So making effective change in a timely manner is tough. Move too soon and you could be out ahead of the market with no customers. Move too slowly and your existing customers flee to smarter competitors. Underestimating the scale, complexity and challenges of change often catch out companies even when they make the call at the right time.

IBM's legendary turnaround from a hardware company to become a software and services company when many of its rivals disappeared could probably not have happened but for the inspired leadership of Lou Gerstner. Without such leadership, companies just go round in circles and eventually disappear (we look in detail at the importance of leadership as a critical success factor in Chapter 6).

Innovating from within is really hard

Clayton Christensen's book *The Innovator's Dilemma*[70], has become a standard reference on why many companies fail to adapt properly to market changes. Although he wrote it principally from a technological change perspective, many of his principles apply to the kinds of market change that the digital world is ushering in. Steve Jobs had this on his required reading list and he certainly seems to have absorbed the concepts when he returned to Apple and achieved one of the most impressive turn-arounds in technology's history – or indeed in that of any sector.

In Walter Isaacson's biography of Jobs[71], he describes the time when he returned to Apple after a string of managers, including John Sculley, had led the company towards disaster – at the time it had only 90 days' working capital on hand and was facing imminent bankruptcy. He identified the root cause of Apple's problems: the previous management had let profitability outweigh passion: "My passion has been to build an enduring company where people were motivated to make great products. The products, not the profits, were the motivation. Sculley flipped these priorities to where the goal was to make money. It's a subtle difference, but it ends up meaning everything."

Christensen recognized the same mechanism at the heart of the many business failures he observed: "The best professional managers, doing all the right things and following all the best advice, lead their companies all the way to the top of their markets in that pursuit... only to fall straight off the edge of a cliff after getting there because they can't adapt to what comes next." That's exactly what had happened to Apple under Sculley.

[70]Christensen, Clayton M. (1997), *The innovator's dilemma: when new technologies cause great firms to fail*, Boston, Massachusetts, U.S.: Harvard Business School Press, ISBN 978-0-87584-585-2
[71]Walter Isaacson, *Steve Jobs: The Exclusive Biography*; Little, Brown, 2011. ISBN 978-1408703-48

There are many reasons why companies fail to adapt to change – hubris, complacency, bureaucracy and short-term investment horizons; inadequate skills and resources; hiring the wrong people; and sometimes just bad luck. Christensen focuses on some common factors and by looking at a diverse range of companies across many industries came up with three main findings:

- disruptive markets (that is with a new concept of value) are very different to sustaining markets (that is the incremental improvement of an established business segment) and need to be managed very differently;
- the pace of progress often runs ahead of the market's awareness of the need and can often catch out players who leave it too late; and
- structures of companies color the choices and investments they make – very often their history holds them back.

All three of these apply very well to the digital world, which uses many technologies that could be considered sustaining, but uses them in highly disruptive ways. The market winners of these disruptions *should* be the big established companies. They know these technologies better than anyone and could leverage them to profitably disrupt established value chains in a broad range of industries, in the way that Apple has disrupted the music business and Amazon the book business. I say *should* rather than *will* because unfortunately, history is against them.

The digital world is not just about new ways of delivering stuff online as opposed to in a cardboard box. It's about a fundamental realignment of how value is created and significantly lowering the barriers to entry from new 'left field' players. So existing computing, communications, software and hardware players *should* be the big winners in this shift from conventional ways of doing business to the digital world, but they may end up being among the casualties as new entrants disrupt *their* markets and value chains.

The digital world is a planet's worth of market
The concept of economies of scale is well known and refers to reductions in unit costs as the volume and usage levels increase. 'Diseconomies' of scale are the opposite. There are many sources of economies of scale, such as taking advantage of returns to scale in:

Production costs – for example mobile handsets.
Purchasing – such as the joint purchasing agreement between Deutsche Telekom and Orange.
Financial – like the borrowing at lower interest rates than smaller competitors.
Marketing – spreading the cost of advertising over a greater range of output in media markets.

The basic ingredients of the digital world: communications networks, cloud computing and storage, and device manufacturing are all highly leveraged through economies of scale and all become cheaper to deliver the more they are used. For example, an empty network or data center costs much the same to run as a fully loaded one. There are other, less obvious advantages of scale that operate as well – the Internet world shows the huge advantage of size – if all of your friends are on Twitter, that is where you want to be; if you want to get maximum exposure for your products, get in the top 10 on Google and so on. Thus scale is of benefit in two very important ways in the digital world: your costs go down and your appeal goes up.

When you can address a market of 7 billion people – the Earth's population – in one go, which is where the digital world is heading, this advantage becomes absolutely critical: it's how you can sell an application or a game for pennies via iTunes but still make huge returns because the market is so big. As I said before, even when you charge nothing, the digital 'real-estate' of large numbers of users is still very valuable. Skype is probably the most obvious example of this – being recently valued at over $8 billion but with comparatively tiny revenues and probably miniscule profits.

4

WHAT DO YOU WANT TO BE WHEN YOU GROW UP?

Within an ecosystem, there's only a certain amount of profit available – the difference of the price the customer pays and the sum of all costs incurred– and the various players will try to get a higher proportion of this margin. In an ecosystem as volatile and dynamic as the digital economy, players will constantly jostle and reposition themselves to maximize their competitive advantage. Put simply, someone will put one over on you if they can.

If the digital world offers so many opportunities and yet contains so many threats to current business models, what should you do about it and where and when should you move to in the ecosystem? To misquote a well-known American phrase – that is, of course, the 64 trillion dollar question.

We're talking about multiple industries worth trillions of dollars repositioning themselves to a greater or lesser extent to capitalize on or shield themselves from the impacts of the digital world. Where and when to play are (or should be) questions preoccupying management teams and boards the world over as they juggle with the chances and dangers it brings.

As we saw in the last chapter, moving too slow can be fatal. Many of the opportunities and threats are only now beginning to emerge and will take many different twists and turns as the digital world evolves. 'Betting the farm' on any particular outcome is high risk and, not surprisingly, many established players who are still making good growth and profits are very cautious.

Not so for those companies who were born into the digital world and know nothing else, or for others who have learned to adapt exceedingly well. They aren't sitting on their hands: they're planning their next moves, not suffering from paralysis by analysis.

I'm sure that when we stand and look back at the digital revolution, we'll see that although huge investment in technology infrastructure and standardization created the conditions for the digital world to take off, it took the spark of genius from Apple to ignite the firestorm with the global success of the smartphone. I am not known as an Apple fan: I had Windows Mobile-based phones with my email, calendar, browser et al for years before the iPhone, but it took the Apple to take us from geek to sleek.

So what is the next 'iPhone moment' – when will you open the newspaper on your iPad and read in horror of a move that will badly damage your company, or will it be *your* company that has made the bold move to give countless other CEOs indigestion that morning?

Repositioning to a different business model or niche in the digital ecosystem depends on where you are starting from, where you want to be next – it's crucial to remember that the digital world doesn't stand still and the name of the game is constant experimentation, innovation and reassessment of the market and your place in it. Then you need to figure out the competencies you need to get to your immediate destination, with one eye always on the horizon. The number of industries being inexorably sucked into the digital vortex is increasing all the time and the transformation route for every industry and individual company is likely to be different.

For many companies it's fairly easy to assess where they are now, but much more difficult for them to articulate where they would like to move to next. Many can tell you where they *don't* want to be but can't really describe where they would like to be because they find it nearly impossible to visualize what the world is changing to. They often hide behind a "who can predict the future" shrug of the shoulders.

Most CEOs of communications service providers seem to share a common fear of being reduced to a 'dumb pipe' provider. This worry is in inverse proportion to executives from application services players whose great hope is that the communications companies *will* simply provide the pipes – after all, the digital ecosystem depends on there being ubiquitous, cheap and reliable broadband services everywhere and they certainly don't want to have to invest in infrastructure themselves.

What *do* we know?

Nearly every senior executive I speak to in either communications, computing or applications businesses seems to feel that being at the top of the stack – facing the end user (or *owning* them in some minds) – is the best place to be. Being buried deeper in the ecosystem, as anonymous infrastructure providers, gives rise to the great fear of being commoditized. Of course, it's also easier to explain to a Wall Street analyst or your friends over dinner what a company does if it's a brand they see every day: rather like sausages, people love them when they are on the barbecue but prefer to overlook how and of what they are made. For much the same reason, the underpinning and enabling capabilities behind the scenes in the digital world are much less fashionable and command far fewer column inches in *Forbes* magazine.

Figure 10 shows some of the important movement trends. If you were watching a migration of wildebeest, you could say that the herd is generally moving north.

Google, having observed Apple's success in exploiting the synergies between users' buying behavior and the device they use to consume those purchases, has positioned itself in service retailing and devices, first through the Android operating system, then the Google Play digital store. Certainly its move into device hardware, through the purchase of Motorola Mobility, is a very different type of move for this service and software innovator. As I'll explain shortly, when discussing core competencies, this may prove a step too far.

Amazon has similarly been strengthening its position in digital retail by exploiting device synergies as well. Its success with the first Kindle e-reader had a big impact on e-book downloads and the company continues to expand the range of Kindle products while extending its online store to cater more and more for digital goods (while simultaneously becoming a successful sales channel for apparently limitless kinds of third-party physical goods). It is very well positioned to be the dominant e-retailer and has cleverly positioned Kindle as both a physical device as well as being an application on other makes of tablets and smartphones. With Kindle reputedly being sold at or below cost, its move seems much more about having some control over the ecosystem for digital goods than a great desire to be a device player.

Figure 10 – Companies try to position themselves near to the end customer

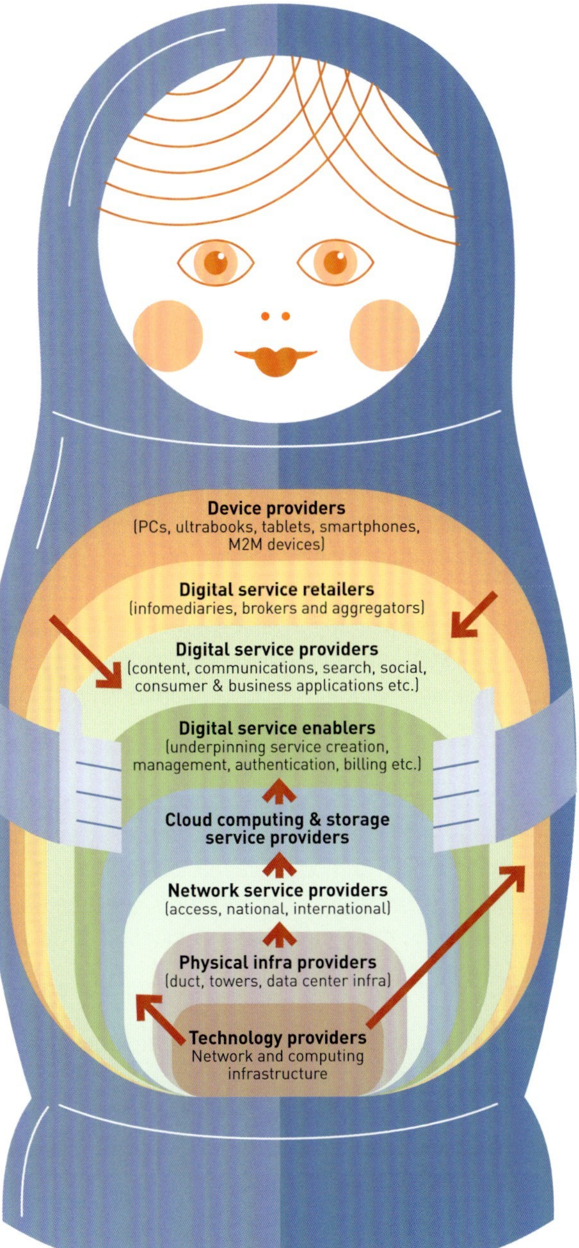

Both Amazon and Google are also active at the other end of the ecosystem, providing infrastructure services including cloud computing and storage capabilities. Time will tell whether this ultimately makes a good bedfellow with a combined device and retail business. Maybe we'll see their various business units float off as separate companies.

Apple of course is moving in the opposite way, growing back along the ecosystem from devices to exploit opportunities as a digital retailer and store provider. Initially viewing the digital store as simply a lever for device sales, its success as the world's dominant music store must have come as something of a surprise. Such is the confidentiality around that company, we'll probably never know what was down to luck and what was careful planning.

Microsoft probably gets the most arrows on the chart for simultaneously 'carpet bombing' numerous sectors. It is becoming highly active in the cloud services area as well as providing its traditional software products on a cloud basis. The purchase of Skype puts it firmly into the digital services provider sector and its fight-back on mobile devices has been marked with the launch of Windows Mobile and the ever closer relationship with Nokia. For good measure, it seems to be using its vast war-chest to vacuum up any available patent relevant to the digital world – as we have seen with the once free and open-source Android, patents are a great way of monetizing the digital world through indirect means.

The strategies of other major software companies are emerging: such as Oracle's Public Cloud offering, an integrated suite of Platform-as-a-Service applications like enterprise resource planning, human resource management and customer relationship management under its Fusion brand.

Computing infrastructure players have been moving away from reliance on hardware technology and into services for some years: IBM started this trend and this move has subsequently been followed by others including HP (although it's fair to say that HP has followed quite a few different and rather confusing strategies of late!). IBM's latest iteration of this is to target cloud-based services as well as the more traditional outsourcing of data centers, consulting and systems integration (see Chapter 7).

In the communications sector, the major network equipment suppliers Ericsson, Alcatel-Lucent, Nokia Siemens Networks and Huawei have all moved, in recent years, to providing a range of Infrastructure-as-a-Service managed network services and about one fifth of all mobile subscribers are now hosted on managed service networks operated by these network equipment providers (this is discussed in some detail in Chapter 2 as well as in Chapter 7).

Digital children are born

Many communications companies are moving to provide cloud-based services and some have established separate or arm's-length digital service companies. Telefónica is one of these and has launched a 2,500 people-strong global division called Telefónica Digital based in London, U.K., under the leadership of Matthew Key. It has regional centers in Silicon Valley, São Paolo, Madrid, Barcelona and Tel Aviv.

Its mission is to exploit opportunities in the digital world and deliver new growth through location-based advertising, eHealth, mobile money, venture capital, global partnerships and digital services such as cloud computing, mobile advertising, M2M. The division will run Telefónica's Skype-style Internet telephony service Jajah, the Spanish social network Tuenti and the Latin American Internet broadcaster Terra.

It's too soon to say how successful Telefónica will be with this departure, but certainly it is making substantial resources available and clearly it has done some thinking outside the box, and not for the first time. Telefónica was the Spanish incumbent, and the first former monopoly to generate greater revenue from outside its original territory (through expansion into under-developed Latin American markets) than from its domestic market way back in the 1990s.

SingTel Optus is another good example of the trend for former telcos to disaggregate into focused business units. In March 2012, it announced the formation of three business units, including one call Group Digital Life with similar aims to Telefónica Digital and aiming to become a leading player in the digital ecosystem, with innovative and cutting-edge digital services. SingTel also has the fast-growing mobile advertising and marketing industry in its sights to graft onto its new structure, recently signing an agreement to acquire U.S.-based ad specialist Amobee: SingTel wants to become the leading mobile advertising company in Asia Pacific and one of the top three worldwide.

Maximizing profit in the digital ecosystem

The concept of value chains and ecosystems isn't new – it's been around for a long time and was first described and popularized by management guru Michael Porter[72]. He described how supply chains and distribution networks sometimes work with industry-wide, synchronized interactions to create an interconnected system which he termed a "value system" – these days more frequently called an ecosystem. When he first coined the term, Porter could probably not have conceived the incredible level of interaction and interdependency of the digital world.

A value chain creates value along the flow and the most successful players will be those who manage to capture the maximum value generated along the chain. An important point here is that within an ecosystem, *there's only a limited amount of profit margin to go around*, that is the difference between the final price the customer pays and the sum of all costs incurred in the creation and delivery of the service.

[72]Michael Porter: *Competitive Advantage: Creating and Sustaining Superior Performance*; Free PR, 1998 ISBN-10: 0684841460

So it's not surprising that the various players will constantly jostle and reposition themselves to maximize their proportion of this margin. In an ecosystem as volatile and dynamic as the digital economy, we can expect an extreme amount of movement by companies trying to leverage their competitive advantage, bypass intermediaries, create new business models and generally trying to out-do one another.

This is somewhat of a paradox, however, as everyone in the ecosystem depends on everyone else for their success, so competitive jockeying will sometimes have unintended consequences. It's a classic 'co-opertition'[73] situation since the players need to elbow each other for maximum profit but can also all benefit by cooperating to improve their efficiency in the ecosystem, thereby reducing their costs and achieving a higher total margin to the benefit of them all. A good example would be everyone using common standards at all the points of touch in the chain for trading issues such as order management, problem resolution, billing and settlements, and so on.

With that as a backdrop, where is the ideal place to be in an ecosystem? Where should you aspire to be if you are not already there? Plenty of management consultants will always advise being as near to the end user[74] as possible and the market movements of many of the big players bear this out. For example, the advice from CapGemini[75] is: "A firm client relationship is key in acquiring the sweet spot in the value chain: companies with direct end-consumer contact are in control and able to capture client's desires and will finally result in a reinforced brand image and more revenues."

The fear of having your market dominated and controlled by someone else, and being commoditized into a low-margin business, seems to be the main driver of companies that want to 'move up the value chain' to be as close to the end user as possible. This notionally means you have more control over your destiny or, as Jack Welch once famously put it, "When you're number four or five in a market, when number one sneezes, you get pneumonia…"[76]. As I pointed out in Chapter 1, the communications companies are also huge retailers today but, just like record and book retailers, they are under the threat of disruption from the digital infomediaries and need to watch their backs very carefully.

Undoubtedly the player at the head of the value chain has some advantages but perhaps not as many as in the past. In an open, connected digital world many well-established rules of business aren't what they were. For example, the old marketing dictum of asking your customers what they want and then giving it to them has definitely been turned on its head. Customers in innovative markets usually don't know what they want and numerous recent technology leaps would definitely seem to confirm that.

---

[73]Simultaneous cooperation and competition
[74]The end user is not necessarily the customer who pays the bill
[75]Jaco van Zijll Langhout and Eric Bun, *Business Innovation*: www.shakingupthevaluechain.com/2008/08/revaluing-your-position-in-the-value-chain2/
[76]*Nikkei Business*, February 21, 1994

So while getting close to your end customer to develop what they want may have conventionally been a strong advantage, in the digital world it probably translates into giving customers a vast array of what they might want and see what sells, then refine the offer and get rid of stuff that doesn't work, and quickly. Amazon has been very successful with this approach. Since it made a strategic decision to let third-party resellers use its trading platform its range of products and services has increased dramatically, along with its revenues.

Can leopards change their spots...quickly?

When jockeying for position in the digital ecosystem, successful players will be those who can move more quickly than their rivals to spot and exploit an opportunity, but who are also smart enough to know when not to bite off more than they can chew. For instance, I might want to be a heavyweight boxer or a ballet dancer but it's never going to happen because no matter how hard I want it and how hard I try, I'm not built that way. My point is that picking your position (or positions) in the digital ecosystem is partly about figuring out where you *should* move to but also being intelligent enough to work out where your organization *can* move to, and a constant willingness to experiment, to test your thinking in the market.

Changing spots it is often harder than most organizations think, especially those with a long-established culture and fixed set of core competencies that often causes them to badly miscalculate the complexity and difficulty of radical change. Core competencies are very useful assets in stable businesses but often prevent easy movement in times of change. Many business writers, including C.K. Prahalad and Gary Hamel[77] have written extensively on this subject and they describe core competencies as: "The collective learning in the organization: unlike physical assets, which deteriorate over time, competencies are enhanced as they are applied and shared. Core competencies are difficult for competitors to imitate."

Put simply, changing core competencies is a bit like the old saying, 'it's hard to teach old dogs new tricks', but the inverse is also true: it's also hard to teach new dogs old tricks! For example, it's difficult for companies that have built their competencies around running large-scale infrastructure day in, day out to suddenly become successful and serial innovators. However, it's just as difficult for a start-up company of bright young things to immediately know how to run a high-scale, high-reliability infrastructure well because of the huge mix of skills that are required. It's a matter of horses for courses.

I'm absolutely not saying that companies should stay in a rut, simply cautioning that it pays to recognize your strengths and weaknesses before you move. There were lots of people who scoffed at Apple when it announced (or should I say leaked, Apple doesn't do forward announcements) that it would design and sell a mobile phone because of the complexity of the technology and the fact that Apple had never been in the market before.

[77]Prahalad, C.K. and Hamel, G., *The Core Competence of the Corporation*, Harvard Business Review

Ed Colligan, CEO of Palm, was quoted saying at the time: "It won't be easy to create a good smartphone that works on networks worldwide – Nokia, Motorola have worked on this for 25 years and still have only partially succeeded"[78]. Steve Ballmer, Microsoft's CEO, was characteristically more blunt, saying: "There's no chance that the iPhone is going to get any significant market share: no chance."

Apple had the huge advantage of having a leader who knew the company inside out, knew its strengths and weaknesses and knew how far he could push the envelope. Companies can and should evolve but not everyone has a Steve Jobs at the helm.

So how *should* the companies who aspire to take a big stake in the digital economy go about positioning themselves and where necessary transform their business models, culture and competencies to meet that goal? The larger and more established the player, the harder that transformation is to achieve and Christensen as well as other writers describe why – not least of which is that large existing companies get fixated on their core business and this sucks investment and talent away from fledgling ideas.

Christensen, like management writer Peter Drucker before him, says that key changes always start with a company's non-customers and the "new" should be developed separately from the old and should be nurtured and sheltered. That, hopefully, is Telefónica's logic for establishing Telefónica Digital – I write a lot more about this in Chapter 10.

Table 1 – Core competencies in each segment of the digital ecosystem

Digital ecosystem sector	Core competencies and characteristics
Infrastructure providers: • Data center / hosting providers • Network service providers • Cloud computing and storage service providers	Access to capital; long-run business model, operational excellence; reliability / quality; geographic coverage; scalability economies of scale; hardware, software and integration skills
Digital service enablers	Innovation, software skills service management ethos and capabilities, partnership management
Digital service providers	Innovation; customer empathy / market knowledge; speed; development skills
Digital service retailers / infomediaries / brokers and aggregators	Customer and market empathy; packaging / pricing skills; advertising; partnership management; customer experience management; core competency in building / operating high-scale IT systems

[78]Source – Christopher Meinck – www.everythingicafe.com

So what *are* the core competencies required for success in each of the segments in the digital ecosystem? At a very high level, I think the core competencies defined in Table 1 are the characteristics that will define successful players.

As an example of who might dominate where in the ecosystem, let's take my friends the communications service providers. The deep competencies of the larger, more established providers often lie in building and operating large-scale network infrastructure while many others, especially newer market entrants, have excellent marketing and packaging skills. Few communications companies have a strong competency in both and even fewer have deep competencies in innovating new services that are highly in tune with target customer segments and getting them to market fast.

Is it better to stick with areas that leverage your core competencies and concentrate on honing them to be the best at that? Or is it better to reposition to a new part of the ecosystem where you perceive better growth prospects, but where you need to learn or acquire new competencies?

I'm sure Rupert Murdoch thought that he could buy his way into new competencies and business models with the acquisition of MySpace. Until early 2008, MySpace had been the most visited social networking site in the world, surpassing Google as the most visited website in the U.S. and was probably worth $6 billion at its peak, but eventually MySpace was sold in June 2011 for just $35m to digital media firm Specific Media. The gamble didn't work and mainly because the hard-edged revenue growth model of News Corp drove users away and destroyed value rather than creating it, letting Facebook through to become the $100 billion gorilla. As Rupert Murdoch, Chairman and CEO of News Corporation, said[79]: "I made a huge mistake – we proceeded to mismanage it in every possible way..."

It's a good case study in what happens when you try to manage in the digital economy using the operating tools and metrics of the old world – Murdoch just didn't understand the Oklahoma Land Grab model of building a base and monetizing later. As a former MySpace executive[80] put it: "Rupert took his eye off the ball...he got obsessed with Dow Jones – that's when all the trouble really started... word came down from News Corp that if our revenues dropped we had to offset them dollar for dollar in cost reductions and the team became focused [on] cutting costs rather than thinking about driving the business." So just like Apple under Sculley, the passion felt by MySpace's founders was subsumed by the drive for early profit first and foremost and customers abandoned it.

All kudos to News Corp for trying because doing something is better than doing nothing, which is what most companies faced with market changes unfortunately do and history is littered with their remains. Sure, they do enough to put a nice paragraph or two in their shareholders' annual

[79]News Corporation Annual Shareholder Meeting, October 2011
[80]*Financial Times* Dec 4, 2009: www.ft.com/cms/s/0/fd9ffd9c-dee5-11de-adff-00144feab49a.html#axzz1qELambte

report, but in the main, many take a 'wait and see' attitude. The real danger is that the market moves much faster than the time needed to execute a proper and thorough change strategy. Just look at the rate of penetration of smartphone and tablets into the market – 25 percent market penetration in a year in the U.S. for tablet computers from more or less a standing start.

As I say in more detail in Chapter 10, the evolution of a market (just like evolution of living things) doesn't go in smooth, straight-line progressions – it goes in fits and starts. The early stages of the digital world were relatively slow but now we are in a spurt that will rapidly accelerate the pressure behind the digital tsunami of more users and devices, giving rise to more application services demanding more capacity, which encourages more users and on we go. At the same time, the machine-machine uses of the digital world are so economically attractive that they will explode and push enterprises into a digital approach very quickly, as we discussed in Chapter 2.

Big company: big problem

Plenty of experience also shows us that the odds are stacked against most market players moving quickly and decisively and plenty of CEOs know this. Failing to be in position to transform or to take a stake in new opportunities should trigger a red warning light on every CEO's desk or more particularly on their shareholders' desks: inaction, indecision or apathy when markets are changing rapidly should seriously worry investors.

Christensen noted the phenomenon of the difficulty of getting investment in new innovations into large, established companies when he said that "small markets cannot fulfill the growth need of large companies" because innovative ideas in new markets often deliver comparatively small revenues at first, which are not even a rounding error to a large company with sales of many billions but needing to deliver 10 to 20 percent growth rates – so they stick with leveraging the current business.

"We could make more money on one TV phone-in program than you're going to make in a year" was the response I once had in front of an investment committee for one of my brilliant ideas. The very term 'investment committee' says it all – after all, as the saying goes, a camel is a horse designed by a committee. A committee usually takes a safe route, which is often perceived as doing nothing.

Meanwhile, those small but high-growth opportunities are very attractive to start-ups and small companies, so new entrants automatically have a built-in advantage when it comes to exploiting new ideas. Big companies are often the result of an inspired individual's vision, a lot of luck and venture capital. Big companies often miss those opportunities because the revenue growth doesn't move their needle enough. Unless they are led by a charismatic, visionary leader who is prepared to back hunches, new ideas are often left in the 'pending' tray.

Communications companies suffer from this problem in spades: after years of stunning growth in mobile, market saturation has made them fixate on cutting costs and generating growth from their existing business model, which means that so far, most have missed out on the wave of innovative new digital services. For the past decade or more, industry conference after conference and analyst report after report has predicted "the next big thing" and everyone gets excited for a year or two.

Location-based services, music, games, entertainment services, mobile money were all going to be the next killer app. One by one they have appeared, but usually delivered by an over-the-top provider, denying the communications service provider that future revenue stream and weakening its link with the end customer who more and more identifies with the device and digital store provider, or the application provider. The game is not over yet of course – empires can and do fight back, but every day the costs of that fight-back rise and winning back intimacy with end customers becomes more difficult. A Kodak moment is coming for some.

If you look back at the 'Matryoshka dolls' ecosystem shown in Figure 10, the dynamics around competencies, investment and risks change considerably. As you move 'up' the model, skills innovation and speed become important characteristics and the need for capital investment is lower. As you move 'down' the model, access to capital, operational skills, reliability, geographic and economies of scale become much more important factors.

Large capital and scale requirements are also high barriers to entry, which ensure there are relatively few competitors in the lower parts of the model: to provide services such as communications, cloud infrastructure and technology there will be accelerating levels of aggregation, mergers and acquisitions. At the digital services layer, the barriers to entry for service entrepreneurs are much lower ensuring that there will continue to be very considerable growth in the numbers of players as the breadth and depth of the digital economy flourishes.

While many players would *like* to control the retail point of sale of digital services because it gives them influence over much of the rest of the ecosystem, I'm not convinced there is room for a large number of them. So we have a diamond-shaped market (see overleaf) with relatively few players at the top and the bottom with a very large number in the middle. These three broad areas: infrastructure; service innovation and service retailing are three different sectors in the ecosystem and will have different winners and losers with different competencies.

While the digital stores and services capture most of the column inches, without the enabling infrastructure – which needs to work reliably and efficiently, first-time, every time – the upper layers can't exist. It's inevitable that infrastructure service providers will somewhat fade from public view and only become visible when something goes wrong. Think about BP's Deepwater Horizon drilling rig – nobody had ever heard of it until it exploded and trashed the Gulf of

Figure 11 – The digital economy is likely to become diamond-shaped

Mexico! Very few people call their service provider to say that their broadband is running really fast, but plenty do the opposite. Consumers' lack of perception of the different layers was clearly demonstrated when AT&T and Apple first launched the iPhone: Apple won plaudits for nearly all of the good things about the product and AT&T picked up nearly all of the bad press for anything that went wrong, despite neither view being fully accurate.

This difference in perception of what users see as important has a very real impact on the value they place on various elements of their service. This in turn translates into factors such as brand loyalty; willingness to pay and ultimately stock-market valuation. This is a classic iceberg picture where a large part of the digital world floats unseen under the waterline without anyone caring too much until that 'Titanic moment' when everything goes horribly wrong.

Infrastructure is unloved and unfashionable although it's a sector with great promise. I already discussed (in Chapter 2) how equipment suppliers have moved aggressively into providing network services over the last decade. As the squeeze on communications service providers' business accelerates, more and more of them are outsourcing and will outsource network operations to companies like Ericsson and Huawei. This creates a virtuous circle – the more communications providers outsource to these companies, the greater the economies of scale and market power of the outsourcing suppliers, who don't have the conflict of interest that many communications service providers struggle with concerning providing wholesale services to their competitors.

It seems likely that, left to a pure market economy, the provision of infrastructure services would quickly morph into a relatively small number of very large players worldwide. However, every country in the world has some form of government regulation for communications and in general, governments control the supply of the raw material, radio spectrum, and are likely to continue to distort true market economics, leading to a lengthy transformation cycle for infrastructure provision (see Chapter 5). In the end, economics will prevail and we will see infrastructure service provision in the hands of a small number of large-scale, highly efficient providers, even if regulation slows that move for a while.

What I think technology providers should do

Governments aside, the prospect of almost limitless use of communications, computing and storage technologies to power the digital world should be the source of endless joy among the manufacturers of this hardware and software for years to come.

However, as I've said a number of times, the digital economy is creating winners and losers and some technology suppliers have had a tough time in recent years, hit by technology shifts, the squeeze on operators' margins, driving very aggressive pricing; and sharp new competitors, particularly from Asia. Mergers, acquisitions and downsizing have been commonplace.

The core reason for the lack of unbridled happiness is, of course, that while volumes of data flowing in the digital world are increasing exponentially, the propensity to pay for it is not in line with that growth. While new technology is constantly needed to keep up, prices for it are falling continuously. The civil engineering costs to support networks and data centers now exceeds that of the technology costs by a considerable margin and this trend is likely to continue. So technology providers are in the 'run to stand still' conundrum.

Both network and computing suppliers have diversified into services and many now have substantial outsourcing and managed services businesses. The whole trend of the digital economy is towards an ecosystem of many types of digital service. I expect that the shift from providing physical technology to providing the capability *as a service* to continue and it's a smart way to go since this approach introduces additional differentiating factors to help avoid commoditization. So I would expect the managed services area of the technology providers' business to grow faster than their supply of physical hardware and software.

Where I would be more cautious is taking on the running or even ownership of an operator's legacy technology, particularly obsolescent infrastructure. Of course, this is exactly what a lot of operators want but taking on a patchwork quilt of many different technologies, work practices, labor issues and so on is very difficult to do and make money, especially where the customer demands that you do it more cheaply than they used to do. Running a service based on your own technology or at least a common set of technologies from which you can derive some scale economies is much more likely to be profitable, so as a minimum, you would need the ability to progressively replace the obsolescent technology.

As I say in Chapter 8, if you are in an outsourcing situation where the client demands *how* you do something rather than focusing on the outcome of what you do, almost invariably there's trouble ahead: a managed services supplier providing infrastructure services is a viable way forward, but while running somebody's old junk at a discount price might swell the top line, it's unlikely to do much other than produce red ink on the bottom line.

Done the right way, providing infrastructure services is a viable business for technology suppliers, especially those with large service business already who can leverage economies of scale. The problem is, while some service providers will welcome this, it almost certainly puts the technology supplier on a path to compete with those cloud and communications providers that also want to be in the infrastructure services business. So once again, I think that this is likely to mean that the business of producing the technology and the business of taking it to market as a managed service are likely to need to break apart to avoid serious customer conflicts.

Of course, another sensible outcome might be partnerships between the managed service arms of technology providers and the infrastructure service business units of service providers. That would be a win-win, marrying technology innovation with operational skills, capital, operating licenses and spectrum. We shall see!

At the device level, technology players will also see substantial growth, but again hardware margins have a habit of evaporating rapidly with competition unless you have the brand strength and manufacturing prowess of Apple. As I said in Chapter 2, expect device manufacturers to continue to move to provide services where possible, particularly digital stores to differentiate themselves and maximize margins. I think the jury is still out on whether this works the other way round (Google and Amazon in particular) because it's a big leap from being a service provider to a consumer goods designer manufacturer – but now I'm sounding like Steve Ballmer, which would never do!

Obviously wherever a company sits in the digital ecosystem, being a highly efficient and extremely well-run business will be an essential 'ticket to play' with speed and innovation also being very important characteristics. Economies of scale are important in many areas as well as large capital resources, especially at the infrastructure level.

What should communications service providers do?
Of all the sectors in the digital economy, the communications providers seem at times to be the ones that most resemble a rabbit caught in the headlights. Maybe because it's my background and you always see the flaws of those closest to you the most clearly, but many communications providers have really been a 'one trick pony' for such a long time that learning new tricks is very hard. There is an old saying: "If you don't know where you are going, any road will get you there," but, since the evolutionary path of the digital economy is at best fuzzy and likely to be volatile, overly precise planning isn't a great idea either.

Even so, you do need a general compass heading where the digital market is going and where you are going in it, where timing is everything – how much time do you have to transform before your market position deteriorates to the point that you have no options left?

My strong impression is that, with a few notable exceptions, many communications players are assuming that their current business model has plenty of life left in it, the digital economy is some way off and there's no need to panic. I think they're wrong and the reasons I outlined in Chapter 1: the rapid, global adoption of smartphones provide a platform that will destroy current voice and messaging revenues and the rate of this destruction is accelerating. In addition, as explained in Chapter 2, infomediaries will certainly badly damage, if not kill communication providers' consumer retail businesses, again much faster than service providers think.

I can't visualize any scenario short of turning back time, where the voice and messaging products that have been the mainstay of revenues for communications providers will sustain for more than a few years when faced with very low-cost or free services that are easy to use and work reliably. Voice over IP (VoIP) services have been around for a long time but until recently, haven't been easy to use and certainly haven't worked reliably.

I remember in the early days of mobile telephony, when you'd get a lot of noise on the call, people would say "I'll call you back when I get to a real phone". I can also remember some fixed-line providers taking great comfort from that and the fact that coverage in offices was often poor – relying on your competitor failing is generally a bad strategy. Assuming VoIP won't be as reliable and easy to use as conventional telephony is a badly flawed plan.

Messaging is even more exposed: for years SMS was the highest margin product in the communication provider's portfolio and seemingly unstoppable, yet it is now past its peak and set for rapid decline in the face of more functional products given away for free. Apple, like Research In Motion before it, provides a free message service (iMessage), bundled with their operating system and in many cases users don't even know that it has supplanted SMS. It has the same user interface as its SMS app and Apple made no big announcements about the functionality – it just happened, impacting SMS revenues (and also causing consternation to many users because iMessages operate on a 'best efforts' basis and sometimes the messages don't get through). WhatsApp is another very popular, free product offering greater functionality than SMS.

It's not just the revenues from the services that endanger the communications companies, if you get your device and all of your digital services from somewhere else, why would you come to the phone company to buy airtime when somebody else, with a great brand name and a strong customer ethos, has bundled it into a neat package? So coupled with losing the voice and messaging market is potentially losing the consumer retail market too.

Will communications providers lose their consumer retail business? Yes, even if it's hard to imagine now when communications companies are huge retailers providing a range of services to around 6 billion customers. In the past, communications companies didn't compete directly with digital stores offering applications, music and movies – digital stores were hurting the communications companies' *future* revenues but not attacking their current ones.

That's changing fast and we can expect more moves like iMessage to shift more and more of the customer experience directly to the combined device and digital store provider, weakening brand loyalty or even the entire logic of purchasing from a communications provider. These moves will accelerate by bundling the airtime into the device contract, as Amazon has done with Kindle: the device and digital store provider is offering full airtime broadband services on a multi-country MVNO[81] basis. The fact that the device and digital store providers have not moved aggressively yet or that in places regulation will slow them down does not diminish this threat in the medium term.

The speed of adoption of smartphones and tablets more or less guarantees that these moves will happen and may well happen much faster than communications service providers can reposition. Those that are not actively building a new position in the digital economy could find themselves in a very vulnerable position of being acquisition targets at a knock-down prices. It's a rerun of what happened in the U.S. at the turn of the century when long distance and international carriers were caught napping and acquired for a fraction of the money they had plowed into infrastructure and licenses.

Crucially communications service providers' brand image and customer experience is weak compared to the likes of Apple – as Walt Disney once said, "People spend money when and where they feel good. Apple, Amazon and Google are very successful in positioning themselves as 'lifestyle' providers with an excellent range of services wrapped up in a great customer experience. That a possible goal for many communications players, but it's a big mountain to climb and few will succeed.

The empire strikes back

On the other hand, communications companies have big weapons in their armory and need to use them to play to their strengths. They're excellent at running very large scale infrastructures with high levels of reliability and service quality and can exploit the fact that consumers, especially enterprises, quickly tire of a 'best efforts' type of quality of service, even on 'free' services like Skype. Increasingly, enterprises that run their businesses and shift them more and more to the digital economy will not tolerate 'best effort' because the impact on their businesses is much greater than savings on communications costs. It's interesting to see Research In Motion retreating to its enterprise heartland for just this reason (oh and also for getting whacked in the consumer market by Apple) and we'll see if this succeeds, but at the time of writing, the picture was not rosy.

[81]Mobile Virtual Network Operator – that is, buying wholesale network capacity rather than owning infrastructure

Most communications players also have strengths in the areas of trust, protection of privacy and reliability – this was baked deep into the DNA of the communications industry from the beginning. As I explained in Chapter 3, I think many digital services whose entire business models are based on exploiting personal information are skating on ever thinner ice with users. It's only a matter of time before it cracks, at which point, cleverly positioned communications providers may well be able to exploit customer information as a line of business: for example using anonymous data or information that the customer has authorized.

I don't expect communications providers to easily create such a huge market as their voice, messaging and whole consumer retail business constitute now, but I do think many are sleep-walking and will wake up to find the nightmare is real and the action they take will be too little too late.

As I'll explain in Chapter 12, transformation and repositioning ideally need to take place from a position of strength and although margins and growth for many providers are under pressure, the situation is not yet so bad for most that they lack sufficient resources to effect a vigorous transformation. But they must act now – the situation is likely to deteriorate quickly and there is no time to lose in both defending their current business and capitalizing on growth opportunities.

Communications companies are not used to assessing threats and opportunities from outside their own sector – usually competitive threats come from other licensed operators and direct competition is generally easy to spot because you usually understand where it's coming from, where they can hurt you and how you should react. In the digital economy, different types of rivals appear from many new angles and understanding what they are up to is infinitely harder. Successful defensive and offensive strategies (and I'll come to some examples shortly) will be all the more difficult to execute, and need strong, visionary leaders at the helm (as we will see in Chapter 6).

This is no time for 'safe pairs of hands' types of manager to be minding the shop: it's a time for inspirational and bold leaders to emerge who can really make their mark and take the communications sector into the digital world with energy and vigor. Not all companies will recognize this early enough and while they won't go bust overnight, they will slip behind the pack and the wolves will pick them off one by one in a series of mergers and acquisitions. That's economics at work and, regulators notwithstanding, it will be a healthy, if painful, process.

So what are some defensive and offensive strategies?
Using the old ice-hockey adage of "skating to where the puck will be, not where it is now"[82] is a very important principle. Picking your spots in the digital economy and then moving to exploit them is a fundamental first step, weighing up such factors as:

[82]Wayne Gretzky

- Where are the growth opportunities?
- Where isn't the turf strongly contested so far?
- Where are we best equipped to succeed in terms of our current position and core competencies?
- Where will we be able to maximize profitability for our shareholders and employees?
- Where do we have the best chance to move to from today's starting point?

An obvious and crucial defensive action is to extend your current business for as long as possible, which means being able to drive out operating cost as revenue from the 'cash cows' flattens. As we have seen time and time again, unless this is done in a smart way, cost reduction can trash customer service, drive customers into the hands of rivals and really hamper the agility needed to move quickly on new packages and services. The goal shouldn't be just to keep operational flexibility and customer experience where they are now: both need to improve greatly. Hence maintaining a competitive consumer retail position for as long as possible should be the focus of this thrust and that demands:

- Leveraging and increasing brand strength, especially in enterprise markets.
- Exploiting service quality and reliability (and absolutely not weakening it through badly targeted cost cutting).
- Radically cutting the cost base to withstand or even start a price war.
- Greatly improving customer-centricity and experience to maximize customer retention.
- Broadening the portfolio beyond core products, even if they compete against or cannibalize your core products – better you do it than give up your market position to others – such as introducing innovative new voice and messaging products.

In terms of offensive strategies there are at least three high-growth segments that have real potential. They are:

- Providing an expanded range of infrastructure services, not just networking but the entire range of enabling infrastructure services needed by the digital economy, including processing and storage.
- Providing innovative, enabling services on top of your own or others' infrastructure, such as security, authentication, charging, settlements and customer care services on a 'white label' basis to digital service providers.
- Providing application services to vertical markets, particularly enterprises and particularly leveraging M2M opportunities.

Providing infrastructure services. This is an obvious target for infrastructure-based companies but often it is either not taken seriously or is positively spurned, usually because of lack of clarity over which business the player wants to be in. By this segment, I don't just mean being a wholesale network provider – the so-called dumb pipe – I mean providing an integrated and attractive range of enabling infrastructure services that the digital economy needs.

At the heart of this are a highly reliable, competitively-priced, scalable suite of advanced broadband communications (fixed and mobile services), cloud-based computing and storage capabilities. This is the Infrastructure-as-a-Service (IaaS) market, providing capabilities needed by a wide swathe of digital service providers as well as enterprises. There will be consumers at the end of the value chain but this is primarily for an enterprise, not a consumer play.

Infrastructure-based businesses can be grown incrementally with demand, are less risky than innovative application service businesses and have formidable barriers to entry for competitors. They play to most communication providers' core competencies, and generally provide low-risk returns on investment for the long run that heavyweight capital investment demands. On the downside, the *growth* potential for investors is lower than creating the next Twitter or Google, but neither are they investment risks: venture capital assumes a high failure rate among companies it invests in – the number that make it into the stratosphere like Facebook or Twitter are tiny compared to the number of failures.

Many of today's communications players have the right operational skills and access to capital for this business. They are obviously large-scale network infrastructure providers already but usually have large-scale IT and data center competencies as well. Nevertheless, the computing and storage aspects may require partnerships to bring the necessary skills to bear and sufficient market credibility.

Customers for these capabilities could be: other communication service providers, who choose not to go down the infrastructure route; cable operators; web players; and a broad range of digital service providers, particularly those aiming at or in vertical market segments and enterprises. Connected device providers and digital store 'infomediaries' are also possible customers, including a rise in products that have broadband services bundled with the device, such as those provided by Amazon with Kindle.

There are three primary characteristics for success in this kind of infrastructure-based service business:

- do it big;
- do it cost effectively; and
- do it extremely well.

Economies of scale are obvious and vital as well as widespread geographic coverage resulting from an increasing number of mergers and acquisitions. As Sunil Bharti Mittal, Chairman of

Bharti Enterprises, said:[83] "The bloodbath has started to happen; market caps have halved; companies are making losses. There will only be a few players: six or seven, but certainly not 12. Consolidation is inevitable."

Obviously the best-positioned players will be those who have already built up a portfolio of international operating companies that can be rationalized into a cohesive approach. To gain the necessary speed for further expansion, partnerships rather than more M&A-based consolidation will be a faster way to gain economies of scale, particularly through consortia of collaborating players who can agree on common operating standards to reduce their operating costs (see Chapter 14).

A simple analogy is the code-sharing and co-branding arrangements of a number of major airlines. Collaboration between communications providers, extending this to technology providers who have large-scale infrastructure managed services, also makes a lot of sense for both parties – each brings their relative technology and operational skills to the party.

The "do it cost effectively and do it extremely well" factors also need to be taken very seriously. For example, if you were intent on pursuing this business it would be very odd if you were cutting down your available expertise through short-term moves to outsource operational capabilities to a partner. While that might make sense if you need to maintain obsolescent infrastructure like a legacy 2G network for roaming traffic, otherwise you need to retain as much of your operational skill and expertise on modern infrastructure as possible.

This is particularly important in the IT sphere and software competencies are critical to success in every segment of the ecosystem, yet many communications companies still regard the CIO and the IT group as a cost center to be minimized and downsized rather than as a strategic asset to be nurtured and grown. All the characteristics of partnership management, customer experience management and innovation plus the highly optimized service operations, which I describe in Chapters 7 to 12, are vitally important to succeed in this sector.

CenturyLink in the U.S. is a pioneer of this approach. Through a series of ambitious takeovers, notably Embarq (which had itself previously demerged from Sprint Nextel) and Qwest have transformed CenturyLink from a relatively small, regional phone company in the U.S. to the third biggest in the country. Strategically it has added the $2.5 billion acquisition of cloud computing company Savvis, broadening its infrastructure portfolio and giving CenturyLink a worldwide presence. While growth is impressive, the company still seems to be hedging its bets concerning exactly which sector it is really concentrating on, in common with many other players.

Providing enabling services. This market is a close bedfellow to the infrastructure play but is an important value-added layer on top of the underlying infrastructure – yours or anyone else's

[83]World Economic Forum, January 2010

– so it is not geographically tied to where you have assets. These managed services leverage the internal operational functions that communications companies undertake every day. Their expertise can be offered to a variety of other digital providers who may choose not to perform these services themselves but prefer to contract someone with better economies of scale and expertise.

For example, security management, authentication services, service level agreement monitoring, charging and settlement services, customer relationship management services and so on can be provided on a managed services basis to a third party, provided you can do this more cost effectively and better than they can in-house.

The smart energy sector is an opportunity to provide the underlying infrastructure services of connectivity, computing and storage to transport, process and store metering information from millions of consumers, but also the additional services required to analyze and process information to produce and manage a consumer billing operation and provide additional services such as real-time demand information back to power generators to optimize consumption.

There are many other examples of these enabling services that digital service providers need to support their own services that represent fairly obvious 'low hanging fruit' for companies who already have competencies and scale in this area.

Again, the *do it big, do it cost effectively and do it very well* mantra applies because economies of scale, highly efficient operations and a high-quality customer experience are vital to any organization that is relying on your services as part of *their* go-to-market strategy.

Providing aggregated digital services and M2M capabilities to vertical markets. This market is a major opportunity for communications providers and leverages many of their strengths. Industry sectors such as energy, automotive, financial services, government, healthcare, manufacturing and retail industries are only just fully awakening to the implications and benefits that leveraging the digital world can bring, but that awakening is happening rapidly. Companies like salesforce.com have made a big, early impact but virtually every vertical industry segment will be open to some form of digital service market entry and the market window is wide open right now.

Communications players have huge potential to create packages of services aimed at businesses in specific market segments to help them serve their own customers more effectively. These could be achieved by aggregating a mixture of their own services (covering infrastructure, enabling and sector-specific application services) integrated and packaged with third-party services and aimed at specific verticals. In particular, these services fit tightly with M2M applications in these sectors, as I outlined in Chapter 2, where I gave some examples of these services aimed at different sectors and segments, such as small to medium and large, multi-national businesses. They would probably need to be taken to market in partnership with specialist companies established in those sectors.

Success in this market allows communications providers to exploit a number of advantages that they already possess, such as a large customer base, brand strength, large-scale service reliability and trust. The match of competencies to the target market is much better than the consumer sector and where web-based competitors are weaker with few enterprise competencies.

Another area of considerable interest is the market to supply well-packaged business services to small and medium enterprises, for instance, a variety of cloud-based applications and communications services tuned and packaged for a specific sector or customer (as we saw with the plumbing company example outlined in Chapter 2). Communications companies are particularly rich in small and medium enterprise customers and often have a more sustaining ('sticky') relationship with them.

However, it's not a complete home run – market entrants will need to develop their competencies on a number of fronts: brokering and managing relationships with many different partners; understanding the needs of each sector; being able to offer tailored services to each segment; and providing great customer service. These competencies will demand considerable flexibility and agility to cater for the needs of different partners with different business models. Historically, communications service providers are not strong at managing equable partner relationships. We take a detailed look at this in Chapter 7.

Excellent and tailored customer support will also be a significant success factor – many communications companies do this well for their enterprise customers today but they do it for relatively simple products to mass markets. The aggregated services market I've described is far, far more complex. Achieving a sufficiently high level of tailoring and packaging of cloud-based applications so that companies trust them enough to run their business on them will need considerable investment and training in more specialized customer and technical support. To create the packages in the first place will demand first-rate software integration and support capabilities and sector-based specialists who understand each target market and their particular needs.

The entry point in this market will be generic cloud-based infrastructure services plus some application services of generic reuse as part of the mix. Many communications companies are 'cutting their teeth' on being a channel to market for more established cloud services such as Microsoft's Azure service. However, the real prize is to move quickly into more valuable and focused service bundles for specific industries, which will be much more 'sticky' than merely reselling single standalone services.

A number of communications companies have already established divisions focused on vertical sectors that will expand massively through M2M applications and therefore have high potential for early movers. However, many of the key characteristics outlined earlier will be vital for success – particularly developing an innovative and customer-centric approach. These markets are immature and a huge amount of learning will need to go on through small-scale pilots and trials, learning from mistakes and building on successes.

Beware the Murdoch/MySpace syndrome of heavy-handed management coupled with premature expectations of high levels of profit. Setting such priorities is likely to be counter-productive. The web player model of grabbing market share and learning as you go is the key.

In addition these markets will be about successful partnership management and empathy with the specific customer segments being targeted – a Henry Ford-type response of "any color as long as it's black" won't work. Since it will be virtually impossible to develop all of the necessary competencies and understanding of each vertical sector, selective partnering with specialist providers on a case-by-case basis will be very important.

I do want to emphasize that any of these moves will require significant expertise in IT and software integration. Most communications companies completely misunderstand the need for software centricity in the digital world and continue down their traditional path of seeing IT as a supporting activity to the 'real' business of running a network that dates back to the days of clockwork switches and copper. Modern networks are software. Cloud-based services are software. Peel back the coating of Google, Amazon and Apple and you'll see masses of advanced and highly skilled software developers – they *are* the business, not merely supporting it.

Communications providers who want a future in infrastructure provision and who are downsizing or outsourcing all of their current in-house IT skills are making a big mistake. Outsourcing the maintenance of legacy junk makes sense, but don't throw your babies out with the bathwater – you're going to need every one of them. If fact, you almost certainly won't have enough in-house expertise and will need to look at more innovative software development and integration skills either through acquisition of companies or aggressive recruitment. Systems integrators have this kind of skill today and partnerships, mergers or acquisitions between communications companies and systems integrators may well come back into fashion because of this.

Action this day

I can't stress the importance of grabbing turf in the digital economy quickly, even if early moves are not as yet as profitable as the existing cash cow business that they are designed to replace. Early action moves you up the learning curve; makes it clear to customers that you are open for business and informs stock markets that you are not fiddling while Rome burns (see my advice to market analysts in Chapter 5).

Different parts of the world and different market sectors are evolving at different rates but as the time taken to effect change is nearly always longer than the time for markets to develop, it is vitally important to act decisively and determine the market segments you want to be a major player in, those you don't and those you want to exit.

The reason for action is not just to capitalize on opportunities or address threats; it will also help you make the right short-term decisions. As I said above, you would be unwise to take short-term actions that would damage building up strong software competencies – yet companies are doing this every day. If you want to be in the infrastructure business, don't damage those competencies. If your path is going to concentrate purely on services and not on infrastructure, then start to move in that direction as quickly as possible before you get caught up in the whole 4G spectrum and infrastructure investment cycle.

One major impact of the digital economy is it enables companies to unbundle their activities and concentrate on specific areas with much greater clarity and intent. We will see a continual reduction in the number of companies in the infrastructure space and at the same time a continued explosion in the number of product innovation businesses (such as the many thousands of applications developers, games developers and so on), which are likely to exploit low barriers to entry and to be characterized by large numbers of small businesses. Product innovators need speed and flexibility and to be highly creative – all of which tend to favor smaller organizations.

This concept of tight focus, M&A in some market segments and unbundling in others, will cause many painful decisions in the transformation process to realign businesses and face the opportunities and threats in the digital world. Time is not on the side of companies who shy away from bold decisions – the digital economy *is* having a big impact and opportunities open today may fade very quickly. At the same time, threats that are not clear now can loom out of the mist with amazing rapidity; sources of strength can turn into sources of weakness almost overnight and even the most successful company can swiftly find itself in an untenable position.

Clearly the infrastructure service provider segment will appeal to players that already operate large-scale infrastructures in either mature or developing markets, or both. The most likely candidates for the business enabler model include providers that have already begun opening up their networks and assets to third parties, or plan to do so, and new challengers who have embraced the concept and can now build on their partner management and wholesaling capabilities.

The enterprise service aggregator role is likely to appeal to those providers who have a strong enterprise customer base already and particularly those with service and software integration skills in-house. That should not exclude acquisitions to make good any shortfall in competencies or reputation. Enterprises which rely on these services to run *their* business will do a lot of due diligence on your competencies to ascertain you are the right supplier. The deeper the competencies and the longer the track record in providing sophisticated enterprise level services, the better.

The consumer services retailer role will be the most difficult for communications players to succeed in the long term (even though they start with a massive retail customer base) because of the narrowness of their consumer service portfolio and lack of experience in understanding the needs of consumers and their lifestyles. Brand and image are also very important here and in the fiercely competitive digital retail market it may be all too easy for communications company brands to be painted as out of touch by the fickle nature of market fashion, particularly among younger consumers.

One thing is obvious – if communications companies want to be big market players in the digital world, outside of the infrastructure segment, they have to solve the market fragmentation problem I have referred to several times. They must ensure that the rules of the game are not dictated by a small number of closed digital worlds dominated by infomediaries who control the route to market and how services are delivered, their terms and conditions; technical interfaces and so on. No single communications company has a big enough market reach to rival Apple, Amazon and Google but together they are bigger than everyone else. So they *must* play the card of offering, creating and fostering an open digital economy that allows open trading between any part of the digital ecosystem in a federated approach where the common currency is open standards.

They know how to do this: after all they created the world's largest 'machine' – the global communications system where a small number of standards link anyone to anyone. The open digital economy must, of course, go further with standards such as those covering security, authentication, onboarding services, service level agreements and revenue management. The standards are the easy bit – getting the understanding that it needs to be done and making it happen is much harder.

Reach beyond your back-yard
The digital economy means the market will be almost entirely borderless, apart from those

countries who seek to impose Draconian controls. The whole nature of cloud-based services relies on economies of scale and utilizing under-loaded infrastructure in different parts of the world on a virtual basis. Whether you achieve global reach through infrastructure directly under your control or through a federation of partners using common standards will be a decision downstream, but the vision needs to be global even if you initially enter the market on a more limited basis.

Providing enterprise application services will require economies of *scope* – in other words you get economies from a broad portfolio of services rather than a narrow one. Again, a global market vision will be very important because if you aren't global, it will be difficult to compete with companies that are. Service aggregators that limit their focus only to those geographies where they have physical infrastructure will be much less successful for the same reason that operator-based app stores failed – they simply don't provide originators of services with enough reach.

Many communications companies have successfully built up large global footprints with the mobile market being the most proactive and successful. Vodafone is the most obvious (and now that it has moved ahead with acquiring Cable & Wireless will be by far the largest) but others such as Qatar-headquartered Qtel Group; UAE-based Etisalat; Russia's Vimplecom; the Malaysian Axiata group and Indian-based Bharti are among those who have been very active. Telefónica, Orange and Telenor have also built up or acquired an impressive international presence.

Today many of these groups are often loosely coupled operations and brands under a holding company with different infrastructures and operational approaches in each country and inconsistent customer experience across the group. To fully leverage the global aspects of the digital world, communications service providers needs to integrate their operations much more tightly to offer a uniform portfolio, similar look and feel features, a common customer experience, constant quality and be able to offer a big market footprint to partners. They must also rationalize their infrastrucure to leverage procurement muscle and run operations on an international, not a national, level, in order to exploit cost advantages over smaller players.

Again this can be a slow process, so a fast-track route would be to use a more federated approach within and possibly between groups using common standards and common data as the 'glue' at the trading points of touch in the ecosystem.

Make radical simplification a core competency
If unbundling and focusing on core business is not challenging enough, another key requirement for success among communications players is the radical simplification of the way their businesses operate. Whichever segments are chosen, the business of creating, delivering and monetizing digital services is relatively straightforward. Complexity tends to creep in over time.

This isn't just confined to communications service providers and I'm sure that the first waves of employees at Facebook, Google and Microsoft would be astounded at how quickly corporations can develop layers, complication and duplication almost as fast as they recruit users. Indeed, on being appointed CEO of Google, co-founder Larry Page instituted a number of changes to simplify what he regarded as an overly complex and bureaucratic structure that had grown up.

As Ray Ozzie, creator of Lotus Notes and former Chief Software Architect at Microsoft, once said: "Complexity kills". In a large company, it is not at all unusual for processes to be so convoluted that nobody understands them all end-to-end. The same goes for systems where there may be hundreds or even thousands of separate systems handling billing, customer care, planning, order management, fault management and so on.

How does this happen? There are lots of reasons, but the most common is the proliferation of departmental-level processes and systems with little or no overall control exercised. It comes and goes with management fashion – centralization of decision-making can be very effective at reducing duplication and fragmentation but it also means that decisions are too far removed from the people doing the job and what they need to do it well. Companies typically go through cycles of centralization and devolution.

Time is another factor: the greater the length of time you have been in business, the likelihood is the business becomes more complex – and some communications players have been around for many decades with many arcane and complex processes and systems that grew organically. For others the problem has been compounded by growth: rapid growth causes people to implement systems and processes as quickly as they can with the intention of going back and optimizing them at some future stage, but they rarely do.

Growth by acquisition brings another set of challenges as the acquired parts of the company generally have their own culture, processes and systems and rationalizing them can be a huge challenge. This is especially true if they are spread across countries with different traditions. So to be successful, M&A programs need to be supported by the routine, repeated, radical simplification of processes if operating costs are to be continuously driven down. That demands setting clear goals for business processes and blueprints for systems, as we explore in Chapter 7. Without that, the spaghetti will just get more tangled, operating costs will rise, customer service will decline and time to market for new innovations lengthens. I'll focus on some of these tools and techniques in Chapters 11 to 14.

Whatever the underlying cause of complexity and whatever the business model, the fact remains that the companies that are going to win are those that deliver great services, representing good value to the customer, while delivering better profits than their rivals. Market economics and stock markets always favor the lowest cost (not price) provider who can provide consistently attractive services because they create the best returns to shareholders. Apple stands as a testament to this – everyone looks at the great design and customer appeal but the real secret of Apple's success is its prowess in highly optimized manufacturing and supply chain management.

Winning doesn't need to be absolute, if your results are consistently ahead of the pack, your stock price will rise relative to your competitors and you'll be like a lion looking for an antelope with a limp. That's how the U.S. communications market re-consolidated after the breakup of AT&T – the various regional operating companies didn't go bust – some just weren't performing as well as others and so were prey to acquisition.

As the global market consolidates and large players hunt for ever more scope and scale, the strong will pick off the weak: becoming efficient isn't like tidying up your guest room, something you'll get round to when you get time. Being a bit less efficient doesn't normally mean a fast track to bankruptcy (although the airline business worldwide might not agree), it's about not being at a *relative* disadvantage to your competitors and being open to absorption by another company or perhaps worse, a slow drift into irrelevance.

Most communications service providers have had a golden decade since the turn of the 21st century when the fantastic growth of mobile revenues masked operating inefficiencies. In the few cases of fixed-line only operators the problem has been clear for some time. In the 1990s, BT was among the largest and most profitable companies in any business sector in the world, but the multiple effects of a very open market with brutal competition, haphazard regulation, the lack of a mobile arm and some questionable management decisions have seen it slip down the global rankings. By 2010, only 20 percent of phone calls in the U.K. were made over BT's network[84] and profits were roughly half the level they had been 20 years previously[85]. It's not the first and certainly won't be the last player in such a position and like any stragglers behind the main pack, it is vulnerable to being swallowed up.

The aim has to be a set of highly automated, highly integrated business processes that operate at least cost with the maximum business agility and deliver the highest level of customer experience. Those three factors are often seen as being in conflict and many companies fail because they focus only on the cost reduction aspects.

That's the much quoted 'three legged stool' that I first used in *The Lean Communications Provider* – get one leg of the stool longer than the others and it falls over. The aim of radical simplification is to produce a sustainable, agile growth business, not just to improve financial results over the next few quarters. For sure, moving to high levels of automation and integration will eliminate expensive labor but the focus should be on the agility and improved customer service benefits even more than the operating cost reduction.

[84]Ofcom Annual Communications Market Report 2011
[85]Publicly quoted results: www.fundinguniverse.com/company-histories/BT-Group-plc-Company-History.html

Many large companies tend to want to build their own custom business processes that need customized software systems to automate them. This in turn leads to highly inflated IT budgets, typically with customization and integration costs being at least five times the cost of packaged software. Naturally, everyone would like to drive a handmade Rolls-Royce but not everyone can afford it and in highly competitive markets, the luxury of high levels of customization cannot be justified. I'm not saying don't differentiate, I'm saying build differentiation into the small number of places where being different generates value, not cost.

A radical simplification program needs to be seen as a totality and I give a lot more detail in Chapter 11 onwards. If attempted in a piecemeal fashion, by one division of the company or without proper commitment and backing, then it is likely to fail. Success demands huge energy and drive, especially from corporate leadership because organizations are hard to change – remember that your competitors, many of whom you don't even know about yet, have a whacking great advantage in not having the deadweight of legacy culture, processes and systems.

And culture is perhaps one of the hardest areas to change because the thinking behind the phrase "this is how we do things round here" goes very deep: it is only when a disruptive force comes along that cultures face serious challenges – and the digital economy is a massive disruptive force.

5

JOKERS IN THE PACK: EXTERNAL FACTORS

Some things you can control, but governments aren't one of them. There's a place for regulation, but the market is a powerful mechanism for sorting out what is needed. Regulators need to move from their former role of breaking down monopolies to encouraging market development and investment. Market analysts have a significant role to play here, too.

As former British Prime Minister Harold Macmillan[86] once said when describing the greatest threat to fulfilling a strategy: "Events, dear boy, events." Even the best-laid plans can get wrecked by uncontrollable, external factors. Players navigating the choppy waters of the digital world will also face numerous challenges that they can't control and perhaps the greatest of these, particularly for heavily regulated communications companies, is the action of governments.

The communications industry as we know it today is largely a creature of regulation: governments have wanted to intervene in this market as far back as the early 20th century. In 1912, the British government took over supply of all telecoms services in the U.K. (except, weirdly, for one city, Hull in northern England) and in 1913 AT&T was granted a monopoly in the U.S., but remained in private hands. The monopoly approach spread across the world and was based on a fundamental principle formulated by AT&T President Theodore Vail in 1907 – that the telephone by the nature of its technology would operate most efficiently as a universal service.

Interestingly, the U.K. and the U.S. were also the first to break the monopolies of their communications industries over 70 years later. In 1984 they started a global trend, which has resulted in truly enormous growth for the industry and huge success, but the regulatory processes that still surround the communications industry are imperfect in many ways.

A regulatory framework was an essential tool to dismantle powerful monopolies, but regulators seem to want to continue regulating even when it's time to stop and let market forces take over. Of course there is a place for regulation, but it should be the minimum required to ensure that communications are open and available to all on reasonable terms, and avoid the abuse of power – be they market abuses by large companies or the abuse of privacy and information by companies and governments. Outside of those sorts of areas, market economics are pretty good at dictating what is needed and when, especially as we are entering a whole new phase of the digital world and the critical role that communications play in enabling it.

Unfortunately, as we've explored already, not many communications companies have yet grasped the full realities of the digital world and, sadly, even fewer governments and regulators.

In the 1990s, when the big deregulation wave was happening around the world, the communications industry was highly vertically integrated and it was almost impossible to separate the various aspects of providing services. The network *was* the service and different services needed different networks. The early days of deregulation had little choice but to force competition on this vertical basis, in other words to stimulate multiple, competing networks to generate competing services to drive down prices for customers. This worked well, especially for mobile, which took off dramatically with everybody winning from the basic economics of elasticity of demand: competition drove lower prices; lower prices drove more customer demand; more customer demand drove more investment – fantastic result all round.

[86]Maurice Harold Macmillan, 1st Earl of Stockton, was British Prime Minister from January 10, 1957 to October 18, 1963

However, things happened that caused investment in infrastructure to become progressively less attractive. First the price of spectrum went through the roof as governments got greedy and used spectrum auctions as a way of dealing with debt and taxing the industry. Second, as markets started to saturate, prices and margins fell sharply on core products such as phone calls. Third, the advent of fixed and mobile broadband meant many other digital service providers can exploit the infrastructure investment of the communications companies without investing themselves, and crucially, the astronomical rise of the over-the-top companies generated unprecedented amounts of traffic, without communications providers getting a direct share in the revenue generated by their investment.

The revenue mix of communications providers was historically made up of line rentals and the cost of phone calls and messaging. With increasing competition, calls and messaging have been bundled with data packages and, as smartphones have proliferated, the mix has altered the revenue picture dramatically. While it varies considerably around the world, charges for data bandwidth now approach 50 percent of average revenue per user. This is likely to continue to grow towards 100 percent as traditional circuit switched voice and messaging are displaced by IP-based alternatives.

I am not presenting a 'bleeding heart' petition on behalf of communications companies – they can do that very well themselves – but just at the time that the digital economy needs a major escalation in infrastructure investment, regulation often seems to point the other way, reducing the appetite for building the technology base from which everyone will benefit enormously. Sure some governments are giving grants and handouts, but in the main these are a sticking plaster on a wound, often just giving back some of the money they took in the first place. A serious rethink is needed separating infrastructure regulation from service regulation, and bringing it into line with the realities of today rather than basing it on the needs of the latter part of the last century.

Infrastructure regulation: focus on encouraging, rather than smothering, it
Theodore Vail was right in the early 20th century, from an economic viewpoint. He would have seen the lunacy of multiple competing railway lines and realized that basic infrastructure like water pipes, gas mains, roads, railways and communications infrastructure is at its most efficient when you have one fully loaded network rather than many lightly loaded ones. So while deregulation stimulated the market and consumers benefited from technical advances and competition, a hidden tax on every communications user has been the price of building out multiple networks.

The economic reality of a small number of large networks rather than a large number of small ones, plus a small army of citizens angry at so many cell towers around their towns and countryside, has forced regulators to at least consider allowing infrastructure sharing, even if they have been reluctant to come right out and say that infrastructure-based competition was misguided. In recent years we've seen the acceleration of shared infrastructure on various

Short-term greed versus long-term prosperity

Governments can take credit for fueling the digital economy through breaking up the old telecom monopolies but that hasn't stopped them trying to swell their coffers through ham-fisted raids on the market's profitability.

In early 2000, the lessons of a disastrous auction of the 3G radio spectrum in the U.S. were not learned by the German and British governments, who pressed ahead hoping for a big tax windfall. Unlike the U.S. they allowed their telecoms industries to take the full risk of heavy speculative borrowing against the hype that 3G would instantly kick-start the digital economy. Of course, it did, but only after billions of dollars of R&D, network build-out and almost a decade later.

The sealed bid, online auctions offered a limited number of licenses and I well remember the quandary operators were put in: if they lost the bid, stock markets would punish them severely because they would be perceived as being locked out of the digital future, so they took massive risks with high bids, incurring enormous debt and it raised around ten times more than originally expected. In the U.K. auctions raised around $34 billion and around $45 billion in Germany. British finance minister Gordon Brown[87] was unmoved by the argument made by Nicholas Negroponte in his famous argument against this approach on the grounds it was "condemning our children to an information poor society".

In any event, government hubris blinded them to understanding the realities of the market, the complicated engineering and the huge investments in technology and applied punitive taxation at just the wrong time. What had initially looked like a quick win in tax revenue turned sour and damaged the European industry, which was at the time technologically ahead in the world markets. Stock markets lost confidence in the telecom industry and share prices tumbled. Operators' previously rock solid credit ratings slipped, meaning they could no longer borrow to fund the license fees and the costs of 3G rollout. They promptly exported their capital freeze to suppliers who felt an icy blast that cost 100,000 jobs within a year in telecoms support and development across Europe, with 30,000 coming from the U.K. alone.

The intervening years have seen much interesting regulatory behavior around the world, usually consisting of an elaborate dance between service providers and legislators in which the providers offer to increase investment in return for regulatory concessions while legislators threaten more regulation unless providers invest. Meanwhile the players who use that infrastructure, often at marginal rates, have been enjoying massive growth rates and have been trying to ensure that it continues through lobbying for Net Neutrality with debates ranging from informed to downright scaremongering – and I'll give my opinions on that vexed issue later in this chapter.

[87]Brown later became one of the least popular British Prime Ministers in recent history

commercial models and it is probable that almost all 4G networks will have to be the basis of shared infrastructure for economic as well as planning reasons.

Installing multiple optical fiber broadband networks, where each fiber in its own right is capable of almost unlimited bandwidth would be the height of folly, especially in access networks that would require multiple companies to dig up the same street. Countries like Australia and Singapore have recognized this in forming specialist organizations to run such networks on behalf of *all* of the service providers on an equal access and universal service basis.

Digital service providers need ubiquitous, fast and low-cost infrastructure to deliver their services to market. If the infrastructure is not there, out of date, too slow or doesn't cover enough of the country, it's bad news for everybody – for macro-economic development, for individuals, for enterprises and for the digital economy itself. Regulation needs to become much more attuned to the different segments of the digital world laid out in Chapter 2. Making investment in infrastructure unattractive helps nobody and mandating infrastructure competition is pointless – if players *do* want to compete on infrastructure, let them but don't force everyone to pay for an uneconomic model.

Of course, if there are only a few or even just one infrastructure player, safeguards need to be put in place to make sure they provide a universal, first-rate service at as low a cost as possible and that they don't abuse their market power. It is certainly not rocket science to come up with a formula for this and it doesn't have to be enforced by a government department. A not-for-profit corporation owned and/or funded by the service providers which use the infrastructure would be a sensible model with sufficient 'light touch' regulation to ensure privacy, security, open access and universal service. Provided that the operating license for such a utility provider is long enough to get a return on investment, money will flow.

Even if governments and regulators take no notice of these points, it's going to happen anyway: fighting the laws of economics is like fighting City Hall, you can't win and ultimately the infrastructure base is going to tend towards singularity as it's the most economically efficient way of doing it. Far better for that to be recognized and appropriate safeguards built in rather than letting it happen haphazardly, possibly with unforeseen consequences.

Digital service regulation: focus on letting the market run free but protect privacy

Generally speaking, I would not advocate any kind of heavyweight regulation of digital services and I agree with some of the founding principles of the web that it should be an open highway for everyone. However, highways attract highwaymen and we need some policing, particularly over the protection of personal information and security. As Roger McNamee said recently,[88] "the web has become rather like Detroit – look hard enough and you can find really useful things, but if you're not careful, you can get mugged!"

[88]www.ted.com/talks/roger_mcnamee_six_ways_to_save_the_internet.html

I wouldn't want to draw a line on what is and what is not acceptable content from a moral viewpoint because this is down to individual tastes and cultures and these things change over time. However, I *do* think it is unacceptable that people's personal privacy can be invaded without their knowledge or explicit approval. When I hear of things like smartphone apps that quietly raid your contact list without your permission or knowledge, I find it outrageous and believe that there must be some basic regulation and legislation to prevent such abuses. Beyond that, I think we should leave digital services to normal free-market principles and let the creativity of their innovators run riot.

An intrinsic problem here is that while governments may be sympathetic to curbing the ability of *private* companies to use information, they actually want to increase their *own* ability to penetrate the privacy of people using digital services. One might expect authoritarian governments to want to do this but, as an example, the U.K. government – home of the so-called mother of Parliaments – is progressively increasing its ability to spy on any and every transition in the digital world. Its *Regulation of Investigatory Powers Act* already allows the government and a wide range of other public bodies to:

- demand that an Internet service provider (ISP) provides access to a customer's communications in secret;
- undertake mass surveillance of communications in transit;
- demand ISPs fit equipment to facilitate surveillance;
- demand that someone hand over the keys to protected information;
- monitor people's Internet activities; and
- prevent the existence of interception warrants and any data collected with them from being revealed in court.

The benign-sounding *Digital Economy Act*, goes further and established a system of law aimed at making it easier to track down and prosecute persistent copyright infringers, but it also opened the door to further invasion of privacy by introducing "technical measures" which allow, among other actions, the legal termination of Internet connections. Readers familiar with George Orwell's novel *1984* will remember his fictional totalitarian government being able to make people non-citizens and while it may sound overly dramatic, this is the digital economy version of the same thing.

It seems this still is not enough. The U.K. Government has announced plans to introduce legislation that will require all digital services companies to install hardware that will allow the Government Communications Headquarters (Britain's electronic 'listening' agency), to gain real-time access to communications allowing it to trace who an individual or group is in contact with, how frequently they communicated and for how long by any means – phone, text, e-mail, Facebook, Twitter and Google.

So, while I hope that governments will turn their attention away from over-regulating the digital economy towards protecting the freedoms and privacy of their citizens, it seems they have the opposite in mind.

Net Neutrality regulation. This topic runs and runs and I have written about it a number of times, but not as clearly as Dr. Hossein Eslambolchi, some of whose thoughts[89] I draw on here. The basic issue is this: 'should all information flowing around the digital economy be treated equally?' The principle of fairness goes back 150 years to the days of telegraphy where laws in many parts of the world required that all messages were to be treated equally and managed on a 'first in, first out' basis.

Fast forward to the present day and on face value, those principles would appear to be still valid but some understanding of the technical issues is needed to grasp the consequences. The underlying transport mechanism is based on packet technology (typically multiprotocol label switching) for all digital services. All well and good except that some services in the digital economy are more affected than others by quality of service problems such as bandwidth limitation, latency[90], jitter[91] and packet loss[92]. For 'real-time' services such as voice, video conferencing, streaming video and some cloud-based services, this shows up as distortion or cutting out, jerky or frozen pictures and in the case of gaming applications, multiple players simply can't compete because of the delays.

So if all packets are treated equally, e-mail for example, which is not affected by delay, is treated the same as a voice call which would be badly impaired by even a tiny delay. The reality is that what seems like a simple and 'fair' rule isn't simple or fair at all because it creates unacceptable degradation of real-time services and an unreliable customer experience that ultimately dampens competition and puts the brake on the growth of the digital world. It's another of those well intentioned ideas (like having unbridled spectrum auctions) that has unintended consequences.

Of course there have to be safeguards and traffic management approaches should not be abused to discriminate against certain companies (which would almost certainly be illegal anyway under anti-trust or restraint of trade legislation in many countries). However, most countries to allow different grades of postal service where, if you pay more, your letters or parcels get there faster. If you wanted to travel from one city or another you could choose a car, a train, a bus or a plane and each would have different costs and different arrival times.

We allow choice in many areas, so why do we want a 'one size fits all' approach to communications? What's intrinsically wrong with having different grades of communications

[89]Dr. Eslambolchi's blogs: http://www.2020vp.com/hossein-blog/2011/12/net-neutrality-versus-net-fairness/
[90]Latency is a measure of time delay experienced in a network
[91]Jitter is a measure of the variability of the latency across a network: a network with constant latency has no jitter
[92]Packet loss occurs when one or more packets fail to reach their destination

service at different prices? Is it fair that everyone ultimately has to pay for the cost of over-engineering the network infrastructure when many people's needs are such that they wouldn't even notice a few milliseconds delay if they were web browsing or downloading content? On the other hand, you might be quite happy to pay a bit more for guaranteed quality of service if you were an avid multi-player gamer or to avoid a poor quality connection when performing surgery via telemedicine!

Providing credible, comparable information about service provider's traffic management policies will better serve the digital economy than more laws or forcing all information to have to wait its turn like a 19th-century telegram. Transparency, not more regulation, is the answer.

We can't regulate the digital economy by looking backwards. If we do, the rate of innovation is likely to be inversely proportional to the rate of regulation. That would hurt everyone – taken to its logical conclusion, we would need to eliminate traffic lights on roads, ban bus and taxi lanes and make everyone wait the same length of time in emergency rooms, regardless of whether they are bleeding to death or bumped their toe.

For anyone who knows anything about IP-based network technology, Internet traffic management is essential and non-negotiable. A policy of transparent, optimized and fair traffic management is needed around the world, not the dead-hand of more regulation.

It's not just communications regulation that is hindering the progress of the digital economy, which has immense power to do good for a huge number of people – mobile payments being a very good example. So I can't see why (apart from appeasing powerful interests) some governments, from India to Indonesia and the U.S. want to insist that mobile payments must be controlled by established banks. They have successful examples of pioneering services such as M-PESA in Kenya (see Chapter 9) as proof that simple mobile payments can transform lives and a country's economy – about a third of Kenya's GDP is flowing through M-PESA annually. And surely, if the last five years have taught us anything at all, it's that banks are not invincible, necessarily trustworthy, or always understand the consequences of their actions. Although it's not impossible, we have not yet seen a communications service provider being feckless with other people's money.

It's another example of regulating by looking in the rear-view mirror rather than accommodating and adapting to circumstances, needs and perhaps most importantly, the vast opportunities of the digital world. I wholly agree with the comment made by Paul Donovan, CEO, eircom Group, that, "I'd like to see a sign in the reception of every regulator's office stating the conditions for when they will no longer be necessary."

Financial analysts – another set of jokers in the pack

Governments (at least democratic ones) often come up with policies designed to fit the cycle for their re-election rather than the right thing to do because the time needed to make real change is longer than the usual period an elected government is in power. Too often, they concentrate on short-term tinkering rather than long-term structural change.

Short-termism also influences the behavior of investors and companies and is usually geared around quarterly or at best annual reporting cycles. The influence of analysts – particularly financial seers – shapes the thinking and behavior of investors and in turn the decisions of chief executives since their opinion translates directly to stock valuations and therefore is the *de facto* measure of success and ultimately the net worth of the CEO. It follows then that if the analysts are measuring the wrong things in the wrong timeframes, then the likelihood is high that those CEOs will make the wrong moves.

Like governments, CEOs are forced to make decisions that will boost quarterly results rather than concentrating on the kind of risky and long-run structural changes they need to make to ensure that the business transforms and avoid the Kodak moment described in Chapter 3.

Today, the staple measures of a communications company's performance include:

- **Earnings Before Interest, Taxes, Depreciation and Amortization (EBITDA):** This is a standard indicator of a company's financial performance calculated as revenue less expenses (excluding tax, interest, depreciation and amortization).
- **Average Revenue Per User (ARPU)** is used universally as a measure of growth or decline and monitors the revenue generated by one customer per unit of time, usually per year or month. Typically ARPU includes fixed charges plus revenue generated from incoming calls.
- **Customer numbers**, that is how many 'subscribers' as a proxy for size, which might well have little to do with profitability.
- **Churn rate** measures the rate at which customers leave for a competitor. The communications industry suffers the highest customer churn rate of any industry. Strong brand name, good marketing and excellent customer experience tends to mitigate churn. Increased churn exerts a downward pressure on ARPU.

These are reasonable measures for a market when it is in a steady state but the market is increasingly volatile and changing rapidly. Measures like customer numbers or ARPU don't measure the profitability of those customers and the metrics encourage CEOs to push towards running an unprofitable business. For example, if a company tries to maximize profit by shedding unprofitable customers in saturated markets, they are criticized for incurring high churn rates and reduced customer numbers.

In addition, revenues from current services are so large that they mask new revenues from new sources, so although the company may be carrying out good innovation or transformational change it won't be given any credit by analysts for some time, so why divert resources if the market, your stock price and personal bonus package is focused on the short term?

Financial analysts must do better at understanding the market dynamics at play and weight their analysis much more around moves to increase and sustain shareholder value in the mid term by making the kinds of strategic changes necessary rather than encouraging CEOs to squeeze one more quarter's results out of a business model and set of services which are on their way to becoming irrelevant. To do this, they should be asking CEOs tough questions about their strategy, what moves they are making towards attaining their goals and figuring out if the strategy adds up. Instead they too continue to look in the rear-view mirror and reward short-term fiscal engineering.

Cutting costs in huge business isn't that hard and you can milk that goat for a long time if you aren't worried about making the kinds of investments in technology, people and culture that the business will need to sustain and grow in the coming decade. Analysts and markets should not be encouraging that behavior, quite the opposite; they should be punishing it for what it is – short term and short sighted.

It's also worth noting that none of the major financial analysts or the ratings agencies, whose power has grown out of all proportion in the last decade, saw the global banking crisis looming, and the odd voice that warned against impending doom was ridiculed. You can't get any clearer evidence that analysts of all stripes are not all-knowing, so it's a surprise they remain so powerful and have such a massive impact on share prices.

6

THE CRITICAL IMPORTANCE OF STRONG LEADERSHIP AND CLEAR GOALS

"Play it safe, leadership by committee" kinds of people didn't win the Oklahoma Land Rush: they never left home for fear of being trampled. Neither will they be winners in the rush to stake out territory in the digital world – those that do will be typified by visionary leaders at the helm of companies that are brave, bold and far sighted but with teams who can also execute well by setting clear goals and directions.

Strong leadership, in the form of enthusiastic involvement from the CEO and the top management gets rated consistently as among the most important factors in successful transformation. This is self-evident – you won't get very far if senior management are not particularly interested in the program, or even worse, some top managers are actively trying to undermine it.

I remember once being involved in a major business reengineering program that selected the company's top 100 'best and brightest' people to lead it, only to find that some of the divisional presidents were skeptical about the program on the grounds that engaging in it might not be the best career move. It disappeared without trace after a few months.

Leadership is a quality which is hard to define but you know it when you see it and its importance has been recognized since the dawn of civilization. History's greatest philosophical writings such as Plato's *Republic* and Plutarch's *Lives* have explored the question of 'What qualities distinguish an individual as a leader?' Leaders are not the same as managers – managers are good at managing the status quo. As agents of change, leaders want to take the organization to where it needs to be next.

The terms leadership and management are often confused because both may have the organizational power to direct and take big decisions. In fact, they are different types of people, perform different roles and have a part to play at different times in a company's evolution. Good leaders aren't necessarily good managers and may not even be particularly likeable people. Steve Jobs was a brilliant leader but his refusal to suffer fools is legendary. Winston Churchill had the same reputation and showed that while he was outstanding as a leader in the crisis of wartime, his management of a country in the aftermath of war was less exemplary.

I was introduced to the work of Dr. Meredith Belbin many years ago and his ideas on the subject have stuck with me throughout my career. Today Belbin is Professor and Honorary Fellow of Henley Management College in the U.K. He and his team developed some interesting research on the character traits of individuals that make up successful teams[93]. He identified nine types of role that make up highly successful teams – all nine are important even though they have very different characters and contribute differently towards the team's success.

Belbin doesn't use the word leader, but defined two types of role in a successful team whose attributes are critical to providing the leadership of and direction to the team. These are the *Plant*, people who are highly creative and good at solving problems in unconventional ways, and the *Shaper.* They are challenging individuals who provide the necessary drive to ensure the team keeps moving and doesn't lose focus or momentum.

[93]R Meredith Belbin, *Management Teams: Why They Succeed or Fail* (Butterworth Heinemann, 3rd ed., 2010) ISBN: 978-1-85617-8075. www.belbin.com/rte.asp?id=8

These attributes are often found in leader types, but they often lack some of the other characteristics that are important to execution. For example, *Implementers* are needed to plan a practical, workable strategy and carry it out as efficiently as possible and *Completer Finishers* are used at the end of a task, to 'polish' and scrutinize the work for errors, subjecting it to the highest standards of quality control. Belbin's fundamental point is that it takes different types of people with different character traits to make up highly effective teams – recruitment in your own image tends to build very lopsided teams, only good at certain tasks.

If you have ever seen one of those team-based game shows on TV or been involved in some management team building, you'll know that teams consisting only of leaders tend to fail miserably because they spend all their time arguing over the right direction. Equally, teams comprising good implementers also fail because they lack the vision to know what to do.

In his seminal book, *Leadership,*[94] James MacGregor Burns defined the two types of leader: first, *Transformational* leaders who focus on the big picture, needing to be surrounded by people who take care of the details. Throughout World War II, Churchill famously employed red stickers of his own invention labeled: "Action This Day", which he affixed to memos in the corner of a paper sent to the much put-upon coterie of people who made things happen for him. The leader is always looking for ideas that move the organization to reach the company's vision; usually brilliant communicators, this leader is highly visible and uses a chain of command to get the job done. The second type, Burns called *Transactional* leaders, who I would call managers, are given power to evaluate, correct and train subordinates when productivity is at the desired level and reward effectiveness when the outcome wanted is reached.

People take their direction from true leaders because they believe in them and *want to* follow them whereas the more conventional 'boss' type of manager gets people to follow them because they *have to,* to keep their jobs – they may be very good at managing stable companies but are not much help and may be a constraint in times of change.

However you wrap it up, transformation of an entire company or an entire market is a complicated and sometimes scary journey into the unknown for most people. Imagine a column of people marching through the woods in the dead of night who have no idea where they are going; they just know they need to follow the person in front of them. Their morale and belief they will come out safely and not be eaten by a bear is greatly improved if they have faith in the judgment of the person at the head of the column, who they believe knows where they are going.

A transformation journey is not so very different. People shouldn't be in the dark because the communications from executive management will be frequent and illuminating, but the same basic story applies that a leader who can inspire confidence, loyalty and get people to follow their direction is a huge asset in undertaking this journey.

[94]Burns, J. M. *Leadership*. New York: Harper and Row Publishers Inc, 1982. ISBN: 978-0061319754

Many leaders aren't the right people to face the digital tsunami

Industries like the communications sector have needed good managers to ensure they delivered results when the competition heated up – driving sales up and driving costs down relentlessly for as long as the 'gravy train' continues to run. Many may be former chief financial officers because they can attack the cost base to keep margins up, even when the top line starts to fall. Many may be great sales people who can squeeze every last drop from revenue.

The chaos of the digital economy and the need to radically shift position means that many people at the helm today are not the right people. There's no shame in that, it's just that at different stages of a company or a market you need different skills. Geoffrey Moore described it well in his books that have become Silicon Valley bibles[95] – Google's investors brought in Eric Schmidt to turn the founders' dreams into a successful business but he in turn handed over to Larry Page when Page had gained enough experience to kick-start Google's next phase.

The dangerous time is when change is needed and the manager types and/or their boards don't recognize it's time to move aside. Periods of change – and the digital economy is bringing more change than we have ever seen faster than we have ever seen it – need visionary leaders who can foresee what the future shape of the market will be and know how to steer their company to maximize the opportunities that it can bring. Ultimately it's all about innovation in the products and services that you create and inventing a delivery machine that can provide a great customer experience at an economic price. Today, too many companies that are about to be engulfed by the digital tsunami don't have the right kind of leader to reposition their company to take advantage of it or know how to defend against it.

Jobs railed against 'milking the cash cow' when he was quoted in Isaacson's biography saying, "The company starts valuing the great salesman, because they're the ones who can move the needle on revenues." IBM and Xerox, Jobs said, faltered in precisely this way. The salesmen who led those companies were smart and eloquent, but "they didn't know anything about the product".

Commenting on Jobs' views, the *Wall Street Journal's*[96] Peggy Noonan makes some good observations, which apply well to the communications and computing giants chasing a premier spot in the digital ecosystem. She extended the argument beyond a sales focus to accountants and the money men "who search the firm high and low to find new and ingenious ways to cut costs or even eliminate paying taxes. Because they appear to be adding to the firm's short-term profitability, they are celebrated and well rewarded, even as their activities systematically kill the firm's future."

To push the point home further, Noonan sums up much of what is wrong with large, sclerotic organizations and it's not hard to recognize these symptoms in many companies:

[95]*Crossing the Chasm* and *Inside the Tornado*
[96]Peggy Noonan, *Wall Street Journal – On Steve Jobs And Why Big Companies Die*, November 2011

"Because it's easier to milk the cash cow than to add new value, the firm forgets how to play offense. Basically, the firm is dying, as it continues to dispirit those doing the work and to frustrate its customers. As the managers find it steadily more difficult to make money, they become desperate and start doing ever more perilous things, like looting the firm's pension fund or cutting back on worker benefits or outsourcing production in ways that further destroy the firm's ability to innovate and compete."

To me the value of a visionary leader is summed up very clearly by Jobs: Apple's success was a night and day difference with and without his leadership. He showed conclusively what happens when a company plays offensively and focuses totally on adding value for customers. Not only did he reverse the decline of Apple in spectacular fashion, steering it towards being the world's most valuable company, but it's worth remembering that in his career he transformed four industries – the computer industry through the original Apple; the movie industry through Pixar; the music industry through the iPod and iTunes; and of course the phone business through the iPhone and App Store.

The qualities of the leader must match the period you are in: at times of financial constraint, maybe you do need a good CFO-type at the helm and in a start-up, good inventors always help. Most definitely at periods of intensive change you need an inspirational visionary who is an excellent communicator and motivator.

I have a dream… communicating exceptionally well
Having a clear vision and well thought out goals are academic if people in and around the organization don't know what those goals are or don't understand what is required of them to achieve that vision. Being a good communicator is a vital task of a leader but is also an important hallmark of the guiding coalition driving the transformation because you want to ensure that people understand and accept the vision and know what they need to do.

Doing this well is very difficult: if you have ever played the game known in Britain as Chinese Whispers (called 'Telephone' in the U.S. and I'm told, 'Air-phone' in China) you'll know how easy it is for even a simple and clear message to become hopelessly distorted when passed from person to person. When trying to explain a vision to an entire organization, communication must be exceptionally good and as direct as possible to avoid the message being messed up by people who are less able to communicate or don't really understand it.

Many organizations fail to grasp the importance of clear and regular communication – Dr John Kotter[97], perhaps the best-known authority on leadership and change, estimates that most companies under-communicate their visions by at least a factor of 10.

---

[97]Dr. John Kotter is a Professor at the Harvard Business School; *Business Week* magazine rated him as "the #1 leadership guru" in America. Author of 17 books, his international bestseller *Leading Change*, Harvard Business Press, outlines a clear process for implementing successful transformation

These days there really is no excuse for poor communications: even the smallest company has access to low-cost and effective communication tools through videoconferencing, YouTube, blogs, social media, conference calls and so on. The tools are there but often senior executives either lack the skills or the understanding that it needs to be done consistently and regularly. You can go too far though – it has to be balanced against unduly distracting those individuals charged with keeping current operations functioning while the program is underway. Nevertheless, if in doubt – communicate!

Forbes magazine called Jobs "the world's most inspiring communicator"[98] and in an editorial that described his presentations said: "They were simply astonishing – a Steve Jobs presentation doesn't just deliver information – it informs, educates and entertains."

Few are as gifted as Steve Jobs, but anyone who can't communicate effectively shouldn't be in the role of leader in the first place. There are plenty of training courses, books, coaching and guidance available to anyone who really wants to improve their communication skills but after a lifetime of doing this for a living, it's worth keeping a few things in mind.

Simplicity. Remember that, as a senior executive, you can often see a much broader landscape of the market and your company than many of your employees can. They often just see a small slice of the bigger picture. It's what I call the 'elephant and the slotted fence syndrome' – in other words if you put an elephant behind a slotted fence you would just see a series of grey stripes. The job of the leader in communicating the vision is to describe the elephant (the vision) but also clearly communicate the value of each strip of grey (the role that you want divisions and groups to play). The vision and goals should be communicated in terms that are as simple as possible. It's a hackneyed phrase but the 'keep it simple, stupid' principle is really worth bearing in mind. Jargon doesn't translate[99] well, especially from the boardroom to the people who actually run the organization.

Visual and vivid. The clearer the picture of the future, the more people will understand it. You should try to paint a vivid picture that will capture imaginations and stick in the mind – I like to use metaphors and analogies all the time when I'm speaking and find that these help tremendously in getting across ideas with people from other cultures or countries. CEO Stephen Elop's analogy of Nokia standing on a burning oil rig with the only course of action available being to jump into freezing water was brilliant – people might not have liked the message but it was certainly vivid and sticks in the imagination.

Repeatable. Communications should also be highly repeatable, that's to say they are simple and arresting enough to be passed on through the organization and stay intact – avoiding the 'Chinese Whispers' problem. And because misunderstanding is all too frequent, communication

[98]www.forbes.com/sites/carminegallo/2011/08/26/steve-jobs-the-worlds-most-inspiring-communicator/
[99]It's why I've tried very hard to use the minimum number of acronyms and jargon in this book

should not just be in one direction – wherever you can, invite questions and feedback so that people really understand what you're saying and what you want them to do.

Walk the talk. Communicating isn't just about what is said – most people judge someone by what they do rather than what they say. So the actions of the leadership team can be even more important than the communications messages they send out. As they say in America, you need to "walk the talk" because nothing inspires more than the senior management team behaving in a different way and embodying the changes that they preach. At the same time, nothing undermines a transformation program faster than inconsistent actions by the top team.

Positive and personal. For people to really get behind turning a vision into reality, it needs to make people want to do it. Put crudely, that means there is some reward for individuals when all the hard work is done. If the vision paints a picture of someone else getting all the rewards, then expect your vision to hit the rocks when it comes to implementation. I'll talk more about reward systems later in this book but a vision should score a hit in the mind of the person receiving the message and be something that will benefit others personally or directly (not just abstractly or 'it seems like a good idea').

Possible and believable. Finally, the message must convince the listener that the vision is possible and they can believe that success is achievable. That doesn't mean it should be 'dumbed down' – there's nothing wrong with the vision being inspiring, stretching and implying a lot of hard work but if it seems too fantastical or crazy then many people won't take it seriously. This is a difficult balancing act since true transformation is often about implementing ideas that seem crazy on first hearing.

Life in the digital world is full of ideas that conventional wisdom said couldn't be done. Marketing used to be easy a couple of decades ago – you went out and surveyed what people wanted and then got on and built it. Today it's all about innovation, 'thinking outside of the box' and making big leaps of faith to put a product in front of customers that they didn't even know they wanted but, quoting Matt Bross's mid-Western best, they "know good when they see it". Being visionary is good, but the goal needs to be explained with sufficient clarity and passion that the people who have to implement it believe it is possible and a good idea.

Nothing I've said here is revolutionary; the average politician does it every day. Politicians tend to be very good communicators because if they aren't, they don't get elected and won't be politicians very long. Business leaders can learn a lot from watching how top-notch politicians communicate complicated ideas to large numbers of people by being direct and clear. The best of them inspires and unlocks passion and energy: former British Prime Minister Tony Blair arguably wasn't always a good judge of policies or even a great prime minister but he is a superb communicator and could carry an entire nation with him at times.

To achieve successful transformation to the digital world, you'll need all the help you can get and a critical element of good leadership and communication is setting clear, achievable goals. This has long been understood: Publilius Syrus, a first century BC Syrian, certainly understood this. One of his many maxims was: "Whatsoever you attempt, consider your goal" and since he started life as a slave but by his wit and talent won the favor of his master, who freed and educated him, he seems to have had a clear goal and executed on it.

It's the word *clear* that is the important one here: lots of people set goals but if they're not clear to the people who have to execute on them they're a waste of time. Fuzzy goals – ones that can be interpreted in different ways – send people off in different directions and usually the net sum of their efforts tends toward zero.

Lighthouse goals
I call these overarching aims 'lighthouse goals' because like a lighthouse they should shine a clear beam to guide people to their destination. Many vision statements and goals are crafted by committees who want to throw a bone to every department and function in the organization and consequently these politically correct but practically useless statements have little effect. They remind me of the scene from Monty Python's *Life of Brian*[100] where the leaders of the People's Front of Judea are trying to decide what they stand for – hilarious, but forever going round in circles.

By having clear goals, people know what they are striving to achieve and a sense of accomplishing them. Workers are much more motivated to achieve goals if they have a reason to want to achieve them and particularly if they feel they have been given a degree of personal responsibility for their achievement.

John F. Kennedy's famous 'Man on the Moon' speech[101] was a model of lighthouse goal-setting – a compelling vision for a nation which, at the time, was very much an 'also ran' in space technology. He said: "We choose to go to the moon in this decade and do the other things, not because they are easy, but because they are hard, because that goal will serve to organize and measure the best of our energies and skills, because that challenge is one that we are willing to accept, one we are unwilling to postpone, and one which we intend to win."

Lighthouse goals must 'speak' to everyone involved in their achievement otherwise there will be little personal identification or motivation with the goals. They must be specific, measurable, attainable, realistic, time-targeted, evaluated and re-evaluated.

Big visions need big goals
Kennedy's 'We choose to go to the moon in this decade" goal was big and daring. He didn't clutter the clarity or enormity of it by a lot of implementation detail. Jim Collins has written

---

[100]*Monty Python's Life of Brian*, Dir Terry Jones, 1979
[101]Address at Rice University on U.S. space goals, September 12, 1962

some highly influential business books[102] and coined some great terms in his time. One of them is the *Big Hairy Audacious Goal* to stimulate companies to define visionary goals that are strategic and emotionally compelling.

Some good examples of Big Hairy Audacious Goals that have the 'lighthouse' effect for me are:

- **Amazon:** To be Earth's most customer-centric company; to build a place where people can come to find and discover anything they might want to buy online.
- **Skype:** To be the fabric of real-time communication on the web.
- **Microsoft:** A computer on every desk and in every home.
- **Google:** Organize the world's information and make it universally accessible and useful.
- **Apple** has never published one, but this from the new CEO Tim Cook comes close: "We believe that we're on the face of the Earth to make great products…we're constantly focusing on innovating. We believe in the simple, not the complex. We believe that we need to own and control the primary technologies behind the products we make, and participate only in markets where we can make a significant contribution."

Many of these may have evoked a snigger or even a 'yeah right' from complacent competitors when they were formulated by relatively unknown companies, but each went on to fulfill their goal, or get close to it, and in the process became mega corporations.

Of course, they were fortunate to start with a blank sheet of paper and weren't held back by decades of history and culture, unlike many others. When focusing on change and transformation, the sheet of paper is usually far from blank – in fact it's likely to be full of illegible scribbles because the organization is so complex, it's hard to understand it, end-to-end. In Chapter 13, I lay out some thoughts on radical simplification: simplicity should be the aim not only of the message itself but also a practical end-goal. If people can't understand how a company works, then they are unlikely to be in a position to ensure the transformation program runs as efficiently and effectively as possible.

Simplicity also needs some qualification: a goal like "we want to be number one" sounds good on the surface, but what is it a measure of? Does it mean number one in profitability or number one in earnings-per-share or number one in a customer survey or number one in terms of the size of the customer base? The ideal is to have a simple core to the message that everyone can buy into, supplemented by a balanced scorecard of broad, company-changing goals that will sustain over time.

Stretch the organization out of its comfort zone
Lighthouse goals are not short-term, tactical targets, they represent the big moves that the company needs to take. If necessary, they can be broken down into steps, but the point of

[102]*Great by Choice; Good to Great; How the Mighty Fall; Built to Last; Beyond Entrepreneurship*

lighthouse goals is that they aim to stretch the organization and to get people to see that they cannot possibly achieve the goal by just tweaking the way the business currently operates – transformation starts inside people's heads by encouraging innovation and driving new ways of thinking about issues.

That is why transformation and innovation go hand-in-hand – you can't have one without the other. I delve into innovation in Chapter 9, and it's worth bearing in mind that new kids on the block generally excel at innovation because they don't have the baggage of an existing business and ways of doing things to weigh them down.

Having the vision and talent to look beyond today and envisage the market as it will become, or indeed as you could make it become, is the interplay between vision, leadership and clear goal-setting. It's where the difference between a charismatic leader and a manager (or worse a committee) are likely to be sharply in contrast – a leader might 'bet the farm' on a deeply held personal view of the future whereas a manager or a committee will probably play it safe.

The 'play it safe' fraternity would examine the rate of market saturation of cash cow products and services and consider the historical impact of this on competition and margins. They might plot a time window in which transformation must be completed, but have no idea which innovative new markets could be exploited and instead point vaguely to whatever seemed to be in vogue at industry conferences.

The core of the strategy would be right – in the communications or computing industries nobody questions that the market will continue to drive providers down a 'more for less' route (that is, prices in real terms will continue to decline) and that gives a strong steer on how the business should be run, but where is the 'aim for the heart' idea – the soaring concept that will truly transform the company's position and *grow* revenues and market share, not merely ensure survival?

As I go around the industry worldwide I hear a lot of people talking about having set out to build a transformed company with substantially and continuously lower operating costs to maintain margins as service levels increase; continuous improvement in their customers' experience to maintain or grow market share; and continuous improvement in time to market for new services and innovations. The key question though is this – is it enough? Is being lean and mean enough to win a big slice of the digital world? Or does it provide a 'ticket to play' in a market where everyone has moved in the same direction and those that haven't are out of business.

The rapidity of which new services, new business models and new players are building the digital world is staggering and we have already seen a handful of companies take dominant positions from which they will be hard to shake (although not necessarily impossible as we explored in Chapter 3): Apple is the dominant smart device player, Google the dominant search player; Facebook the premier social networking platform; Amazon the biggest digital shopping mall; Skype the largest international phone company; and eBay the greatest marketplace.

Dominance brings some significant advantages but it can't be taken for granted. Also as discussed, relying on your competitors failing is not a great corporate strategy for communications, media and information companies.

Ensuring a lack of conflict

Having a clear process that everyone understands and can follow greatly increases the probability of transformational success because it reduces the overlaps, duplication, fragmentation and intra-departmental conflict which arises when different parts of the organization use different approaches that often contradict each other.

The fundamental scope of a transformation program and the sheer size of the organization can often have a paralyzing effect on the people involved. Where should they start? What and how should they prioritize? Who should do what and when?

As I'll expand much more in Chapter 10, transformations tend to fail more often in companies already under pressure and for good reason – in a failing company people are often too busy fighting fires to think about what is needed to transform the company. This frenetic preoccupation with the short term is common, especially in the parts of the world where recession is biting deeply and where the business culture focuses on short termism.

This is one of the reasons players in fast-growing markets such as Southeast Asia and the so-called 'BRICS' countries[103] have an advantage over their European and American counterparts. They are culturally geared up to take a longer-term view and the financial pressures on them are not so severe.

To really get people behind the lighthouse goals, they not only need to be inspirational, clear and stretching, they also need to be supported by more detailed themes whose objectives will move the company in stages towards the overall aim. In turn, themes need to be broken down into clear initiatives, which should be clearly sequenced and leaders need to explain how they will relate to one another. There are a number of techniques that I'll review in more detail in later chapters.

I drew heavily on the Lean approach (which has many merits) in my last book and over the 15 years that have intervened, many practitioners have fused the Lean approach with the Six Sigma process. While Lean and Six Sigma processes are primarily approaches to improve current business they can help considerably in giving a disparate organization form and structure to look at the transformation process end-to-end to help keep everyone synchronized.

[103]Brazil, Russia, India, China and South Africa

Breaking down goals into themes and initiatives within a common process like this helps make transformation more manageable because it allows individual teams to focus on particular aspects of the task at a level of implementation detail, whereas the lighthouse goal is very high-level and lacking in any clues as to how to get there. This detail makes the corporate plan much more realistic, personal and exciting.

Articulating exactly which functions, geographies, product lines, processes and systems will be impacted by the transformation also helps reduces unnecessary anxiety in the organization. The number of themes will vary but there should not be too few (because they will of necessity be very broad if they are few in number) or too many because they will overlap and be confusing. Three to six themes appears to be about the right number and each should have leaders and be as distinct and self-contained as possible to avoid overlaps.

Focus of transformational goals

It's vitally important to know what is to be transformed and what is not. This comes back to having a clear vision of the business(es) you want to be in and the type of company you want to become. This is much harder than just improving the operations of your current business because there are often a number of "unknown unknowns" that get in the way. In reality you usually want to do both with a twin track approach:

- exploit your current business fully, which although it may be slowly sinking into the sunset could probably have its life extended by improving business efficiency and effectiveness;
- develop new business areas in parallel using different business models and approaches.

Many people – usually those who either lack vision or are going to retire shortly – will often try to obstruct a twin track approach, muttering about the folly of large-scale transformations and claiming life isn't as bad as people say. They will frequently want to move the current business forward *en masse* calling on the rather hackneyed analogy of trying to change the engines of a Boeing 747 while it is airborne. The problem then is two things tend to happen – the needs of the current business suck the life out of the effort to build the new business and the whole thing moves so slowly, the company misses the window of opportunity.

Competitor goals and benchmarks

Setting goals to drive a transformation program is difficult when viewed from an internal operational standpoint. It is often much easier to see if you stand outside the company and look from the viewpoint of the market – as a customer or even a competitor might. It's also tied up with first and second mover advantages (see Chapter 9): maybe you're the first and you have no competitors – yet. This thing is that in a globalized economy, competitors are coming fast and furious from countries and regions that aren't on many companies' radar. Or perhaps you are trying to take a market from someone else.

Either way, who *are* or who are or *might be* your competitors? Where are you vulnerable? In other words what kind of innovative services, positioning, pricing/packaging and quality might they offer to attack your chosen position? When and what would you do about it if they did? If you are the challenger, how exactly are you going to defeat them?

In uncertain times and when the market is immature, it's easy to view everyone as a competitor. Many companies I come across seem to be frightened of their own shadow and avoid partnering on the basis that the potential partner may turn into a competitor. The inverse is just as bad where the competitive threats are underestimated and a partner learns a lot from working with you before attacking you.

Competitors fall into two groups – those you can see and those you cannot. Of these, the competitors you can't see are by far the most dangerous, because you don't know they exist or even worse, because you have not understood the implications of their moves.

Perhaps they come from a different enough industry or starting point that they are able to take a radically different position than you. For example, British Airways tried to compete against companies like Virgin Atlantic by offering higher-quality wines and more comfortable seats. In the meantime, in Europe, the upstart low-cost carriers like EasyJet rewrote the rules of running an airline, catching everyone by surprise through offering super-low prices and no-frills service. Ryan Air, one of these players, is now the seventh largest[104] in the world by passenger numbers – considerably larger than British Airways.

Competition is all about relative strengths and weaknesses, not absolute measures. You need to be better than the competition so that you have more and happier customers, as well as happier shareholders. To do that you need to really understand your competitors – where they are in relation to you, how you are going to beat them, and how you are going to keep beating them?

Goal-setting also needs to take into account where competitors are now, where they might reasonably be expected to go, and where they could attack you if they changed the rules of the game – and changing the rules is fundamental to success in the digital economy. Benchmarking can be a very valuable tool in helping quantify key points but obviously difficult when you are pioneering in greenfield markets. Nevertheless, as much comparative information as you can gather is always useful, particularly if you can benchmark yourself against companies that excel in other fields and have the potential to enter your market.

For example, customer satisfaction and experience measures can help you understand the art of the possible and are not specific to any one business area. As I'll expound in Chapter 8, a customers' benchmark of a good experience with a supplier transfers across sectors and they compare everyone with their favorite. If one provider stands out from the rest, but appears to

[104]Based on International Air Transport Association and individual companies' published figures

be structurally similar to you and operating in similar markets, it may represent a reasonable stretch goal to beat that competitor.

These types of benchmarks and metrics continue to grow in importance for service providers that have to manage more and more components and partners. With so many moving parts involved in short-term, high-margin services, it is extremely important that service providers pinpoint where flexible joints are necessary in their infrastructure to accommodate important services. Creating agility requires a true understanding of how migrations and changes impact what is in place. Only through sophisticated metrics, devised and tested by peers, can that impact be understood.

Benchmarking exercises are often run by consulting firms who can help advise on where to focus efforts to improve or beat the competition. They can be expensive but can also produce good results. A helpful, anonymized source of data for communications providers is from the industry group, TM Forum, which offers a Business Benchmarking Program to participating members, providing detailed benchmarks on operational processes across a large number of other providers. In addition, the Forum generates *Business IQ* reports on various aspects of transformation, which are free for members to download from its website.

7

CREATING SUCCESSFUL PARTNERSHIPS

As the digital economy evolves, partnerships are becoming as inevitable as breathing and if you can't manage partnerships, you're not going to succeed – it's as simple as that.

Viewing suppliers as partners in an equal, respectful relationship isn't about 21st-century political correctness; it's much more pragmatic than that. Very simply, if one of you fails, you both fail: trying to screw the partner on unrealistic, unprofitable and unsustainable business terms might look good in the short term, but in the real world it will hurt you as well as them – and probably sooner rather than later.

At one time or another, management gurus Peter Drucker and Tom Peters have both been quoted as saying, "Do what you do best, and outsource the rest." It has a nice ring to it and has the right notion of focusing your energies on your core competencies, but it says little about how to make that work. In the digital world, partnerships are an essential factor – you rely on others and they rely on you in an ecosystem. So the business of creating and sustaining successful partnerships is another core competency that you need and is a critical factor to success.

So far, I've painted a picture of the digital economy upsetting some established wisdoms, business models and creating winners *and* losers. For sure, focusing on what you do best is likely to be an important factor in success but in the process of doing that you become critically dependent on others to do the things that you need but choose to use somebody else to deliver– the end user gets the sum total of all of the activities of all of the partners in the ecosystem and if they don't deliver, everyone gets hurt. So I use the term *partnerships* a lot here rather than *suppliers* or *contractors* because of the mutual dependency that working in an ecosystem brings.

A good definition of a partnership is "an arrangement where parties agree to cooperate to advance their mutual interests and benefit" and in the digital economy context, partnership describes the position where a company concentrates on adding value where it excels and where they need a capability but don't need to own and run it, in other words, partners that are good at that aspect. Since each is dependent on the other, this is not a 'master-servant' type of outsourcing arrangement, both parties have to make it work or both suffer the consequences.

Throughout this book I stress that building partnerships and making them work is a critical core competency. They could include partnerships with technology suppliers, infrastructure service providers, other service providers of various sorts (who perhaps provide specialist services or geographic coverage) and with channels to market. This is because in a connected, digital world the whole market is…well, *connected!*

As the digital economy evolves, it will increasingly become a service-oriented world where all the capabilities that you need to run your business and provide services to your customers are founded on an ecosystem of cloud-based virtual services, provided by partners of various sorts. Partnerships are becoming as inevitable as breathing because of this mutual dependence factor and if you can't manage partnerships, you're not going to succeed – it's as simple as that.

The trouble is that a lot of big companies aren't good at it and that's a big disadvantage. So this chapter is about some tips and ideas needed to make partnering a success, as well as things to avoid and some new thinking on the subject.

The end user sees the net sum of all of the component services in the ecosystem that are strung together to deliver the solution that the user needs: such as connectivity, processing power, storage, application functionality and capabilities that manage the customer interaction such as billing, care and so on. This is a federated approach, requiring clear business and technical interfaces and trading relationships across the 'borders' of these providers so that it can work in a harmonious whole and deliver the right solution to each end user.

For communications companies, this federated approach isn't new – they've been providing international communications services in a federated model for decades but the level of interaction across the 'trading borders' was highly regulated by the International Telecommunication Union and pretty much limited to signaling connectivity and financial settlements between the parties with virtually no end-to-end management of the customer experience. So although they *should* be good at it, I'm not sure they are.

In the digital world, services are more complex, user expectations higher and the global nature of the market infinitely greater – applications can be on any server anywhere and so can the user. So everyone is pretty new to managing this but there's little doubt that being able to manage complex partnerships seamlessly for the benefit of the user and to keep operational costs within sensible bounds is going to be a key weapon in the armory for aspiring digital services players.

The reason big companies that have been in a dominant position over a long period of time often struggle with partnerships is because they have been used to dominating the companies that supply them with the underpinning technologies. The habit of demanding the lowest possible price runs deep and is one of the main causes of problems when structuring sustainable partnerships. Another reason is almost everyone in the ecosystem is simultaneously a buyer and a seller, and most aren't used to this peer-peer relationship.

Although the Drucker quote rhymes, I'm not going to use the *outsourcing* term much. To me outsourcing (as opposed to in-sourcing or doing-it-yourself) belongs to a world of business models where one party dominates in the relationship and where the balance is stacked in favor of the buyer.

We can learn a great deal from looking at the outsourcing market and how it has developed over recent decades, especially to take stock of why some outsourcing deals work well and why others fail. The promise of outsourcing makes a lot of sense, ideally allowing companies to concentrate on their core competencies while leveraging someone else's better skills, geographic location and/or economies of scale. After all, why run the staff dining room or your own vehicle fleet when somebody else can do it better and cheaper than you?

In recent years, a lot of outsourcing contracts have been based on exploiting arbitrage in labor rates by employing people on lower wages in emerging economies to take over jobs previously done at home in developed countries. Lots of manufacturing jobs moved around the world along with service functions such as managing call centers. This practice generated a lot of negative political debate and public opinion. It has tainted the term outsourcing as something unpleasant and sneaky, often focused on roles where large numbers of people are needed (catering, cleaning and so on). It became synonymous with people being exploited for lower wages.

Added to that, a lot of outsourcing contracts have failed to live up to their promise and many people have their favorite outsourcing horror story. All too often, the problem has been just as much with the buyer of an outsourcing service as with the supplier. In any event, it's a big mistake to view outsourcing as getting 'out' of anything.

Just as a manager may give some task to their staff but doesn't stop being responsible for it – they set objectives and have ways of checking on progress. You must remain in control of your own destiny and continue to be responsible to your employees, customers, partners, shareholders and other stakeholders for how well that function performs, whether you run it yourself or you use the services of a partner to provide it.

It's no wonder that the term outsourcing is being replaced by *managed services.* Whatever they're called, all of that good and bad experience is a goldmine of information about what works and what doesn't in helping to define best practices for creating a win-win situation. It's highly transferrable knowledge to the digital world of using managed or cloud-based services to provide the capabilities you prefer not to operate yourself.

Of course people are still involved, but managed services are usually technology-centric and rely on specialization and economies of scale to work. For example, rather than running a billing operation yourself, many providers used managed billing services to do this for them. Networking is the original managed service: stick voice or data in at one end and it comes out the other without the user having to worry about capital investment, operations, maintenance and so on.

As I've said several times, in the digital world, everything that can be digital, will be – in other words a huge number of functions become virtual managed services that are currently performed in-house with people and physical products. Cloud computing, cloud storage, cloud-based applications, M2M automation of previously physical manual tasks are becoming the norm, offering the potential for a huge growth in players offering specialized, niche services that because they can exploit some advantage of place, scale or skill, means they can do it faster, cheaper and better than it can be done conventionally.

Opinions change all of the time on what to do yourself and what to source from someone else. For example, just a few years ago most mobile network operators viewed the suggestion of outsourcing the maintenance of their cellular base stations as heresy – they believed that this function was critical to operating a mobile business and therefore a crucial asset and a corresponding set of competencies were needed to look after them. Yet in just over a decade, offloading base stations into someone else's care has become the industry orthodoxy. The growing array of digital services will accelerate this trend and change these perceptions much more profoundly, restructuring business as we think of it today in many ways.

Kick starting the managed services market in the communications sector

The 'telecom crash' of the early 2000s revised thinking about what was important to retain in-house and what to outsource. Often confused with the dot-com crash, which happened at around the same time, the telecom crash led to the first real focus on optimizing costs in what had, until then, been an unstoppable engine of growth and stock-market confidence. As I explained in Chapter 5, various governments, including the U.K. and Germany, extracted enormous sums from the industry for 3G licenses, triggering a massive capital freeze that sent shudders through the entire communications value chain, speeding up the consolidation of suppliers and wiping out what was left of the U.K. telecom technology base.

People in England have had centuries of experience of governments screwing them financially: in 1487, the then Lord Chancellor of England, John Morton[105] devised a very nasty tax regime for King Henry VII based on a choice between two equally unpleasant alternatives – it became known as Morton's Fork. Service providers bidding for spectrum came to understand the concept very well – if you don't invest, you risk trashing your market company by missing out on the growth of the digital economy or make the investment and risk trashing your company by saddling yourself with debt mountains for years to come.

The telecom crash didn't start the practice of using managed services in the communications sector but did give it a big boost, which has considerably changed perceptions of what was vital to keep in-house. Many sacred cows were sacrificed, including the idea of getting somebody else to run your network. Many suppliers were only too happy to oblige because they needed to keep revenues flowing and telecoms equipment providers like Ericsson and Alcatel-Lucent began offering managed services to operators for network equipment operations and maintenance. This has grown over the subsequent decade as cost pressures on operators have mounted through competition and market saturation.

In recent years, the managed services market has continued to grow rapidly. Ericsson probably now manages more network capacity supporting more mobile subscribers than any operator including China Mobile. New Delhi-based Bharti Airtel has become the 'poster child' for the concept, exploiting it to the point where all of its network and IT infrastructure is provided on contract by suppliers like IBM, Ericsson and Alcatel-Lucent, often through local joint venture companies. Bharti's success has influenced many other providers to take this approach as they rush to cut costs and become more operationally agile.

---

[105]John Morton: Lord Chancellor of England in 1487, under the rule of Henry VII

Consuming or supplying managed services, the divestiture of functions or assets, or both, has short-, medium- and long-term implications for both buyer and supplier and considerable and careful thought is needed before embarking on a partnership-based approach of managed services.

Beware the quick fix

All too often, short-term cost cutting on the current business model is still the primary driver for choosing managed services: drivers like operational and business agility are still a long way behind. Alarmingly, these short-term drivers are often against the company's strategic capabilities required to succeed in the digital world and can damage competencies that will be essential for a provider to retain. So careful balancing of tactical and strategic goals is needed to work out which functions you can give over to partners as well as how to get there and how you're going to succeed once you've arrived.

If short-term cost reduction prevents you from being able to capitalize on future high-growth markets, you're ultimately going to fail. I'm not saying that minimizing operating cost is not essential, just that you have to be very smart about the way you do it. If it destroys your ability to grow into new markets or worse, it hurts your short-term interests too – for instance, damaging other important aspects of your business like customer retention – then you will come to bitterly regret the quick fix.

As digital services like M2M and eHealth become the norm, your customers' lives might literally depend on how well the service is delivered. A shrug of the shoulders and pointing the finger at your managed service partner when a failure occurs won't get you off the hook because you chose them. Part of the responsibility to your customer is to ensure that your partners are up to the job and that they do it well, through proper monitoring and evaluation. Yet on many occasions, the choice of partner is often driven by muddled priorities that result in decisions being made for the wrong reasons.

Partner-based services must be aligned with your business goals and revisited frequently to make sure they stay that way – if the contracts and service objectives within them are not aligned or are not changeable, then the value of the relationship will almost certainly diminish. And approaching them solely as a way of cutting costs is unrealistic and likely to end in failure: the aim is to establish a long partnership that yields sustainable economic and operational benefits for *both* parties.

Kathleen Romano, Director – Bill Print, Payment and AR Operations, Verizon puts this point well, saying, "I don't ever want a partner that just saves me money because I need to add value to the business. I can only manage a certain number of things and as our business is moving so fast, I need to add value, not simply stand still."

This equilibrium is very important to a sustainable relationship and viewing suppliers as partners in an equal, respectful relationship isn't about 21st century political correctness; it's much more pragmatic than that. Very simply, if one of you fails, you both fail: trying to screw the partner on unrealistic, unprofitable and unsustainable business terms might look good in an episode of *The Apprentice*[106] but in the real world it will hurt you as well as them – and probably sooner rather than later.

Market realignment is driving partnerships

As I said earlier, the digital economy is causing monolithic, vertically integrated businesses to break up into horizontally focused companies working in partnership. For example, in the communications sector the rising cost of spectrum and the much smaller cell-size of 4G networks will ensure that an increasing number of digital service providers will shy away from building and owning 4G infrastructure themselves, instead relying on infrastructure provider partnerships for the mobile broadband connectivity that customers need.

This trend is happening with increasing regularity but not without some bumps and casualties along the way. For example in Russia, Yota was set up to provide the four biggest network operators with broadband access via 4G, but it has hit disagreements between those involved. In the U.S., LightSquared's wholesale 4G plans have seriously been zapped on Capitol Hill over interference with GPS coverage. In Australia, the National Broadband Network that is under construction has been hugely controversial while in calm and well-ordered Singapore, Nucleus Connect seems to be smoothly providing ultra-high speed access to its owners and partners alike.

This realignment isn't new. In Canada, Aliant, Telus and Bell Canada decided some years ago to share a single mobile infrastructure so they could better use their resources to compete against Rogers Communications, but the operating model has become complicated and multi-layered. In the U.K., T-Mobile and Orange joined forces to create a single entity running both their brands called Everything Everywhere and became the U.K.'s largest mobile network operator at a stroke. It expanded again as the new company formed a 50/50 joint venture with Hutchinson's Three business in the U.K. In January 2012, China Telecom Europe announced it would launch a mobile virtual network operator (MVNO) on Everything Everywhere's network – the first time a Chinese operator has launched MVNO services outside China.

We are seeing numerous partner based business models – for example, infrastructure providers offering 'white label' services to third parties who brand it as their own and add value , such as Amazon's Whispernet brand. The network provider may also decide to provide other infrastructure services, such as cloud computing and storage, in conjunction with partners to offer a full suite of capabilities. Further expansion to offer global services would also be a likely course through either acquisitions or further partnerships with other infrastructure providers.

---

[106]Reality television show hosted in the U.S. by Donald Trump and syndicated in other countries. Business people compete in an elimination-style competition and typically 'stab each other in the back' to win

Many players will simultaneously be users and providers of managed services as companies expand their digital service portfolio and rely more and more heavily on partners, so we will see an increasingly complex 'value web' of partnerships emerging. For example, AT&T provides Amazon's Whispernet connectivity in the U.S. while Amazon's EC2[107] services partner to deliver cloud services with companies such as Tata Communications, currently one of the top cloud players across India and Singapore.

Microsoft is both a huge customer of communications services partners and at the same time is focusing on communications companies being go-to-market partners for its cloud-based managed services, such as Office 365 and Azure. Others may appear from 'left field', particularly large enterprises such as banks or pharmaceutical companies who could become managed services providers as well as users. This duality of both user and provider is interesting and those that succeed will have mastered the art of how to thrive in a world where you never quite know which end of the value chain is which.

Referring back to Clayton Christensen, his firm view is that as companies specialize and spin up new service business that differ from their core original business, they are much more likely to thrive as separate 'spun out' businesses and we'll have to see whether companies like Amazon and AT&T actually do this. I'll dive into Christensen's ideas a bit more in Chapter 9 and will also draw on other writers such as Henry Chesbrough and Andrew Garman, who have successfully taken many spin-outs to market.

So what exactly are managed services?

Unlike outsourcing, managed services extend beyond simply transferring people and/or infrastructure and responsibilities to a third party. Managed services are generally a 'black box' type of service where you don't get concerned about the detail of *how* something is delivered, you just focus on *what* is being provided. Perhaps the simplest example is an electricity service – it just arrives and all you care about is that the current, the voltage, frequency and price are as agreed in the contract, not how it is generated or transmitted.

Managed services increasingly include the option of using Software-as-a-Service (SaaS), cloud-based solutions and virtualization so a managed service provider can be of many types – including cloud storage or computing providers, network providers, application service providers or it could be much more tangible, such as the provision of physical capabilities like cell towers or data center infrastructure. The easiest way is to regard managed services as clouds, as shown in Figure 12 overleaf, which can be used in any combination.

For example, in the network service provider area, services could be aimed at a retail user that needs fully outsourced network management and providing features such as IP telephony, messaging and call centers, virtual private networks, managed firewalls, and/or monitoring and

---

[107]Elastic Compute Cloud

Figure 12 – Examples of managed services and providers

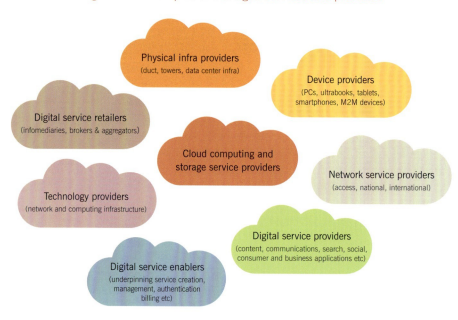

reporting of network servers. These may also be much more closely tailored to specific market sectors such as specialized business services for the connected home, connected car, eHealth, smart energy and so on. Put simply, if there is a market that needs a service, somebody will pop up offering an online digital/cloud version of it before too long.

What is the goal of a partnership?

I talked a lot about setting clear goals in Chapter 6 and the same concepts apply to being clear about the goals and motivation behind using a partner to provide a managed service. If these are unclear, you're unlikely to achieve them – perhaps as Charles Granger once wittily observed it's a case of "we lost sight of our objectives so we redoubled our efforts".

There are numerous reasons why you might choose this path – for example, in addition to allowing you to focus on your core business, other possible gains could include access to new knowledge, talent and operational expertise. Managed services can also help by being a catalyst for change, for example by helping drive innovation, restructuring the cost base, improving quality, helping to reduce time to market and smoothing your path towards standardization. They could also offer better risk management, greater access to venture capital and tax advantages.

One lesson in particular is worth learning: seeing managed services simply as a way of getting rid of a problem is foolhardy. The issue won't magically go away because it is no longer in-house; if anything it will be compounded and almost certainly cause more trouble further down the line. The perception might then be that the managed service approach failed, but in fact it couldn't do anything else in such circumstances.

Whatever function or part of a business that you entrust to someone else to run doesn't mean you no longer have responsibility for ensuring it is delivered. If it's an ancillary service like your office cleaning, then if it doesn't deliver, it's an inconvenience. If you have built your product on top of those provided by partners, it may be catastrophic if the partner lets you down – it's *your* customer base and *your* brand that is damaged.

The nub of the issue is what functions or infrastructure elements does a company want to move to a managed service and why? What are the strategic goals you are trying to achieve, and what is the value proposition of the managed services? Is it the best way of providing faster, better, flexible, more innovative services?

The theory that using managed services should be cheaper because of the partner exploiting geographic labor arbitrage and economies of scale is rapidly becoming out of date. This is especially true when you place highly customized requirements on your partner – the more they have to customize their approach for you, the more it costs them, so the more it costs you. Getting involved with how the partner performs a function is generally not a good idea – they may do it differently to you but what really matters is the results they deliver and how the managed services partner's processes interact with yours for seamless delivery.

You have to stop thinking about partners as just a convenient way to cut costs – if that's possible then all well and good but remember – lowest cost usually means lowest quality and least flexibility. Partners should be treated as you would any other critical part of your service delivery model because that is exactly what they are – your priorities should be focused on gaining competitive advantage, enhancing the customer experience, gaining agility and flexibility and sustainable operational efficiencies.

Where do managed services and partners fit into your strategy?

Moving towards using managed services is a big strategic decision – particularly if it is an integral part of your own service delivery to customers. It fundamentally changes your business model and the way you need to organize and manage your own operations. So it's depressing to see that all too often, senior executives allow the shift to managed services to be done on a piecemeal basis, department by department, frequently in response to short-term pressures on one part of the business, rather than part of a well thought-out strategic shift or transformation program. Managed services should be tightly integrated into your corporate and individual business unit strategies guided by answers to the following five straightforward, but often hard to answer, questions:

- Why is a managed service partner being considered for the corporation? Define the problem that this approach will solve.
- What are the expected business outcomes of the managed service and what are the targets that will define success?
- Who should perform the services? Which services will be retained in-house and which will be delegated to which partner? Who will be responsible for the end-to-end delivered service and how is assurance going to be engineered in this new operating model?
- How should the managed service be delivered to ensure maximum value? The degree of customization in a managed service will drive cost, affect partners' ability to meet your business goals and determine the ease of innovative.
- Where should the managed services be performed? How should the delivery of services be distributed and what are the implications?

If serving your customers is going to be partially dependent on a partner or partners, it raises these types of fundamental business questions and it's much better to have worked them out before the ink is dry on the contract(s) rather than find out that different parts of the delivery process have negotiated multiple contracts, all set up with different service level agreements (SLAs), contractual terms and length of contracts. That creates an operational and business nightmare but it is common when departments act autonomously.

To avoid that fragmentation nightmare, all departments need to be acutely aware of the impact on the end-to-end service delivery chain and ensure that commitments to the end user can be delivered. It is essential that managed service contracts are tied to that end-to-end service delivery view rather than a blizzard of incompatible contracts that are expensive to change and difficult to exit.

Using managed services is likely to have a major effect on your organization achieving its corporate goals, so decisions about deploying them must have very senior level approval and support to ensure they match corporate business objectives – and continue to meet them. They cannot remain solely the responsibility of departmental heads.

That fragmentation problem gets much worse when trying to provide services across an international group of companies. International provider groups are increasingly common in the communications sector as providers want to be able to deliver a consistent portfolio of services across large geographic areas. They want to package the services they provide in their home market to sell overseas, for themselves and other customers, including in countries where they don't necessarily own infrastructure. If they have a disparate, fragmented policy governing the use of managed service partners as part of the overall service delivery mix, the operational and service quality challenges multiply rapidly.

Large organizations, especially the trans-national groups, need a strongly coordinated approach to avoid that kind of fragmentation, which can be so damaging. Imagine trying to offer consistent service quality to your end customers if your managed services partners all use different approaches for measuring service quality or escalating problems. Likewise, trouble is inevitable if they have different definitions of service level guarantees, different contractual terms, conditions and applicable laws governing liabilities, rebates and so on. Looked at individually, these contracts may seem reasonable. Put them together and you have anarchy.

Central governance is essential to avoid this nightmare situation, perhaps through a center of excellence for control of how managed services will be used, how contracts will be set up and the operational characteristics agreed and measured. This shouldn't be a bureaucratic, old-style procurement department function but a proactive group that both understands how to make partnerships work and can 'normalize' terms and conditions so that end-to-end service flow is manageable.

Establishing long-term partnerships with managed services suppliers is a highly desirable aim, rather than chopping and changing on a price-driven basis because any change to a partner that's embedded deeply in your service delivery chain is bound to be disruptive, and the bedding down process time-consuming and expensive. At the same time, don't succumb to the temptation of signing a long-term, inflexible contract just to get a better price – develop the partnership together and extend and renew the contract as you go along. Contracts *do* need to be flexible from the outset – typically five or seven year contracts abound, but nobody can be sure what the market need will be even three years from now, let alone double that time.

Shared responsibility and trust

Many readers will have had experience of being on motivational management courses and playing team 'games' such as the one where an unfortunate participant is asked to close their eyes, lean backwards and trust their colleagues will catch them. It's a hard thing to do but developing partnerships is a bit like that – unless there is a trusting relationship between the parties, the relationship won't work and will end quickly and badly.

If there isn't complete trust, companies are reluctant to hand over control to the managed service provider and don't give them the necessary information to do their job properly. Thus begins a vicious circle where the managed service provider cannot perform very well, which erodes trust more. This is particularly prevalent in situations where the managed service provider is taking over a function previously carried out in-house and where you are likely to encounter the mentality of 'no one can do it as well as we can'. Starving the managed service provider of important information or advice and being critical when problems occur can start the rot in a partnership from the earliest stages of the contract.

You can't just trust to luck and blindly assume that the managed service provider is going to perform. Going back to the team game analogy, a wise person would establish that their colleagues are there and both willing and able to catch them before falling backwards. So a strong governance model is needed; when performing due diligence on a managed service provider, a structured approach should be taken to ensure that they are capable of the task, have the appropriate skills, training, resources and information to succeed.

It is a prudent idea to build in incentives to succeed in making the relationship work that are more powerful than harsh punishments in the form of penalty clauses, but the most important aspect is building a fruitful, mutually dependent partnership with an open and honest flow of information in both directions.

There are many good examples of how such mutually dependent, trust-based partnerships work. Some 20 years ago Mercedes Benz thought they were the only people who could make a screw good enough to go into a Mercedes and the company nearly went bankrupt. Now, like many others in the manufacturing industry, it has very well thought out, long-term partnership arrangements but it went up a steep learning curve to get it right (as any Mercedes owners out there will know, there was a sticky period where the legendary Mercedes quality definitely suffered through weaknesses in their supply partnerships).

The Mercedes brand and customer loyalty is totally dependent on the performance of those partners so it is vitally important that promises in the form of SLAs for quality, timely delivery and so on are kept because everyone in the ecosystem knows that they will only profit in the long term if those partnerships work. The ideal goal is that penalty clauses are never invoked because both sides of the relationship will suffer if they are.

In the digital world, managing service levels can be more complex and dynamic than in a manufacturing supply chain. Both sides of the partnership have to be very clear about what constitutes the right performance and work off a common set of terms and conditions. This becomes even more critical if there are multiple contracts with multiple providers because if you don't manage contracts closely together, you have no way of knowing if they contradict or overlap each other or comply with service level or operational level agreements.

Date a few times before you get married

Building business partnerships is a little like getting married: building a trust-based partnership that is beneficial to both parties over a long period of time is helped greatly if you choose the right partner in the first place. It's always a good idea for both parties to understand as much as possible about the other and this means an in-depth, all-round assessment of the proposed partner including an analysis of the risks involved: what is their organizational structure, financial position, competency track record, culture, business drivers and so on. Such an analysis should not be rushed – hurried tactical decisions inevitably result in long-term pain and the old adage of marrying in haste and repenting at leisure applies as much to business partnerships as personal ones.

Price is obviously very important in a business partnership, but it needs to be balanced against numerous other criteria, including the cultural fit between the parties – indeed my great friend and industry veteran Bill Ahlstrom goes so far as to say this is the single most important factor – and a commonality in the strategic objectives of both. Also, it's always valuable to benchmark price levels in the marketplace to figure out what you want the price to be before you start negotiating.

When choosing a partner, it's also a good idea to ask for 'bad' as well as good references from customers where things have gone wrong and been fixed. All partnerships will experience difficult times and understanding how a partner addresses these issues will better prepare both parties in advance.

If there is the likelihood that you or your potential partner will change strategy or direction, especially in very good or very tough economic conditions, opt for a shorter contract. Extending or renegotiating longer terms with a satisfactory partner is much more cost effective than terminating an agreement that is no longer working. In particular, beware of contracts and pricing based on the prevailing economic climate – in boom times contracts are often erroneously based on the premise that the volumes will always increase and thus pricing will always fall – the recessions of recent years have shown this to be an unwise assumption, catching many service contracts out.

For example, when Nortel found itself in trouble, its problems were made worse because its managed services contracts didn't allow for scaling down and it was expensive to extract itself from its contractual obligations. In financially unpredictable times, it is always a good idea to remember that what goes up often comes down; it's usually just a matter of when.

This exploration phase should be both ways. It's not just a matter of checking out the potential partner – the buyer needs to be very open about their needs. So you too have a duty to be clear about what you want to achieve and when, not only at the start of the contract but throughout the relationship. Too often from the managed service provider's point of view, it seems that a client may want to change their requirements every second week, which leads to stresses and strains in the relationship and often changes to prices in the contract.

During the initial mutual exploration, if there is a need to regularly change critical levers or other rapidly altering operational needs, these need to be captured in the scope of work and governance model that is embedded into the contract, otherwise when a request comes up, both parties end up aggrieved. Again, Bill Ahlstrom feels that good governance is a crucial success factor, yet in practice is often sketchy at best. This 'scope creep' can be a major source of problems in a partnership and if the buyer pressures the supplier into accepting contract terms or racks up additional unforeseen demands within the contract price that they cannot deliver economically, they are then very likely to look for ways of restoring reasonable financial margins.

This can be through exploiting loopholes in the contract, such as punitive costs for undocumented changes or possibly worse, reducing service levels, skill levels and staffing volumes. One-sided contracts may make the 'winning' negotiator look good with their boss but are generally bad business and very often quickly fall apart.

Getting it right can have a highly positive effect for both parties: the buyer gets what they want at a fair price and the supplier gets long-term business and good reference accounts. As an example, Sally Davis, when she was CEO of BT Wholesale, explained how she had helped drive the company to become a substantial managed services supplier through a strategy of developing deep, long-term relationships with customers and working out how their products and services could be tuned to best meet customers' needs – one size does not, and never will, fit all in managed services. That approach has enabled that division of BT to build a base of more than 1,000 wholesale customers and move from accounting for less than 10 percent of its revenue from long-term contracts, to over 40 percent and rising.

Finally, a word about 'offshoring'. When selecting an offshore partner or creating a captive office – often for cost reduction reasons – it pays to be cautious about the 'headline' price quoted because managing the relationship with an offshore partner can have a lot of additional costs as well as challenges such as different cultures, working practices and time zones. The process to secure this type of relationship is similar to other managed services arrangements, but greater emphasis is required in the areas of governance, integrated process definition and collaborative means of communication.

Negotiation

As with the partner selection stage, don't be tempted to rush the negotiation process – the time and resources spent up front will pay big dividends later – you can't build a stable structure on shaky foundations.

You need input and involvement from all management levels and affected departments by the introduction of a managed service partner during the negotiation and transition phase. Take time to absorb their input and insist on a conservative transition that matches the size and complexity of the scope to be transferred to your partner. Run it as a properly planned and managed project, and ensure active management participation and that the transition budget is not spent elsewhere.

You must build flexibility into the contract and anticipate change. Structure the contract so that you can move the initial emphasis on cost control and cost removal towards innovation and market expansion to allow for shifts in the economy and the markets you serve. Build in appropriate contractual levers to facilitate changes and anticipate that a point will come where you need to re-open negotiations to accommodate more fundamental changes.

The most difficult part of a contract to get right is defining the service requirements and measures of quality that the supplier needs to provide. Too many contracts focus on SLAs that use the metrics the buyer managed *internally* rather than business impacting goals. For example, a contractual requirement on a partner to guarantee server availability 99.99 percent of the time is much less useful than a service level goal of specifying the buyer must be able to process transactions such as an order. After all, if server availability is 99 percent and there are 100 servers, the one unavailable server might be in the critical path to complete the order, but its lack of availability will not invoke the service level failure. The buyer should focus on the *what* and leave it up to the supplier to figure out the *how* of achieving it.

Applying an analysis of critical business needs when defining service level goals allows a clear focus on the right things: for example Michael Lawrey, a senior executive with Telstra, gives a good example of shifting a managed network services contract with airline operator Qantas from a preoccupation with network operational metrics such as phase errors and jitter levels to measuring how many people couldn't board their plane if the network wasn't performing. Contracts should be very clear about the process for recovery from any shortfall or failure in meeting the service level goal and should specify measures such as mean time between failure and mean time to restore services as well as how to properly manage issues such as scheduled down-time. The problem reporting process, problem ownership, time stamping, escalation processes and so on should all be clear because if they are not there will be endless arguments and finger-pointing when something does (as it surely will) go wrong.

The carrot and stick elements of the contract are very important as well but remember that over-use of the stick can de-incentivize partners whereas incentives, when used properly, can encourage the right behavior from the supplier. Penalties, often enforced through reductions in fee levels, must be painful enough to ensure that the cost to assume the risk is greater than the cost of the failure. Contracts rarely have penalties on this scale so that success is never having to invoke the penalty clauses in the contract. Incentives in a contract often reverse the penalty model in that the base amount awarded is augmented with bonuses for meeting business outcome defined by metrics. Regardless of how the carrot or stick is implemented, the goal should not be to punish but to prevent problems from occurring in the first place and, failing that, should produce changes that fix the problems and increase the probability of repeatable successes in future.

The carrot *and* the stick is often a successful strategy and is designed to enable partners to receive penalty/credit earn-backs. In this approach, penalties for underperformance can be offset by credits for over-achievement but it is just as important to set goals against critical issues that affect the business. Beware of agreeing to incentives or credits in areas that sound good but don't positively impact your business.

Contract negotiations from the outset should embrace the process for managing what will happen when the deal comes to an end. Incorporate a comprehensive exit clause in the contract including termination for convenience and termination for cause. If you omit such things, you are bound for chaos but proper negotiation of this will minimize the risk of costly disputes and pave the way for a smoother exit. In first-generation deals, clients often opt for the limited-risk, fixed-fee contracts but renegotiate pricing models and move toward more flexible, usage-based pricing for second-generation managed service deals.

As Mary Whatman[108] says, "No matter how difficult, if something isn't working, change it." The longer a problem is allowed to continue, the greater the ramifications, which could be falling customer satisfaction rates leading to churn, and/or lost revenue, failing to leverage maximum value from assets and resources, or not being able to respond to changes in the market. Verizon's Kathy Romano agrees with this: "The first thing I negotiate on any deal is what's going to happen when there's a failure – if I can get through that and know how we'll deal with failures, then we can build a deal that works."

Managing the transition
A very common failing in the setting up of managed services partnerships is that the buyer doesn't immediately build a close working relationship with the provider. Close cooperation, such as initially embedding people properly with each partner, makes it much more likely to get success in conveying what is required, how interim processes will work throughout the transition and ensuring the service level goals are met or perhaps tuned in the light of joint experience.

A properly thought-out transition period and clear governance are essential for long-term success. Where staff transfers are part of the arrangement, ensure that not all of the key skills reside on one side of the partnership. If there is nobody left at the buyer or seller's end who really understands the issues, then contract management will become a sterile process of reading the contract. This can get even worse if the supplier decides to redeploy those people onto other projects too early in the contract cycle (perhaps to cut operating costs) because

---

[108]Founding Partner at Parhelion GCA and an expert on negotiation of managed services

Service level goals and agreements case study

Service level agreements (SLAs) are one of the most contentious areas of managed services and are usually more of a black art than a science. One of the main problem areas arises from measuring the wrong things – putting too much emphasis on how a service level goal is to be operated rather than the outcome itself. Beth Polonsky, Distinguished Member of Technical Staff at Bell Labs, has an interesting case study on this subject after consulting with a broadband services provider offering services to banks and other corporations in the Asia-Pacific region.

She says: "The SLAs in the provider's contract included typical measures such as mean-time-to-repair sliced in various ways. With hindsight it wasn't clear why these metrics were included in the SLAs in the first place because they didn't provide any insight into customer satisfaction but we think they were probably metrics that had been used by the organization internally.

"We thought that they were doing great and the SLA reports showed that everything was a green light but the provider's customers weren't happy. So one of the main things we recommended was to change the SLA structure and to concentrate on a business objectives hierarchy that focused on the service's health and the quality of interaction between us and the end (provider's) customer. It changed the relationship with the provider and we became more of a partnership with them".

The learning points here are:

- If the SLAs don't match the scope of the contract or the business needs of the customer, the provider can't control something against the level that has been set for them and in the end, the real issues aren't even talked about.
- Low level, operational SLAs just get in the way. If the provider wants to make a creative change about how they are doing something, they find they can't because the metrics will start to be called into question.
- SLA metrics must have a sensible relationship to each other – for example, if they overlap you have a 'double jeopardy' situation where you can be either incentivized and penalized for the same root cause, and depending on how that equation goes, either party can end up feeling like they've been taken advantage of, which isn't how to get the best out of anybody.

This problem becomes more acute when a number of different managed services contracts are in place, that overlap and/or contradict each other, as discussed earlier in this chapter.

then there is a complete absence of any real knowledge and skill regarding the service being provided. One option to consider is making it a contractual obligation to retain certain people to work on your contract alone for a defined period of time.

Another good reason not to deplete in-house skills completely is as an insurance policy if the contract just doesn't work out: even after taking all of this good advice into account sometimes managed services contracts fail. If the approach is unsuccessful for whatever reason and you have nobody in-house who can take it back, then you are in big trouble.

Mary Whatman observes from her experience that the extra things suppliers promise during the sales and negotiation phase often don't materialize in the transition phase. She singles out the commitment to scale up new skilled resources, which in practice often means moving the existing staff around to where they are needed most. As the perceived promises are translated into contractual terms and conditions, more often than not the relationship between the parties becomes adversarial.

To counter perceived broken promises, she counsels, "You should have a different team for the negotiation of terms than the one that will work with the outsourced services provider once it is in place." Staff who weren't involved in the negotiations and who haven't worked closely with the supplier's team in the set-up phase will be less forgiving and more objective. It is paramount, however, that the knowledge gained during the sales and negotiation phases be transferred to both partners by their respective teams to ensure proper continuity.

Some rules of thumb for partnership success
Here are some rules of thumb as a general guide to partnership success. They are based on my own experiences supplemented by that of Mary Whatman and research by Kate Vitasek[109] in her recent book[110].

Do: focus on the what, not the how. Performance partnerships let each player do what it does best, so don't try to tell your partner *how* to deliver your service – it's their core competency after all, so give them the flexibility to bring their skills to the job. Focus on the desired outcomes instead. These should be quantifiable, such as targets for availability, reliability, revenue generation and customer satisfaction. Ensure that outcome targets are well defined and measurable and ideally, there shouldn't be more than about five high-level metrics. All parties need to spend enough time collaboratively during the contract negotiations to establish explicit definitions for how success will be measured.

Do: use incentives and proper governance to drive the right behaviors. Penalties are necessary as well but get the balance between the carrots and sticks right because if the only tool in

---

[109]Faculty member at the University of Tennessee's Center for Executive Education
[110]Ledyard, Manrodt & Vitasek, *Vested Outsourcing – Five rules that will transform outsourcing,* Palgrave Macmillan, 2010. ISBN: 9780230623170

the box is to punish missed targets rather than encouraging ever-better performance, the partnership probably isn't built to last. A governance structure should provide insight, not merely oversight and solve problems in the spirit of a partnership because all parties will benefit if you get it right.

Do: make sure you have commitment and involvement of senior executives when establishing a managed services partnership because it's imperative that your strategy is aligned with your organization's business goals and contributes towards them. It helps a lot if they explain to the troops what you're trying to achieve and why.

Do: expect resistance: someone will always think they can manage a function better in-house than using a partner – and after all, it might be their job at stake.

Do: revisit the terms of the contract regularly to ensure ongoing value and assess if it is still meeting your business needs. No matter how difficult, if something isn't working – fix it.

Do: ensure key people are embedded with your partner and vice versa, making sure that those people will continue to work for you as part of the contract. Beware of letting go of skill sets in-house. Who will know enough internally to manage those working externally and what happens if the contract is brought back in-house? This dilemma is an all too familiar scenario.

Do: use standardized business processes and interfaces between you and your partner because it will save you time, money, effort and resources concerning integration and subsequent testing and, if the worst occurs and you have to change partners, changing will be very much easier.

Do: ensure you negotiate flexibility into the contract, without giving away the family silver. If you don't, you may discover that the anticipated savings disappear in the process of renegotiating terms and conditions. It is imperative that your managed services can quickly track changing market conditions.

Do: consider your customer's experience at all times – don't sacrifice it at any price, it will cost you dearly in the long run. Never establish a partnership which, while it may be cheaper, damages your brand and customer loyalty. Remember John Ruskin's words: "The bitterness of poor quality lingers long after the sweetness of low price is forgotten."

Don't: be 'penny wise, pound foolish'. When a company selects a partner purely on cost it can lead to trade-offs in quality and service, 'beating up' the supplier plus a vicious cycle of re-bidding and transitioning to a new 'cheaper' partner. Either managed service providers will refuse to work with that firm, or they may bid so low they go out of business.

Don't: use managed services as a quick fix. Remember that managed services are way to deliver customer and business value, not a quick fix for business problems. Don't build your contract around meeting short-term objectives but to address your overall strategy. Ensure your partner or customer has strategic goals that align with your own. If not, it won't work.

Don't: measure minutiae such as 50 or 100 metrics designed to capture every single aspect of the partner's performance requiring overhead on both sides just to manage data gathering and analysis. Most of these will be of little practical assistance, if indeed they are ever reviewed at all. Vitasek calls this the 'outsourcing paradox' where the buyer's 'experts' attempt to define a 'perfect' Statement of Work on how the process is to be performed, down to the last touch. Obviously, there is then no scope for the service provider to bring its own skills, knowledge and abilities to the table.

Don't: play the zero-sum game – in other words don't assume that something that is good for the partner it is automatically bad for the buying side. Look at how both parties can gain from any improvement.

Don't: allow the 'honeymoon effect'. Vitasek defines the honeymoon as where initially all is positive and expectations are met but after a time there is little incentive for the supplier to try harder for the more difficult goals or to renew investment, so the relationship deteriorates. To get over this a buyer might offer bonuses payable on set performance improvements. It may in fact be possible to outperform this, especially in the early years, but be aware the partner may be tempted to 'bank' this potential gain against harder times.

BUILDING A CUSTOMER -CENTRIC ORGANIZATION

Apple and Amazon have built two of the world's strongest brands in a relatively short time. With companies like this setting the bar so high for customers' expectations, providing a great customer experience isn't altruism or something you can ignore. It's a fundamental part of the formula for success in the digital world and needs to be an intrinsic part of your organization's culture and operations.

Turning round a poor reputation for quality and customer service is a Herculean task once the market decides it doesn't want to do business with you.

The digital world is largely a customer self-service one: they see your service up close and personal, and interact with your organization directly. There's no hiding place and as such, the customer is only ever a click away from moving to a competitor. Wherever you position yourself in the digital ecosystem, the next player in the chain is your customer. Even if you don't provide services directly to the *end* customer, your role will have an impact – good or bad – on the person at the end of value chain who ultimately pays the money.

Building a valuable brand and a great reputation is critical to keeping customers loyal and a fundamental competency. A positive and memorable customer experience can set you apart from the competition and enable you to charge premium prices, because it adds unquantifiable value to your service or product. If you don't believe it, why can Apple make profit margins bigger than many of their competitors' retail prices? Clearly, if customers feel they are getting more, they are willing to pay more. If you are consistently good at giving your customers service they like, you should be able to create exceptionally loyal customers. On the other hand, if even a small part of their experience is not to their liking, you will lose them and maybe all their friends too.

Good or bad customer experiences don't just happen; they are the consequence of management's ethos and actions. The term customer experience management is a good summation of the task because the customers' experience is the sum total of all of the interactions they have with your organization – from how they found you in the first place to how easy it is to become a customer; the value for money that the service offers and perhaps most importantly how they are treated when things go wrong.

These interactions can be everything from what, how and when you advertise; your website; the accuracy of your bill; the customer care and administration they receive through your call centers or in your physical stores. Every day in almost every way you have the possibility of upsetting and losing a customer by not getting every aspect of the way you treat them right. The weakest link in the customer care chain will let down even the strongest and best managed company: as the British and American TV show of the same name says, it really is a case of "you are the weakest link – goodbye"!

It doesn't matter if nearly every opportunity of reinforcing loyalty works perfectly – it only takes one bad experience to lose a customer. Even worse, one disaffected customer tells their friends through blogs, Facebook and Twitter, and their friends tell their other friends and before long somebody has started a website dedicated to showcasing all the bad things that people perceive you do. So the digital world has amplification built in.

The good news is that if people are delighted with the service they get from you, they also tell their friends: just ask any of the truly, insanely loyal customers that have made Apple into the world's most valuable brand. Such is that loyalty that they forgive little indiscretions, like the iPhone 4's poor antenna design and overheating iPads! Apart for the odd glitch, Apple, along with Amazon and others who excel at customer service, don't leave things to chance – customer experience is carefully designed and managed so that every touch point with the customer is optimized.

In many ways, managing great customer experience is similar to developing innovation in a company (see Chapter 9) in that people are innately innovative, so the management task is mainly about reducing barriers to innovation rather than needing to stimulate creativity. In the same way, people working in a company generally want their customers to like them and their service – they understand if customers desert them they will ultimately lose their job and anyway, who wouldn't rather be on a winning team? So management's task is to foster that inbuilt desire, not smother it.

All too often, corporations put hurdles in the way of delivering a good customer experience, often to the extreme frustration of the people on the front line and those trying to facilitate a positive customer experience. Getting it right is as much about stopping some things as well is starting to do others. This chapter focuses on how companies whose reputation regarding customer service could be better – and of course, it has to be an ongoing process: even the best cannot afford complacency.

Amazon has done an exemplary job of creating one of the world's strongest brands in what could be considered record time: it achieved brand recognition by realizing the company's real purpose from the start, which is frequently voiced by the company's founder and CEO, Jeff Bezos: "We're not in the book business or the music business – we're in the customer service business."

This is the ethos throughout the company, backed by heavy investment in technology to make it happen. In the digital world, customer's expectations are set by the market leaders like this and they set the bar very high. If you can't step up your customer service to match those expectations, you're probably going to have to trade at a discount, which likely means lower profits for shareholders.

Customer centricity
Delivering a good customer experience comes from the company being customer-centric: it's the art and practice of looking at things from the customer's point of view and making decisions accordingly. To be customer-centric, everyone inside a company needs to gain a thorough understanding of customers' expectations, monitor data from customers that's relevant to their role and use it to make a difference – on a continuous basis.

Ideally, every decision should start with the customer in mind as without customers there isn't a business, yet they often get left out of most decisions because of self-centered, competitor-centered or results-centered thinking.

An overriding aspect of developing customer-centricity is the corporate culture, that is, the way things are thought about, talked about and done. This usually flows right from the very top of the company – often from its founder – and can remain even after the founder is long gone: we'll have to see if Apple's master-class version of customer-centricity survives its leader. At the center of a culture that believes in customer centricity is trust: the basis for any long-term relationship, in business or personal life.

Apple and Amazon are not alone. For example, Cisco Systems has a customer-centric culture and is proactive about solutions at every stage of the customer's lifecycle; Cisco makes a concerted effort to maximize its customers' self-service features, so that their agents can focus on more high-value assistance for their customers.

Another good example is Orange, owned by France Telecom, which has pursued a strategy of customer-centricity by investing heavily in the knowledge level, customer communication and responsiveness of their staff. Customer service agents take at least a month-long course before interacting with customers and have to work closely with supervisors in their first weeks of contact with them. This is accompanied by a formal quality assurance program that puts an emphasis on precision monitoring through speech analytics tools that enable Orange to identify at-risk customers who are contacted quickly to address their issues and move them from being at-risk toward satisfied.

The results are impressive – 80 percent of the customers identified as at-risk through the speech analytics were not picked up as at-risk through the agents or other methods. The results are a 20 percent improvement in first call resolution, a 15 percent reduction in repeat calls, and a 20 percent increase in satisfaction with customer service.

The lesson here is that a proactive approach and people who know what they are doing helps build trust. In personal relationships as well as business, you tend to stick with people that are really good at showing that they sincerely care about you and do what they say they're going to do. When people churn to another brand it's often less about how attractive the competitors are and more about being disappointed with their supplier.

That means having a good understanding of what customers want and how they would like to be treated. If you could slim down good customer experience to a single phrase it might be "getting rid of things that annoy customers". Of course you can do better than that and go way beyond such neutrality to "doing things that delight customers".

Clearly, you need insight into what annoys and delights customers. There are no absolute measures for these things; they do tend to vary around the world with different cultures. Also, people's expectations change all the time – my old Dad was delighted to get an orange for Christmas but my grandchildren would be devastated! Societies and their expectations evolve continuously and the companies that give you a great customer experience are the benchmark against which others are measured.

Customer-centricity has both a positive and a negative ripple effect. Get it right and the positive ripple effect of any of the organization's actions is felt by a provider's customer-facing people; by their customers and by the customers' social and professional contacts – brand loyalty rises, churn decreases, customers are often prepared to pay more. Get it wrong and negative impact manifests itself as customer dissatisfaction, hassles, disappointments, annoyances, unnecessary costs, discounting and ultimately losing the customer and probably their family and circle of friends too.

Companies that invest in and actively manage their customer experience do so not because they are altruistic but because it's good, hardheaded business sense. It costs a lot to acquire a customer and that's money wasted if you lose them, or worse, many others in the process. How often does some executive make a business decision, which when viewed in isolation sounds reasonable, but which has a very negative impact on customers, largely through a lack of understanding? Unintended consequences will happen much more frequently if the customer isn't factored into those decisions.

Turning lead into gold

In particular, business analytics and metrics are at the heart of its operations and Amazon is well known for its recommendation engine. This service provides a personalized store front for every customer, which helps to increase sales by enabling customers to find stuff they didn't even know they wanted. It works by analyzing consumers' purchases by product descriptions, prices, ratings, and other attributes. Then it offers products from Amazon's vast inventory (and those of its partners) with similar attributes, even offering low volume, long tail products if they match the criteria.

Amazon's creative use of analytics to constantly monitor and assess customer service might be less well-known, but it is a huge part of its success. It tracks the performance of its websites, call centers and other interactions and uses constant simulation to model, analyze and predict performance based on predicted workloads. As an example, it performs simulations to help measure website latency across the globe, to identify trends or issues and simulate different website usage scenarios.

These simulations are done on a massive scale, aiming to emulate the activity of almost 100 million active customer accounts across many web properties. Of particular concern to the company is coping with seasonal peaks, such as Cyber Monday[111]: any downtime or slow service would mean unhappy customers, lost sales and perhaps customers choosing to go elsewhere in future.

What Amazon, Google, Facebook, Twitter and Apple do very well is convert data into information. Data are the raw facts but information is something useful that can be obtained from that data if you know where to look and how to analyze it. Contrast that with today's communications providers who generate terabytes of data a day from their customers but have limited information about them, either for their own marketing use or to monetize by selling it to third parties who would pay to access that information (as long as it is legal and appropriate of course).

Why is this? A lack of motivation, fragmentation of data across multiple systems and stringent regulation all play their part, but communications companies can learn a huge amount from the web players about turning data into useful information, like turning lead into gold – the dream of every alchemist.

Can you compete if the customer experience is poor?
Of course and many companies do – an exemplar in my view is Ryanair, the European low-cost airline whose attitude seems to be "stop moaning, it's cheap". Its flights are cheap and have helped make flying around Europe more affordable than it has ever been, plus people know what they are letting themselves in for. On the back of managing low expectation, Ryanair now dominates many point-to-point routes between smaller airports in Europe where it typically faces little competition.

Not only that, the airline is often paid by civic authorities to fly to their cities because the flights bring in tourists and trade. Where the market is competitive, Ryanair fights vigorously on price and its business model is honed to survive on razor thin margins. So while most people that you meet would gladly fly with anyone else if they had a choice, often there isn't a choice or the price is just too tempting.

Ryanair makes a conscious business decision to choose operating cost efficiency at the expense of the customer's experience: it is prepared to leave customers queuing on snowy tarmac at an airport rather than interfere with its aggressive and highly cost-effective turn-around schedules for its planes. This is in great contrast to Amazon, which chooses to provide a great customer experience to cover the cost of providing it in additional sales and higher margins. In both cases, customer experience isn't something that's left to chance, there is a plan and a rationale about it.

I can't tell you what *your* strategy should be or where you want to play in the spectrum of price

---

[111]The Monday immediately following Thanksgiving Day in the U.S., which in 2011 became the heaviest online spending day in history when sales reached $1.25 billion in online spending, according to comScore

and customer loyalty; but you should have a clear customer experience positioning and strategy plus a whole set of actions to turn that strategy into deliverable reality to achieve your desired result. Numerous factors come into play when creating this, such as the competitive nature of your market; price and product positioning; the intended sources of revenue and the sensitivity or demands of how your customer wants to interact with you. You wouldn't have to be a genius to work out that being in a highly competitive market, with premium pricing and awful customer service isn't a recipe for success!

Many segments in the digital world are ones where the barriers to entry are relatively low and therefore competitive levels are usually very high. It's also a customer-centric world with a high degree of personal involvement of the customer in the service delivery – they interact directly with the service and the systems support it so any glitches that are there are literally in your face. And if things do go wrong and you need help but don't get it in the way you want it, quickly and courteously, the frustration level quickly mounts and brand loyalty melts even faster.

Do something about it

The success of companies using a great customer experience to drive growth and profitability hasn't gone unnoticed by companies that haven't always had as good a reputation. Over the past few years, as the communications industry has seen its markets begin to saturate, it has had to fight hard to reduce churn, and previous indifference to customer experience management has started to change. Conference after conference, including many I have chaired or spoken at, talk about the crucial importance of the customer and driving up loyalty. The usual suspects of companies that get it right are lauded as exemplars and usually much ritualistic beating with birch twigs takes place about how everyone should try harder.

The problem is that when many of those conference attendees go back to their day job, normality resumes and little, if anything, changes unless there is a clear corporate mandate to do so and strong, visionary leadership to make it happen. I have talked about the importance of leadership many times in this book (Chapter 6 is devoted to it) and the lack of it in companies which have been able to coast when times were good. But the digital tsunami will crash over businesses and show no mercy: fixing bad customer experience isn't something you can do just as your final customers are walking out of the door. Furthermore, turning round a poor reputation for quality and customer experience is a Herculean task once the market is convinced that it doesn't want to do business with you.

When I first started driving, over 40 years ago, General Motors traded (and still does) in the U.K. under the Vauxhall brand. At the time Vauxhall had a terrible reputation for its bodywork rusting. The company fixed that problem decades ago, but I still have a negative impression and have never bought a Vauxhall car. I might just be a grumpy old man; on the other hand I might be a typical customer!

Given the scope, complexity and volatility of the digital ecosystem and the limitations on investment capital, it makes sense to approach the management of customer experience from a continuous improvement perspective. I talk about the different methodologies for running either radical or evolutionary change programs in Chapter 12: change to customer experience must also be run as a well-defined and managed program. This means that different areas of improvement may move at different speeds, but improvements need to be steered to making the biggest improvements as quickly as possible. Continuous sampling of customer experience as behavior changes lends itself nicely to this approach.

Making this happen on a consistent basis, right across a company or a group, is very hard, not surprisingly given the scope, complexity and organizational conflicts that must be addressed by a customer experience program. The first thing you need to identify is how your customer wants to interact with you in the digital world: the whole way of interacting with devices, across devices and between the roles that we play in life is changing rapidly and what we want from our customer experience is changing.

The coming of the Chief Customer Officer

It's interesting to note there is a gathering of momentum towards the appointment of Chief Customer Officers in companies to bring focus and drive to customer experience management. These individuals generally sit at a senior level in the organization, even on the board and while the position (and job title) varies by company, the concept is usually that the person has responsibility for and the authority to design, orchestrate and implement programs and initiatives that improve customer experience across the customer lifecycle.

The position exists in product and service companies in many industries whose customers are other businesses and individuals, as diverse as Allstate, FedEx, Ford, Philips Electronics and SAP. In the communications sector, Telstra recently appointed such an executive (formerly with HP and Dell) as its Chief Customer Officer. He is responsible for sales and service to all segments including consumer, business, enterprise and government customers.

Whether within some organizations this is just a new name for the head of sales or it really is an empowering role that can make significant change to brand loyalty through customer experience management, remains to be seen. It does seem to work in other industries.

In contrast, some companies have taken a different route and have chosen to deploy smaller customer experience overlay teams that act in an advisory or change management role to other parts of the organization. This approach may have a more limited impact because it usually has fewer resources and may not be able to exert influence over budgets and priorities of operational divisions.

A Chief Customer Officer would seem to be a good investment, especially if an empowered executive is appointed with experience of managing customer experience in companies who are good at it, for the following reasons:

• The retail market for digital services, including existing phone services, is intensely competitive – not just competition from other communications companies but increasingly from the digital stores who have growing brand loyalty and a reputation for good customer service.

• Large companies often have a 'stovepipe' structure, with separate service and operational organizations, and information infrastructures. The problem is made worse across groups of companies under the same brand umbrella. This requires a senior leader with appropriate authority to drive a consistent and common approach across the organization, including operating companies in different countries. While customer-facing policies may need some adjustment to cater for local cultures in different parts of the world, it is very important to build overall brand loyalty in a consistent way – the viral impact of customers either praising or denigrating the service does not respect geographic borders. Where companies starting to create global (across geography) products and services, customers expect to receive similar quality of experience in each location. Hence the consistency in customer experience across operating units is becoming more important.

• Mergers and acquisitions are likely to be more frequent in the digital world. They can badly disrupt customer service unless there is a specific focus on managing the end-to-end customer experience. Customer-facing processes and systems are frequently not uniform, and partnerships and acquisitions (or divestitures) can have a big, negative impact unless someone is responsible for ensuring that they don't.

• New services introductions are much more frequent in the digital world and the customer experience can be damaged unless there is a consistent approach to aligning them, from the customers' perspective, with existing services.

• The digital ecosystem involves greater use of partners (as discussed in Chapter 7) and the customer experience is the sum total of all of the players in a value chain. So the Chief Customer Officer needs to extend their influence over all aspects that can impact customers, including across their managed service partners as part of the overall service delivery.

• Many communications service providers are undertaking operational transformation programs and while this is both necessary and positive, the 'law of unintended consequences' can easily come into play unless someone is responsible for ensuring that the customer experience is not damaged by an apparently more efficient back-office.

Given the authority, (rather than a token job title), Chief Customer Officers have the opportunity to address these issues and reinforce the company's leadership to drive to a customer-centric culture. The downside, however, is a bit like the appointment of Quality Management champions a couple of decades ago: there is a danger that other members of the executive team will see customer experience management as something exclusively for the Chief Customer Officer to worry about, allowing them to carry on as before.

Just as quality is everyone's problem, so is the move towards customer-centricity: you might have 95 percent of your operation working really well and delighting customers, but if one part of the organization doesn't support it, the whole investment can be wasted.

As a first step, the entire executive team must understand the payback from a well-implemented customer experience strategy. The Chief Customer Officer needs a mandate and visible backing from the rest of the executive team to lead differentiation efforts with the customer foremost in mind and make sure it filters right through the company, down to the office cat. The Chief Customer Officer needs a program portfolio that demonstrates payback and success, and a mechanism to win support for these efforts right across the organization. Without this support, they could end up being just another in a long list of management fads.

Eat your own dog food

The danger of an organization paying lip service to customer-centricity is very real. You can't fix this problem just by a paragraph in the company's annual statement or in a speech from the CEO to market analysts. The employees will have seen many management initiatives before and in large companies they often learn to keep their heads down and wait for the fad to pass without making any real change.

It's vital that an intention to improve customer experience is backed up by real change. That's not just putting your customer care agents on a course in how to say "have a nice day" – it means fundamental rethinking of everything the company does that impacts the customer and will permeate all aspects of the company. This doesn't just mean the customer-facing parts of the company, but product management, operational management, procurement, IT, customer-facing operations, finance and so on.

Here's a simple example of how good intentions go bad: if product management is pushing sales departments to promote a specific handset and offering big sales bonus incentives to do so that's the result you'll get. Good – well maybe not if you end up with agents selling complicated and overly expensive technology to people who don't need it, won't understand it and get frustrated with it. At best you'll probably see a rise in the number of customer support calls; at worst you'll probably find yourself the subject of a TV documentary into how your company puts profit before customers.

Beware the unintended consequences of what seem like benign actions. If your starting point is low, then in the first instance, your efforts should be focused on minimizing the most common and simple things that upset customers rather than going to the full Apple level of aiming to have customers love you so much that they want to have your babies!

A very good way of doing this is if all of the staff in an organization – and most importantly senior executives – are customers of your products and services, experiencing them in exactly the same way as a customer would. Instead of using 'back door', informal ways of solving issues when things go wrong, staff must be made to work through normal customer channels and experience what a normal customer experiences: every time someone encounters a problem, they should be obliged to use the web self-service or call the call center or whatever channel is available and go through the ensuing process themselves.

Nothing conveys the irritation (and its effect on customers) better than experiencing firsthand the problems of trying to place an order on a dysfunctional website or trying to find support if you can't figure something out. In frustration, you call the help number and work through five layers of interactive voice response systems and get music on hold for 15 minutes only to be cut off once an agent answers!

The fact that board directors generally don't do this, presumably on the grounds that they are too busy and important, tells you everything you need to know about the real priority put on looking after customers and just how seriously customers are taken by the company – basically they are not as important as the management.

Websites and interactive voice response systems are the most obvious examples of unintended customer annoyance – usually instituted to improve operating efficiency, they often present a terrible start to a transaction or conversation, not only are they tedious, at times they just aren't tested properly and lead you into dead ends. Imagine if the system was a series of doors that you had to negotiate to buy something in a store and how maddening it would be if some of those doors led you back out onto the street – mostly you'd keep walking.

These silly mistakes are common, even in major corporations and occasionally among the best like Amazon, because not enough care is given to their design or testing and the impact on the customer through the product life cycle. My broadband provider has a school-marmish message that says curtly "we're very busy right now…. so you'll have to wait" – gee thanks, I wanted to place an order and pay you some money! Why does this go on? Because everybody inside the company uses back-doors to resolve their own problems. They don't see life as a customer sees it and because too often 'efficiency' trumps customer experience.

Not only should your customer experience be tested day by day, minute by minute by all of your employees, there has to be a way of feeding back that experience and making changes for the better. That would happen if the CEO had a bad experience – they would just bark at the responsible executive and the problem would be fixed quickly. The point here is that you want to benefit from the experiences of everybody, no matter what their job or seniority is in the company. To do that, you need to be able to capture what makes customers unhappy, report it and see that something gets done about it.

This might sound simple but it's not. It's a form of what is increasingly being called crowd-sourcing[112] where the experience and wisdom of large numbers of people get fed into the organization to drive change. So, first of all there has to be a way of reporting, collecting and collating that information into programs and actions. There also has to be freedom from the organizational 'white cells' of resistance that will try and prove that there is nothing wrong with the way they do things.

This is much worse in organizations that encourage brushing bad news under the carpet because they don't tolerate failure. In some of the worst cases, 'whistle blowers' (those who highlight problems) are reprimanded or fired.

A critical element in improving customer experience is to be continually alert and open to new ideas for improving it – even very small steps may have a very big impact on customers. The digital world is immensely competitive, so continual improvement and occasional innovative breakthroughs, either originating from your people or copying your competitors, are imperatives for consistently delivering superior customer experience.

As I point out in Chapter 9, people are innately creative – you just have to find a way of liberating their creativity, not stifling ideas. Teresa Amabile[113] at Harvard echoes this: "There's this common perception among managers that some people are creative and most aren't: that's just not true, as a leader, you don't want to ghettoize creativity; you want everyone in your organization producing novel and useful ideas. The fact is, almost all of the research in this field shows that anyone with normal intelligence is capable of doing some degree of creative work."

Continuing the relationship to innovation, getting things wrong and things going wrong in themselves are not necessarily a disaster, providing that people learn from mistakes – they can be a force for good. Routinely punishing people for failure encourages a culture of hiding the problems, passing the buck and denial. Empowering your people to not only recognize problems but to fix it for a customer can often turn into a positive situation with a customer's faith in the company ending up at a higher level than it was before they had the issue.

---

[112]The concept of crowdsourcing is an open call to a group of people that gathers those who are most fit to solve complex problems and contribute with the most relevant and fresh ideas. First attributed to Jeff Howe: www.wired.com/wired/archive/14.06/crowds.html
[113]Teresa Amabile is the Edsel Bryant Ford Professor of Business Administration in the Entrepreneurial Management Unit at Harvard Business School

The point is that when things go wrong, they need to be fixed quickly and not allowed to fester. As I point out elsewhere in this chapter, sorting things out quickly to the customer's satisfaction is a great way of turning an angry consumer into a far more loyal customer, and yet even if this is understood, it seems to be acted on rarely.

Getting a single view of the customer

While getting direct customer experience flowing back from employees who are also customers can be very useful, there are many other sources of information about the customer's experience of your company that you should be making use of. Deriving a single view of the customer from both internal data sources and external places – such as from social media like Facebook – is a major challenge. It's another aspect of big data and is simultaneously a big opportunity and a big headache.

Virtually every aspect of customer experience hinges upon the accuracy and accessibility of data. As I said in earlier, turning data into information is the 21s- century realization of the centuries old alchemists' dream of turning lead into gold – it is a huge source of wealth if you can master it. Real-time information, at your fingertips, about what your customers are doing now, what they want now and what they might be receptive to is a huge advantage if you can tap into it. It will give you a much better understanding of issues, such as how to package and position your own services or make real-time, context-based or location-based offers. It is also valuable information that can be monetized to others, subject to the relevant concerns over privacy.

Unfortunately, data is found in every nook and cranny of an organization, in every imaginable format and at times in conflict with the similar data from other sources. The issue with big data is being awash with it, but unable to turn it into information gold because it's often held by different departments, on different systems in different formats. This makes it hard to analyze and use in a timely manner and that's a big problem because getting a single and consistent view of the customer is crucial – regardless of the channel of communication.

Proactive analysis of what customers want in real-time (or near-real-time) is essential – reactive customer analysis hours, days or weeks after the event may give you trends, but by then the customer is long gone. Being able to make appropriate offers in real-time (for example, 'customers who bought this also bought' kind of recommendations), real-time customer assistance (such as a customer having difficulty placing an order or wanting to initiate a discussion with an agent on the options available) and real-time performance information (like indicating when the website is slow or call center response times are lengthening and so on) can help deliver a very positive impact on the customer's experience and on your bottom line.

On top of that, customers often have different identities; they may use a number of services together and they may interact with the provider through different channels. Tying all of those back to a single view of the customer is a problem because data is typically held in different systems, from customer relationship management (so frequently a misnomer), inventory and supply chain management to enterprise resource planning, for instance.

Different departments may use differing identifiers for the customer and/or use different formats for their name and address and other factors, which make it very difficult to reconcile a single view. Instead companies are forced to rely on expensive and time-consuming unstructured, manual processes, which can produce highly questionable results.

This problem is significantly worse in providers that have a highly fragmented systems base. It underlines the need to radically simplify the operational platform (see Chapter 12 to 14) and if it's done right, it can both reduce operating costs and improve customers' experience.

Higher levels of complexity require new tools to add speed and consistency to decision-making and delivery. Being good at dealing with customers consistently depends on getting the right information to the right person at the right time. Whether it is a marketeer trying to initiate a campaign, a customer service representative trying to solve a customer's problem, a sales rep trying to close on an opportunity, or a business manager seeking to create the 'killer offer' – they all require rapid access to specified data, or data that can be tailored and presented in a meaningful format.

This messy morass of feedback and manual intervention also makes using analytical tools very difficult. Fragmentation really is a major source of problems for a service provider because you can't manage holistically: an essential ingredient of good customer experience is that the experience is consistent and high quality across every channel of communication with the customer. And it's not just digital service providers who have this problem – in a recent survey by IDG Research, the IT manager at a major European bank commented: "The challenge is understanding what comes into our call centers and website and how to automate it. We have thousands upon thousands of callers all with different subjects and we need to get to the top 10 or 20 issues and automate them."

It's no coincidence that two of the hottest areas in customer experience management are *data analytics*, which help providers understand what is happening, and *policy management,* which helps to consistently deploy appropriate solutions to issues as they arise. If data is the backbone of great customer experience, then analytics is the brain that turns it into useful information and policy management are the hands that do the work.

The lack of joined-up thinking in a multichannel sales operation is usually apparent to customers who generally get annoyed when they get a different experience and information on the website, in a physical store or when speaking to a customer care agent. Often these channels have different prices for the same product or carry different product lines and offers because they are run by different divisions. This is not only stupid because it allows the customer to arbitrage between channels in the same business – it says loud and clear to the customer that the provider is not joined up in any way and has an amateur feel to it.

It gets worse when the customer buys a product from, say, a physical store, then goes onto the website to try to get help. As they can't find the product listed, they call a helpdesk only to find that they have bought a special promotion and need to go back to the store for support. Many exasperated customers simply never return. (My own mobile provider, O2, seems to excel at this frustration!).

An overall, enterprise-wide view of how the customer 'experiences' and 'wants to experience' a provider is a vital part of becoming customer-centric. That view should not need to be constrained by the different systems that may be deployed to support the different channels of communication, from customer call centers and interactive voice response systems to web self-service and social media (see below). Inconsistencies in processes, how they are dealt with, having to start again with a call center agent, say, when a customer is struggling with something online are all sources of huge frustration and irritation – which these days is likely to be vented on Twitter pretty much as it is happening.

For an organization to become customer-centric, it needs to drive both a systemic and a strategic process and not merely be an exercise in ticking boxes or using the right words just to keep the boss happy. In companies that were not built this way, this is a big, hard task, requiring the transformation of people, processes, infrastructure and systems. While there may be other reasons for transformation, such as increasing agility and reducing costs, you should never lose sight of what you are trying to achieve, which is to build loyalty among your hard-won customers, in a sustainable, economic way. Acquiring new customers is expensive: advertising costs, campaign management expenses, promotional service pricing and discounting, and equipment subsidies make a serious dent in profits from new customers, especially where subsidies are given to attract them.

Data management is a core competency

Another critical aspect of data management that is highly relevant to delivering a great customer experience is privacy. While providers have the advantage of a huge amount of customer data, it must be administered properly if the provider hopes to gain and keep the trust of the customer, and avoid punishment from regulatory agencies or perhaps the customer themselves. As numerous players like Facebook, LinkedIn, BT and Sony have found, nothing gets you headlines like losing or abusing customers' data and nothing loses their trust faster. Limp responses like "lessons have been learned" generally don't cut it and repeat offenders will rapidly lose customers. This will become a rising issue in the digital world – it may not just be your credit card details that get lost: it may be your identity, your DNA, your health records and so on. In some societies, it may cost you your life!

A strong focus and investment is needed because excellent data management is a core competency of digital providers – you won't be in business for long if you are not. That must be coupled with smart business analytics tools to help managers and customer-facing people offer highly personalized support to customers, while maintaining profitability. Unpicking the spaghetti-like nature of information is challenging – for example, account relationships are often complicated.

A profitable customer may have a separate account for a business, their second home or another family member, which may appear to be unprofitable. If the service provider cannot relate the two accounts, customer lifetime value is not properly represented and any upset of the apparently unprofitable account may result in the profitable customer churning.

Another way of extracting value from large data sets is the use of policy-based management: policies are operating rules that reflect principles about how the company wants to run its businesses and manage its resources. A rules engine reads and filters the data in the production environment and executes automated responses when it encounters a pre-defined situation.

Policies can be used to manage a wide variety of applications, such as service management, quality of service, personalization, discounts, charging/billing, fair usage and security. For service management, policies can allocate priority to different types of information (for instance, gaming services can't tolerate latency versus email which can), decide which has guaranteed delivery, allocate bandwidth and delay low priority traffic to ease congestion.

An interesting report by Rob Rich[114], who heads TM Forum's Insights Research unit, found that companies are increasingly recognizing the potential of policy management as a strategic enabler of service differentiation, but they are concerned about cost, integration, scalability and ease-of-use. It reported that 45 percent of respondents in a survey of 20 of the world's biggest communications service providers (mobile, cable and fixed) have already deployed some sort of rules-based policy solution. Their main priorities are fair usage for congestion and general traffic management; personalization/offer management; tiered service pricing; and new services introduction, mostly related to pricing alternatives.

A good example is using policy-driven rules on a big data issue to address customer experience problems concerning bills for data usage by pre-paid data users – often a big cause of customer dissatisfaction. While contract customers generally understand their usage and pricing and know what bill to expect, prepaid data users are inclined to use up their allowance and move to an alternative provider, without allowing the usual churn predictors to take preventative action. A rules engine can monitor their activity to establish their likely level of satisfaction.

---

[114]*Customer experience in a connected world*, published September 2011, TM Forum. It is free to Forum members to download from the website www.tmforum.org and for others to purchase

As one of the respondents in the survey noted: "We need to be able to drill into all the big data that is spewing out of dynamic usage to get a clear visualization of the end user's experience, so that we can realistically assess satisfaction. If we don't, they will churn – we need to be proactive and present them with a range of personalized options."

Those personalized options are essential because margins on all types of digital service are much slimmer than communications companies were able to obtain in their growth years. Using tools like policy-driven engines makes a lot of sense to help bring new services rapidly to market and monetize them, while improving the visibility and satisfaction of the customer. Good examples include allowing a person to use a service across multiple devices; a family to share a plan or a wallet; a business to share a fixed monthly volume of data over a large number of users; offloading onto Wi-Fi for a better customer experience and to save congestion; making special offers to increase traffic when capacity is under-utilized; offering an unlimited roaming overseas data pass for a day; or increasing data usage in an underused cell.

Policy management tools can also be used to filter the event data coming from both networks and services, extracting critical or interesting events. They can be aggregated or made into a time series, which could be automatically sent to a business intelligence tool for analysis. The product manager may tweak the policy to see how effective it would be if the rule was changed. Tellingly, one senior executive in the survey commented: "The biggest problem is not managing a policy; it is using business intelligence techniques to identify the best policies to implement at a particular time."

The report found that service providers must be able to measure the performance and impact of these policies, as they implement new services and offers in order to understand their successes, shortfalls and changes in customer behavior.

This approach is very flexible and offers a wide range of possibilities to understand customers' needs, usage patterns and satisfaction and is a good example of applying technology that can help proactively manage the customer experience and offer significant choice, transparency and control to customers, increasing their satisfaction and loyalty while giving the service providers more incremental revenue. It's a win-win situation for smart service providers and their customers. Who is a customer anyway?

The question "who is the customer" may sound obvious but this is not as straightforward as it might seem. I already talked about the difference between a customer and the end user in the ecosystem as not being the same thing. Every step in a value chain is a customer and supplier relationship so there are lots of customers in an ecosystem. The end customer is the person at the end of the chain who sees the net sum of all of the steps in the chain, but might not be the customer in the sense of the person who pays the bill. Increasingly digital services have complex business models where the person who pays for the service and the person who uses the service are not the same thing.

In addition, a single end customer/end user may have multiple personas. By this I mean that a person (whose *identity* would be things like name, address, age, sex etc.) is different from their persona, which is the role they are playing at any particular time. For example, they may be in the persona of a private citizen, or they may be in their employment persona.

The private citizen may be interacting with the service for their own needs, or they might be looking at researching something to help with their kid's homework or they might be buying something for their grandchildren. In their work persona they may have a very different expectation of the price/quality mix than they do in their private persona.

Drilling down more deeply, it might be that the customer's healthcare persona is trying to deal with say, an eHealth service to monitor a heart condition, or it might be their home persona dealing with their home energy system or security monitoring. It might be their financial persona concerned with investments or insurance. The customer's work persona also may have varying needs depending on how important or time critical an interaction is – are they are trying to close a major deal or just sending a quick note to a colleague for example?

Understanding which persona you are dealing with can have a big impact on the customer's perception of their experience and the way they react under different circumstances. The contextual approach to dealing with customer experience management takes it to a whole new level and requires even more information analysis to get it right. People's expectations of customer service is set mainly by those providers who excel at it and is likely to keep rising, so if you are committed to improving your customers' satisfaction, you have to look at issues like this.

Colin Orviss[115] has done a lot of research into the area of evolution of the consumer and Figure 13 captures this multi-role, multi persona concept very well. His premise is that the digital world empowers the customer like never before to control most of the facets of their profile, their social interactivity and with whom and how they engage with those around them. The diagram reflects the fact that we are members of multiple communities and that within these communities we have differing roles and personas.

Being aware of which community and role our customer is in at any given time becomes a critical component of how the customer experience needs to be delivered by a provider for the benefit of both parties. Since they are the ones who know their connections and preferences they need to be empowered to manage interactions themselves. The key for providers is to ensure that the analytics and big data management tools are in place to capitalize on this knowledge.

[115]Founding Partner at Parhelion Global Communications Advisors

Figure 13 – The multi-roled customer

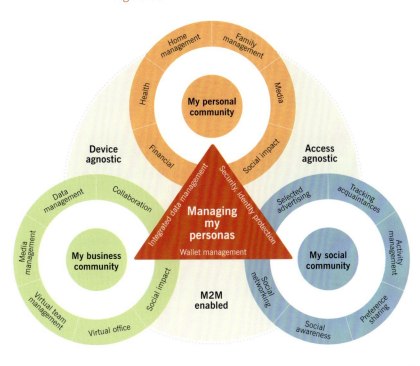

I'm not a number...

A physical retail store is the most personal experience that a digital service's customer is going to get. Here they meet people who should embody the corporate approach to delivering great customer experience. Instead for many providers this is not just a wasted opportunity but often it reinforces the idea that the company cares little for customers.

Who knows if the digital world will all but kill bricks and mortar stores, but for now people selling mobile devices have found they are still an essential part of the sales mix. Apple is the most striking exemplar. Its stores are unmatched in reinforcing a company's unique version of customer experience – shoppers gaze in wonder at its Aladdin's cave stuffed full of goodies. They are dazzled by the glass staircases (patented by Apple of course!) and the staff who look delighted to be there and to talk to customers, and understand the products they are selling inside out, and enthuse their virtues.

In short, Apple stores are less about merchandizing goods than about reinforcing the Apple brand, identity and customer experience. They come close to being seen as a holy place by Apple's true believers.

In contrast, many companies and certainly most communications providers, seem to have a blind spot about the physical interaction with the customer. Their shops are typically badly laid out, cheerless places stacked with a confusing array of technology. Customers are often not greeted (although care is needed with this, see below) or dealt with promptly and employees often know little about the products or service plans. Even worse they typically appear to care even less about how they might fit an individual's needs and/or are unwilling to commit the time and patience to educate customers on complex topics such as smartphones, tiered plans or usage policies.

For those readers who are familiar with the cult 1960s British TV show *The Prisoner* (remade in 2009), the famous line from the show was "I am not a number – I am a free man." Indeed. Customers are real people, with real needs and they are all different. They're not just a phone number. Maybe this would be a good mantra for board members to repeat each morning?

Part of paying attention to customers is to be aware and respectful of cultural differences. For example, North American customers surveyed in a JD Power report found that those who had to wait to be greeted when entering a store registered a much lower overall satisfaction than those who were greeted quickly. This is not the case elsewhere. For example, in northern Europe, people don't like to be greeted by a complete stranger on their way into a store – they feel it is bogus and an imposition to the extent it stops them going into the store.

Wal-Mart discovered this the hard way in Germany, which it exited after nine years of struggling: arguably its failure was mostly due to trying to force its own culture onto a different one ('that's the way we do things around here'). Put another way, it didn't take any notice of feedback from customers.

Cultural differences aside, most customers – wherever they're from – don't like to waste their time. In particular, they don't like to wait to be served. Why should they? They are trying to pay a company money and the company is making them stand and wait for the privilege. What's wrong with this picture? On the other hand, if you are too brisk about the sales process, people don't like that either. They feel that the sales person didn't listen to what they want and that they haven't been treated as individuals, more as a cash till transaction.

A preoccupation with sales revenue rather than sales margin is another unintended consequence that results in poor treatment of customers. It arises, mostly, because one of the communications industry's abiding benchmarks of success is the measurement of average revenue per customer (ARPU – see my advice to financial analysts in Chapter 5). This misguided preoccupation causes many retail stores to miss out on merchandising device accessories which are relatively low-priced compared with devices. Yet they often yield very high retail gross margins, and the selection process can increase the perceived personalization of the buying experience. This in turn increases overall customer satisfaction.

The good, the bad and the ugly impacts of social networking

Everyone loves to listen to what their customers say about them when it's good, but people usually tend to switch off when feedback is less than positive and immediately go into defensive mode about why the customer is wrong. Although it might be painful, listening to the good, the bad and the ugly is an essential part of helping you to figure out what needs to be changed to move customers that next step along the pathway to super loyalty.

Even then you need to keep listening to make sure you don't slip, especially when you are introducing new business models and services and need to understand how to adapt customer experience strategies to accommodate how your customers want to interact, which changes all the time. Understanding what customers want and how they want to inter-relate with us: every single touch point between customers and their providers contributes to customers' perception, satisfaction and loyalty and, ultimately, to the profitability of the service provider.

Perhaps the ultimate example of how to achieve all this is through exploiting social networking channels. We tend to think of the negative aspects of social networks – we screw up and it's all over the web before you can breathe out. Certainly there are a number of stellar examples of just that, such as Molly Katchpole's social networking-led campaign against the Bank of America[116] that tapped into the widespread fury against financial institutions and their role in the ongoing global economic crisis. The Bank had planned to introduce a $5 monthly fee for debit cards, which Katchpole thought was outrageous and so did many others. At the height of the protest, 40,000 people a day were signing up to show their disapproval, forcing the bank to back down and preventing other banks from even suggesting such a step.

In another example of the power of social networking to amplify customer dissatisfaction, United Airlines' bag handlers were unfortunate enough to damage Canadian Dave Carroll's $3,500 Taylor acoustic guitar. The airline refused to pay up and he spent months inside their frustrating customer-service maze making him so angry that he wrote and sang a humorous protest video, made for $150 with the help of his friends, *United Breaks Guitars*[117] and put it on YouTube (you have to see it). It has had more than 11.5 million views since it was posted mid-2009 and the British newspaper, *The Times*, estimated the damage to United's brand and reputation had wiped $180 million off its share price. A case of don't get mad… get even!

But social networking can also be harnessed by companies to influence customers positively about your products and services, as well as act as an excellent vehicle for listening to what the market is saying about you. To get started, see what's being said about your brand name and keywords associated with your solution. Google BlogSearch and Twitter have great search engines to help you follow the conversations underway but also look at YouTube, Facebook and other social media – SearchMerge.com is very useful.

[116] www.washingtonpost.com/local/molly-katchpole-overnight-sensation/2011/11/04/gIQAGzGhtM_gallery.html
[117] www.youtube.com/watch?v=5YGc4zOqozo

A good example of a company that has grasped this is Comcast, the huge U.S. provider of cable TV, Internet and phone services, which turned a social media disaster into triumph with its *ComcastCares* Twitter-based service. Many U.S. cable companies have a history of poor customer service reputation and Comcast's woes got worse when a customer uploaded to YouTube a video of a Comcast technician sleeping on their couch.

Frank Eliason, at the time Director of Digital Care, came up with the idea of using Twitter to interact with Comcast's customers. He discovered that by doing a search for the word 'Comcast' (and occasionally 'Comcrap'), he could find tweeters complaining about things he could address. From a low starting point and by responding directly to the dissatisfied customer and solving their problems, Eliason and his team built a huge amount of goodwill and industry admiration because people saw Frank as their friend.

Eliason has now left the company but one of his team, Bill Gerth, has continued to build on that foundation. His advice is, "Don't delete online criticism, embrace it." Of course, it's ultimately what you do about that criticism that matters but the concept of having somebody who listens, cares about your problem and sorts it out has done wonders for Comcast's image.

John Myers[118] has some interesting thoughts on an increasingly sophisticated use of social media to gain insights into customer's attitudes: "If you've taken information from Facebook; social interaction; media postings from Twitter; social graph data; behavioral and other data coming from all directions providing information on how your customers are linked to other customers – you can identify which customer groups are impacted by your services."

Being proactive on trumpeting customer success stories via Facebook and other social media can help too. Wikis and social networking sites are a good way to involve customers and many leading companies allow customers to post articles, text or video stories, with some companies creating more enthusiasm by tying-in contests to wikis. For example, Dell's creative use of its Facebook page has driven a considerable fall in negative sentiment toward their brand while Microsoft has a program of its sales people uploading 'vox pop' customer videos captured on the spot at customer visits.

Harlan Vold, until recently CIO at Russia's Yota Group, provides some great illustrations of the sort of stuff you can do. Yota Group is made up of several companies, one of which offers 4G Internet services. He says: "We want to look at our customers and understand what they are doing and where they are going, so as a first step, you've got to go into their environment. We provide an app compatible with devices supported by Yota that's linked into social networking sites and lets people give us their permission to use their information.

---

[118]Senior Analyst at Enterprise Management Associates: *Go Where the Customers Are: Using Social Networks to Optimize Your Customer Experience* presented at Management World Americas, November 2011

"Most of our customers are between 18 and 35 years old and it's really increased our outreach into the market – the viral effect is huge, based on that culture, how they pass everything on. We get more information than we give them; you just have to know how to ask for it. You need to be local, because the diversity of the countries we cover is huge, so we set up the channels open to them based on their locality. We get things out there so fast, we now know within days whether things are going to work, down from weeks and months."

...whatever else, customers don't change
One of the main messages of this book is that the digital world will bring massive disruption but the principles of what makes a good customer experience are unlikely to change, because customer needs don't fundamentally change just because of the technology around them.

Digital service providers must be prepared to meet customers' expectations and take an holistic approach to doing so – processes, cultural change and customer-focused leadership are all part of the mix. The situation demands far-reaching changes within those companies that are not there yet. In a technology-based industry, it may be tempting to think that there is a technological solution to this issue through improved data management, the widespread use of data analytics and policy-based management.

While these are absolutely necessary, good customer experience management is at least as much an art as it is a science because you are dealing with human beings, their emotions, their prejudices and their foibles. Unless the customer is central to all of your decision-making right throughout the product life-cycle and at all of the touch points with the customer, you're unlikely to succeed.

Opportunities abound for providers in the digital world, but especially for those who can marry innovation and technology. They would do well to remember that ultimately the customer is king – customers can make or break your businesses. The clearest path to profitability is through maximizing customer lifetime value and that means holding onto them, their friends and families. Delivering a great customer experience isn't about altruism; it's about hard-headed business sense and competing in a tough marketplace that's only going to get tougher. It's about differentiating yourself, building a great brand and making sustainable profits.

I'm indebted to Rob Rich and Annie Turner from TM Forum's Research and Publications team for their help in compiling this chapter.

9

BUILDING A CULTURE OF INNOVATION

"It is not the strongest of the species that survive, nor the most intelligent, but the one most responsive to change"
– Charles Darwin

A corporate culture that punishes risk-taking and learning by mistakes is poisonous to innovation and since innovation is the key to success in the digital world, then companies that reinforce such a culture are both stupid and doomed to failure.

Innovation is the key driver of economic growth and is all about exploiting ideas – Apple didn't invent the MP3 player or the smartphone but it sure put them on the map by being highly innovative about creating better and more desirable products.

So this chapter isn't so much about inventing new things – much of the basic technology underpinning the digital economy already exists – it's about innovating better and more effective products, processes and services to create economic value. Companies that can do this are reaping a rich harvest in the digital world, while those who can't are likely to be condemned to watch the world go by.

Human beings are innately innovative: if we weren't, we would still be living in caves and eating berries for lunch. What companies have to do is figure out how to channel that built-in innovative and creative energy to drive economic value. In other words, encouraging innovation is mostly about *removing* barriers to creativity.

Necessity is the mother of innovation

I said that human beings are innately innovative but they are also innately lazy. If caves had been centrally heated and berries more satisfying, then the history of the world might have been very different.

Inventions and innovations usually arise because people have a problem to overcome. That's why so many innovations have come originally from military sources or from combating natural disasters because the stakes in solving problems when people are being killed are usually very high.

A big necessity that has spurred advancement through the ages is the desire to combat disease. Until the late 18th century, smallpox had ravaged human beings for millennia. It killed around a third of its victims and those who survived were usually subject to terrible, long-term complications and hideous scarring. So when, in 1796, a country doctor called Edward Jenner, who regularly witnessed smallpox at close quarters, observed that milkmaids who caught the relatively benign cowpox virus did not develop smallpox, he realized that deliberately infecting people with cowpox – by inoculating or vaccinating them – could inhibit the spread of the disease.

Another good example of necessity being the mother of *innovation* rather than invention (as the proverb usually runs) is the accidental discovery by the Scottish scientist Sir Alexander Fleming of what he later named penicillin. Before going on vacation in August 1928, he'd stacked together the cultures of staphylococci (bacteria which cause pneumonia, meningitis, diphtheria and scarlet fever, among other diseases – all common killers), whose properties he was studying. On his return a month later, he noticed that one of the cultures had been contaminated by a fungus, and that the fungus had killed the staphylococci surrounding it.

He published his findings in 1929, but they attracted little interest and he eventually abandoned trying to develop penicillin as a medicine.

Meanwhile, Howard Florey and Ernst Boris Chain, both at the Radcliffe Infirmary in Oxford, England had found a way to mass-produce penicillin, which Fleming had failed to do, and after the attack on Pearl Harbor in December 1941 the British and American governments provided funds to enable them to make and stockpile penicillin. By the time the D-Day mass invasion of Europe by Allied troops on June 4 1944, there was enough penicillin available to treat the Allies' wounded. Later, *Time* magazine wrote: "When it was finally recognized for what it was, the most efficacious life-saving drug in the world, penicillin would alter forever the treatment of bacterial infections, spawning a huge pharmaceutical industry that would conquer some of mankind's most ancient scourges." All three scientists were awarded a Nobel Prize for their work but it was the necessity of wartime that enabled the innovation that led to Fleming's discovery being turned into a real solution.

Nearer to our industry, in the early 1980s, Tim Berners-Lee, at the time a contractor at the European Organization for Nuclear Research (CERN), considered the problem of physicists from around the world needing to share data but having no common machines and no common presentation software. He wrote a proposal in March 1989 for "a large hypertext database with typed links", but it, like Fleming's world-changing work, also generated little interest.

Encouraged by his boss – who gave him a NeXT cube computer to experiment with – Berners-Lee began implementing his system and, in August 1991, he posted a short summary marking the debut of the web as a publicly available service on the Internet: "The Worldwide Web project aims to allow all links to be made to any information anywhere and was started to allow high energy physicists to share data, news and documentation. We are very interested in spreading the web to other areas and having gateway servers for other data. Collaborators welcome!"

In keeping with its birth at CERN, early adopters of the Worldwide Web were primarily university-based scientific departments or physics laboratories, but navigating it was awkward until the introduction of the Mosaic web browser in 1993. This graphical browser was developed by a team at the University of Illinois, led by Marc Andreessen – who would later co-found Netscape Communications Corporation and, like so many others, would become a multi-millionaire in the process.

Berners-Lee avoided the path of commercial exploitation and in 1994, founded the World Wide Web Consortium (W3C) at the Massachusetts Institute of Technology, making the web available freely, with no patent and no royalties, so that it could be easily adopted by anyone. This led to the phenomenal growth and success that we see today, as it became the fundamental engine of the digital economy. By early 2012[119] nearly 200 million websites are in active use.

[119]Netcraft survey of web services

Berners-Lee received a knighthood from Queen Elizabeth II and was named Greatest Briton of 2004, both for his achievements and for displaying the key British characteristics of "diffidence, determination, a sharp sense of humour and adaptability". Demonstrating those qualities, he admitted to the *Times* newspaper that the forward slashes (//) in a web address were actually unnecessary: "There you go, it seemed like a good idea at the time," he said in his lighthearted apology.

If necessity drives innovation, what are the drivers of innovation in the digital economy? The opportunity to make vast fortunes is one, but the threat of imminent disaster is perhaps a stronger one. For many communications players, the necessity will be the 'triple whammy' of rising demand for network capacity that is no longer synchronized to increases in revenue, but still requires infrastructure expansion and upgrades; the pressure on traditional services; and the threat to their retail position from digital stores and device providers.

As a report published by Juniper Research pointed out, global revenues billed by mobile operators will likely exceed $1 trillion in annual revenues by 2016, but by then their operating costs will exceed revenues unless they take serious 'avoiding' actions in the meantime. At the same time, numerous other gloomy predictions suggest that the sovereign debt crisis in Europe means that its citizens should not expect their salaries and lifestyles to get back to the levels of the pre-2007 banking crash before 2020 (so please tell your friends to buy more copies of this book!).

So, necessity abounds and that nearly always spurs innovation. But where and how should it be channeled? Paul Berriman at PCCW says: "Communications providers have always thought of themselves as innovators, but almost always in technology terms, which nowadays is just an enabler and far too limiting in the digital world. We MUST innovate in the way we structure our business, run our operations and most importantly, what our role and position is in the digital ecosystem."

Erik Hoving, Chief Strategy, Innovation & Technology Officer at KPN Group, in his typically forthright Dutch style, puts it more succinctly: "Many communications providers are spectacularly good at being spectacularly bad at innovation."

But as I've said, it's not that the *people* that work in that sector aren't good innovators: it's just that the culture and organization of many companies prevents them from innovating. Without innovation, the digital world will pass many of those companies by, as others reap the rewards for getting it right.

Innovation is a strange phenomenon. Many people talk about it, yet it remains elusive because it's impossible to predict the shape that a great idea will take, or how or when it will appear.

Even when ideas with huge potential do come along and are recognized as such, very often organizational structures and company cultures prevent them turning into successes. Remember all of those presentations in the early 2000s about the 3G mobile revolution – all of those wonderful, location-based, smart applications and experiences that it would bring? Well it has come true but, in nearly every case, not from the companies that predicted it – the digital revolution has so far been *enabled* by major communications and computing firms but *exploited* by innovative new entrants.

The dilemma of innovators

I've mentioned Clayton Christensen several times already and it's worth drilling down a bit into his ideas, which are as fresh today as when he first penned them. History is not usually on the side of existing companies when the rules change and the digital world is changing the rules fast over how the market is structured, how you get access to what you want, and what technology is being used. Christensen defines seven 'Dilemmas of Innovation', and taking those and my own thoughts, here are some issues to ponder on the changes that the digital world is forcing:

1 Market progress isn't the same as technology progress

Customers often don't know what they want but 'know good when they see it'. Conventional market research and analysis can be very unreliable and sometimes quite misleading so that companies that make committee-based decisions built on exhaustive business cases, market research and expert opinion often overlook emerging opportunities. The dreaded question of 'who else is doing this' use to haunt me when presenting new ideas to committees in big established companies because if you said 'nobody', they would turn it down because it was risky, rather than getting excited by the fact that we could be the first to market.

2 Innovation requires resources that are extraordinarily difficult to find for disruptive ideas

Unless you have an inspired leader like Steve Jobs at the helm the chances are that in established companies, the needs of today's business will nearly always win against tomorrow's because that is where the power base is and anyway, the company has to satisfy its shareholders on current business each quarter. So resources – money and the best talent – go to the existing business, not the new opportunities. This is obviously a big disadvantage against new market entrants, for whom today's business *is* tomorrow's business – they don't have any existing lines of business that will suck capital and talent away from new ideas.

3 Disruptive ideas need new markets

Old customers are often much less relevant when encountering genuinely new and innovative ideas, so exploiting disruptive ideas is usually more of a marketing problem than a technological one because the market needs to be educated on the advantages of the new idea. Because markets for disruptive ideas are unknown unknowns (that man Rumsfeld again!), managers who conventionally plan and execute may not succeed.

They need to be in 'learn and discover' mode but, as I'll explain shortly, that technique often involves failure and failure is often not a career-enhancing attribute in many companies. So many conventional management skills and approaches are inappropriate in disruptive markets and this can mean that the initiative goes seriously wrong. At the beginning, nobody knows how a disruptive idea will really be used, so customer experience, feedback, experimentation, trial and error are very valuable approaches to learn how to package, position, price and promote the new concept. Sadly, this can be seen as disorganized and amateur when set against the standards normally employed on a 'business as usual' product launch.

4 Organizations have narrow capabilities

New markets enabled by disruptive ideas require very different competencies and capabilities from the ones that went before. However, the 'white cells' that resist change in the way of doing things can be extremely tenacious because they are tied to the existing internal organizational structure, work practices, power-bases, politics and so on. To everyone else, the current processes seem just fine in relation to the existing business, but wholly inadequate for a disruptive new market and a significant dilemma for innovators is how to overcome this. Trying to convince the company to change the way processes work is usually a long, slow battle that ends up with messy compromises. In Christensen's research, creating a new, independent organization usually works best, as I outline later in this chapter.

5 Tolerate failure and learn iteratively

Christensen found that approaches that tolerate failure and learn iteratively are required but, again, these seem counter culture to a successful company at the top of its game in an existing market. In many company cultures, being associated with a failure has a big negative effect on your future career and so smart people shy away from risky or innovative projects. But encouraging risk taking and accepting failure as part of the learning curve are important attributes for companies that want to ensure they are not overtaken by market disruptions. However, risks and failure need to be mitigated and Christensen found that companies had the greatest success when they:

- Planned to fail early and inexpensively using trial and error (like a start-up).
- Embedded projects in small organizations that sought small wins rather than big breakthroughs.
- Embedded projects in an organization that found customers early on to learn from rather than chasing early big revenues.
- Used resources of the larger organization, but not the company's values, cost structure or organizational approach.
- Marketed to new customers and markets and did not search for technology breakthroughs.

6 Don't be dogmatic about always being a leader or a follower

This is a tricky one and, as I'll discuss shortly, there is good and bad about being a 'first-mover', which can confer 'first mover advantage' on the leader, who is rewarded with huge profit margins and a monopoly-like status. But there are many notable exceptions and sometimes the first mover is not able to capitalize on their advantage, leaving the door open for more effective and efficient competitors to dominate the market. This 'second mover advantage', such as Nintendo's dominance over first-to-market Atari, can be summarized by the adage "The second mouse gets the cheese". Amazon was actually a second-mover – BookStacks, founded by Charles Stack, predated Jeff Bezos's Amazon online bookstore by two years but was rapidly overtaken. The point is that each market is different and companies that stick dogmatically to a particular position run significant risks.

But being a follower also involves big risks, particularly in the method of attack against the pioneer – with big companies often hoping that increased marketing budgets will win out against a start-up. A 'me-too' strategy often proves ineffective since the follower may have more resources but may often lack the market understanding and the passion of the pioneer. As latecomer Google showed against the well-established Netscape, there is no hard and fast rule *except* not being a slow follower, which generally results in dismal failure.

7 Innovators get advantages by doing things that don't make sense to the big guys

This last of Christensen's tenets is fairly self-evident: big companies are often stuck in old ways of doing something. Their eye firmly fixed on incremental growth from their current products and lacking the comfort of extensive market research, they can be outfoxed by small entrants they assume are doing odd or even stupid things. Many companies around the world assumed the founders and investors in Facebook and Twitter were certifiably mad because they could not see an obvious route to generating profitable returns. This is because they didn't understand the concept of getting users first and the money will follow.

A cure for innovation indigestion

While hard times are generally the catalyst for the innovative light-bulbs bursting into life, there is also a counterbalance at play, especially in corporations with conservative, inward-looking corporate cultures. Hard times can also produce a cautious, not to say precarious climate: cutbacks and downsizing prevail, stifling innovative spirit as workforces adopt a work ethic of 'keep your head down' rather than put your head above the parapet and draw unwanted attention by putting forward wacky ideas that might be brilliant but risky.

In addition, grand corporate plans and the boardroom are rarely the birthplaces of innovation, especially when resources are tight. But most business leaders aren't stupid: most realize that investments and innovations made in hard economic times will pay back big rewards when markets return to health. The challenge is in knowing how to do that and reduce expenditure in difficult economic times. Andy Garman and Henry Chesbrough bring some fresh thinking on this in their excellent Harvard paper[120]: "History shows that the companies that continue to invest in their innovative capabilities during tough times are those that fare best when growth returns. That's how the U.S. chemicals industry overtook Britain's after World War I, how Sears surpassed Montgomery Ward as the leading U.S. retailer after World War II, and how Japanese semiconductor makers outpaced U.S. companies after the downturn of the early 1980s."

Investing and innovating while resources are scarce is a tough call – you have to focus energies and manage costs tightly while keeping growth options alive for the future. That usually means canceling or mothballing innovations and concentrating on short-term initiatives that fit best with the company's core business. The problem with that is, if the markets around the core business are changing and management concentrates its firepower on short-term initiatives to extend the life of the current business model, then disaster is probably lurking sometime in the future.

That pretty much encapsulates much of the communications industry recently: some companies are seemingly like rabbits caught in the headlights of the digital economy, facing significant pressures on margins of existing services; many face a market slowdown as well, yet few seem to have cracked the code on innovation.

Garman and Chesbrough put this neatly: "Rigorous prioritization halts many potentially promising projects at an early point in their development and leaves them stranded inside the company. Over time, so many projects get abandoned that the company's ability to grow beyond its core business is threatened. If focus is maintained for too long or with too much rigidity, it can become the enemy of growth."

Thankfully, they offer an interesting solution that proposes a better way than putting innovative projects on ice, by using external resources exploiting nascent innovations and not draining management attention and scare resources. More of this later on in this chapter, but even this good idea presupposes that innovation is alive and well in the first place. Sadly, this is often not the case, so I want to return to the core problem of getting innovation flowing by removing barriers to that creative stream.

As I found, somewhat to my surprise, when writing this book, Apple is the best example for so many of the points I wanted to make and of course, one of the best examples of adversity driving innovation. When Jobs returned as its CEO in 1996, following the NeXT acquisition, Apple was having its own 'near death experience' and needed to rapidly change course. Jobs recognized that Microsoft had won the battle over operating systems, so he drove Apple in a different direction, reigniting the innovative culture of the company that had been suppressed

[120]*How Open Innovation Can Help You Cope in Lean Times*, Copyright CT © 2009 Harvard Business School Publishing Corp. Andrew R. Garman is a founder and managing partner of New Venture Partners in Murray Hill, New Jersey. Henry W. Chesbrough teaches at the University of California at Berkeley's Haas School of Business, where he also runs the Center for Open Innovation

by former CEO John Sculley. Again, the sharp difference between invention and innovation shines out: Apple didn't invent the format for storing music as a digital file – the first patent for MP3 was granted in Germany in 1987 – but to quote industry veteran Brian Levy, "Apple made buying music in a digital format easier and more appealing than stealing it by launching iTunes and hugely desirable, beautifully designed devices called iPods."

In another lesson for players stuck in their current market niche, Apple showed that you don't necessarily have to persuade people to find new money to buy your products or services, you get them to shift their buying behavior from the old way to your smarter way – back to the definition that innovation is the creation of *better or more effective* products, processes or services.

So in innovating iTunes and the iPod, Apple simultaneously tapped into the music industry's time-honored, hugely profitable business model. 'Tapped into' might be a bit of British understatement – destroyed the old order might be a more accurate term!

Apple's innovation wasn't just a new solid-state recording device, it was a whole new business model and ecosystem that has replaced the previously very powerful one in just a few years. Free of the tightly controlled route to market, anyone can now put songs out on the web, recorded on their laptops at home and available through digital music stores. Clever use of social networking is how to become a famous recording artist now, not a contract with a big record label. The challenge of how artists make money from their work remains and the sight of more and more sexagenarian rock stars returning to big stadiums suggest that it's not through record sales.

Logically it should have been Sony who came up with the solution, building on its hugely successful Walkman heritage and huge media assets, just like Nokia 'should have' launched the iPhone and kicked off true mobile access to the web, having been the world's most successful mobile phone maker for so long. After all, Nokia had launched its ground-breaking Communicator way back in 1996 – yes I had one too – but as we all know, Apple leveraged its brand position and dominance in music to successfully launch the iPhone and the rest is history. As Jobs said at the launch over and over again: "It's an iPod, a web browser and a phone" – none of which had been invented by Apple – but they innovated to provide an unprecedented level of simplicity and integration wrapped up in a cool and elegant design.

Where were the established, hugely successful mobile device makers? After all they had plenty of cash; good market shares and a booming market. Complacency comes to mind, in the case of Nokia; resting on its laurels at Motorola and maybe some arrogance at Research in Motion, which thought business users would be content to stick with the pioneering, iconic BlackBerry indefinitely. Their joint CEOs resigned while I was writing this chapter; Nokia was under new management and clinging ever closer to Microsoft; and Motorola is now owned by Google: all of which only goes to emphasize the speed of change and the danger of standing still in the innovation game.

Nothing to fear but...

It's deeply ironic that the communications and IT sector is enabling the digital world (and probably has the most to gain from it) but seems to harbor the greatest fear of being eaten by it. It's worth expanding Franklin D Roosevelt's famous 1931 Presidential Address because his immortal phrase "Let me assert my firm belief that the only thing we have to fear is fear itself" had the very telling rejoinder: "Nameless, unreasoning, unjustified terror, which paralyses needed efforts to convert retreat into advance". FDR could have been addressing a group of CEOs from the communications and computing industries to stiffen their backbones. The digital world offers unbounded opportunities but yes, it will change the landscape that has so richly rewarded those companies until now and that is a threat. But turning that threat into an opportunity is what leadership and innovation are all about.

Sadly not everyone will hear, absorb or act on those words and I'm sure that if I'm around to write second and third editions of this book, I'll be including some household names that didn't heed that call and were on their way out. Big established industries often stick to tried and trusted ways of running their core businesses and business models, no matter what the evidence is that the world around them is changing. They tend to focus most of their energies on trying to stem the tides of change rather than exploiting new opportunities, often for fear of such actions hastening the demise of their current business. Apple's demolition of Sony, Nokia and Motorola in the device business; along with Sony, EMI, Decca and other record labels; and HMV, Virgin megastores, Tower Records, Andy's Records and many other stores shows just how powerful the digital lightsaber is in the hands of a determined and innovative Jedi.

The act of sitting and watching your fate unravel was brilliantly described by the business guru Charles Handy, in his book, *The Age of Unreason*[121]. His proposition was that if you put a frog in a pan of boiling water it would immediately jump out. However, if you put a frog in a pan of comfortably warm water and heat it up gradually, the frog is unlikely to take life-saving action until it's too late – it failed to notice the gradual change, rather it continued to accommodate it as best it could (which, incidentally, is why many people don't appreciate how serious global warming is).

Handy explained his experiences of a troubleshooter called in by failing businesses. Obviously, one of the fundamental questions to ask in a situation where companies are in difficulty is, "So what's going wrong?" The answer he most frequently got was along the lines of, "We don't know, we've just carried on doing what we've always done," which of course was the cause of the problem. And many, perhaps most, executives today are truly underestimating the speed of

[121]Charles Handy: *The Age of Unreason* (ISBN 0-09-954831-3)

change, which is accelerating faster than at any other time in our history, so if we continue to simply tolerate the heat, we'll feel the full blast a lot faster than we think.

The opportunities are legion. If my notion of "everything that can be digital, will be" applies, then every business, every consumer and every thing with an ounce of processing power in it will be part of the digital, connected world. That's not just going to consume unbelievable amounts of bandwidth, storage and processing power, that's a shift of huge sections of business life from a conventional way of supplying needs to a digital one – in other words, the process that emasculated the record business applied to every business sector in the world. That offers truly massive opportunities for new players to disrupt markets with a better and more effective way of doing it. Look at the way Salesforce.com is permeating great numbers of enterprises that have a sales team needing support and then let your mind run on every conceivable function that could be digitized and delivered as a cloud-based service rather than a physical set of servers, communications and applications. It's not necessarily new money, the overall size of the pie being spent on such capabilities might not grow but for sure, new players will be supplying them or providing the underpinning capabilities to support others and reaping rich new rewards.

I don't have much sympathy with the growing anti-capitalist sentiment that seems to be mushrooming around the world ever since some head-cases at Lehman Brothers kick-started the global credit crunch that gave way to the sovereign debt crisis in so many countries. But I do look rather benignly at other cultures that don't have the same pre-occupation with quarter by quarter earnings of 'full-on' capitalism. Leaders who have to spend their waking hours with an eye on short-term earnings to protect share prices and their bonuses, don't have the leeway to address the crucial question of where the company needs to be in two or five years' time if it is to survive, never mind prosper. It's sobering to look back 15 years and remember how small the mobile industry was back then, while Apple was struggling desperately to reinvent itself and Google didn't exist.

In another 15 years, things that are small and emerging sectors now – such as cloud-based services in numerous vertical sectors plus the blossoming of machine-to-machine (M2M) communications – are likely to be on a scale we can't imagine now and one that dwarfs what has gone before.

Incubators, accelerators and open innovation

Time and time again, the inevitable story that gets written about a company that failed because it didn't act soon enough to exploit new innovations points to the cause as being the dominating 'dead hand' effect of today's core business. The current business acts like a black hole sucking in talent and resources, especially if times are hard and everyone focuses intensively on preserving it. Not only that, but executives actively kill off any innovations that could negatively impact that core business, fearing it will hurt current sales and conveniently forgetting that competitors can do the same. It's always better to have *your* new product eating the old rather than being eaten alive by your competition.

Several approaches to solving this problem aim to create a level of new business autonomy that helps make the most of the talents and motivation of the 'awkward squad' – those worrisome people with ideas – and helps insulate them from 'help from head office', the arrival of the men in suits.

Incubator projects where the innovators are given sufficient resources and freedom to prove the viability of an idea can be a way of mimicking the freedom that say a Mark Zuckerberg, Larry Page or Jeff Bezos had when they had nothing else to worry about but making their innovation become real. Sure, they had venture capitalists and a million other things to think about but they didn't have to fight head office every day or keep Wall Street analysts happy. A largely separate incubator or subsidiary helps protect innovators and their ideas from the constraints of the parent organization's potentially stifling culture. It also prevents them worrying about failing and losing their jobs, or affecting the company's share price.

The incubator approach needs a strong champion at the executive table who will support disruptive practices and processes to make it work. I've worked with many start-ups and only rarely do they have a crystal clear idea of what they are doing to begin with. A lot of trial and error is needed to see what works and what doesn't and to learn from both. The key is to create an environment that removes the fear of failure – at least up to a point.

Fear of failure is a major inhibitor in many organizations as failure is usually punished by stunted career prospects, lower pay or getting fired. Removing that fear or at least allowing a considerable tolerance of it is a vital factor if you want people to take risks and try new things. Google under Eric Schmidt famously allowed people one day a week to experiment and dream up new ideas and although Page has focused this somewhat, Google is still a far more tolerant and experimental culture than most established communications or computing companies. Amazon also encourages experimentation and risk taking.

There aren't many instances of this to celebrate in more conventional aspiring digital economy players but it can be done given sufficiently enlightened management. Telecom Egypt, still a state-owned operator, has successfully deployed a leadership development program to encourage out-of-the-box thinking and each year selects 25 of the most promising young people to spend 10 months, full-time, on a leadership course and working with innovators. They then return to their employer and apply what they have learned.

The initiative is driven by the CEO, and line managers are not allowed to stop their staff from applying for a position on the program. So far it has been very successful, with more than 150 people having completed it. A key part of this is ensuring that when they return to the company, they are integrated fully into the organization with their fellow employees, rather than allowing an elite, separate 'club' to form, causing resentment and resistance among colleagues.

BT established its Brightstar incubator some years ago and successfully grew and spun out several new companies in partnership with venture capital firm NVP, which went on to successfully develop the concept in a number of other large corporations around the world, including Telstra and Phillips. One of NVP's founders was Andy Garman who, with Henry Chesbrough, advocates that sometimes it is better for innovation to occur *outside* the firm rather than see it suffocated or neglected on the inside.

They call this concept 'open innovation' and I said earlier that I'd return to it in more detail. It's a set of inside-out strategies that may involve opening up projects to outside investment and development by experienced outside firms or spinning off projects as separate ventures that allow the originating company to retain some equity interest in the new company. This approach removes the negative impact that internal innovation can often have on company focus and scarce resources but it can also bring much-needed outside expertise to bear on how to successfully innovate ideas from concept to market success.

New supplier and partner relationships are easier to create as a separate entity, possibly with former competitors who would have found it difficult to deal with the parent, and allowing the creation of innovative ecosystems. Finally, there is the opportunity for the parent to potentially benefit from high-margin licensing income.

As is a consistent theme in this book, Garman and Chesbrough point to the critical importance of leadership by senior executives who are in strategic roles because of the inherent cultural, political and organizational challenges that inside-out open innovation can bring. Navigating the internal politics of such a radical approach needs a determined and effective internal champion if it is to happen.

In the open innovation concept, the parent company does not need to cut the cord completely: in addition to the possibility of continuing to retain equity in the new venture and retaining patent rights that can be exploited, the parent can also be a customer of the fruits of the spin-out. They offer five key moves for making open innovation a success for internal innovations that struggle to get adopted or given resources.

There are none so blind as those who will not see[122]...

The inability of large corporations to seize opportunities because they have institutional myopia is legendary. There are many reasons for this, hubris; familiarity breeding contempt; tunnel

[122]English proverb attributed to Matthew Henry (1662-1714), English Presbyterian minister and writer

Open innovation

Garman & Chesbrough's framework for getting the greatest value from innovation initiatives

Move 1: Become a customer or supplier of your former internal projects

IF your business is pursuing an important capability that it can neither afford to develop itself nor acquire on the open market, and others in or beyond your industry also covet the capability…

THEN join with those others to fund, develop and launch it as an independent business, and become its first customer.

Move 2: Let others develop your non-strategic initiatives

IF your business is refocusing on its core activities and you've identified adjacent, complementary initiatives that drain too much attention, time and capital but that might attract outside interest and investment…

THEN spin them out to investors who can take over the development burden. Others will fund the progress, and you can keep some equity in case they make it big. You can even reacquire the best ventures.

Move 3: Make your IP work harder for you and others

IF a lot of your company's intellectual property sits on a shelf and generates no direct financial benefit and you understand that its value, to you and to others, will dissipate unless it is continually developed…

THEN let outside partners benefit from what you've created, continue its development, and pay you licensing fees. Many businesses recover 10% to 20% of their annual R&D spending in this way.

Move 4: Grow your ecosystem, even when you are not growing

IF your company is an active innovator, continually engaging with its customers, collaborators, industry experts, trade associations, and others to identify future opportunities…

THEN build on your ecosystem of potential innovation partners. Be like Major League Baseball general managers, who always know which team will be interested in which player at what price.

Move 5: Create open domains to reduce costs and expand participation

IF your internal ideas are likely to attract interest from valuable outside communities, potentially creating breakthrough advances or even changing the game within your industry…

THEN consider establishing open domains that either exchange information and ideas or provide shared facilities and services.

vision; denial; and as Jobs pointed out, divisional profit and loss targets breed a singular focus on short-term achievement that sets division against division and causes managers not to see the wider picture.

A good example of this is the story of WorldPay. Its origins can be traced to a small British outfit, headed up by Nick Ogden, who in the mid-1990s launched a single-currency e-commerce site, as it turned out, prematurely. The original business failed to thrive but, based on the principle of necessity driving innovation, the founders spotted that there was big demand from overseas users (who were not even the intended audience) for a cross-currency processing facility.

WorldPay would go on to become one of the largest payments-handling companies in the world, being acquired by Royal Bank of Scotland, who expanded the business by acquiring and merging a number of payment solutions companies from different countries. By 2007, WorldPay had become the largest merchant acquirer in Europe and one of the largest globally, operating in more than 40 countries, 120 transaction currencies and 14 settlement currencies.

Why didn't the banks do this themselves? As a financial services industry veteran observed wryly, "any of the major banks could have set up such a service on a single PC at that time and so could have owned that market themselves, but they didn't because they were institutionally unable to grasp the opportunity – and promptly lost out on a multi-billion dollar market.

It happens time and time again. As I said earlier, Sony absolutely should have dominated the MP3 and online music market – they had an iconic brand in Walkman; a loyal customer base of tape players that they successfully migrated to portable CD players; they owned a major music business; had an R&D machine bar none and incredible financial resources. So why did they let Apple take the market from them? They were blind to the opportunity because they were too interested in protecting their traditional record business model.

As I write, on the same day as Apple's stock value broke through the $650 level – meaning that it represents over 5 percent of the S&P 500 Index – Sony announced layoffs of 10,000 people and forecast its "worst ever" losses. Another Kodak moment!

Bowling googlies
In cricket, a googly is a way of pitching a ball that spins the opposite way to normal, confusing the batsman. The naming of Google is a happy coincidence[123] (cricket not being big draw in Stanford!) but in a market as fraught with uncertainty as the digital economy where nobody understands the rules, bowling and playing curved balls is vital to be able to succeed and launch the kinds of new services that can attract and delight customers while generating new revenue streams and sustainable profits. Many digital success stories started out without any real business plan of how the idea could be monetized, the initial focus was on customer

---

[123]Apparently originating from a misspelling of the word 'googol': Rachael Hanley, *From Googol to Google. The Stanford Daily* (Stanford University)

growth – in other words, the Oklahoma Land Grab. As I write, Facebook is in the process of being floated for perhaps $100 billion and if it reaches that it will make paper millionaires of more than one-third of Facebook's 3,000 employees and founder Mark Zuckerberg worth at least $28 billion.

The desire to generate a stunning business plan that 'proves' how a new idea can deliver a positive return in a known period of time by capturing a certain percentage of the market is deeply ingrained in every conventional business person. But just because you plan for something, that doesn't mean it will happen that way. Sony must have had a grand plan for success in marrying consumer electronics and media, otherwise why buy a major Hollywood studio and record business? Japanese companies share many cultural traits with Chinese and Korean ones, always having a clear strategy and long-term vision. Sony's failure wasn't induced by short-termism but a corporate failure to realize the threat from left field – they assumed that the existing business models would sustain.

In his highly entertaining, but learned book, *Obliquity: Why our goals are best achieved indirectly*,[124] economist John Kay of the *Financial Times* argues that the direct, grand plan approach is generally doomed to failure. This is because the types of problems the human race is struggling with – whether military, economic, environmental, medical or commercial, among others – are too complex to model accurately.

This in turn leads to grandiose but flawed strategies, the very opposite of intuition, feel and insight. Yet these are what successful young digital companies like Facebook, Salesforce. com and Twitter had in bounds in their high-growth stages and still have some of today. The WorldPay team probably used the same intuitive approach: aka 'make it up as you go along'. I explored this theme in Chapter 8 on customer experience and empathy.

Kay wheels out many highly lucid and entertaining arguments to support his theory of obliquity – the principle that complex goals are best achieved indirectly – and explains why the happiest people aren't necessarily those who focus on happiness; how the most successful cities aren't planned (he compares Paris with Brasilia) and how the most profit-oriented companies aren't usually the most profitable.

The googly effect is about doing something that nobody expects and not trying to over-plan the effects of innovation too early. Maybe even the innovator doesn't fully understand it to begin with – innovation doesn't have to be about drastic shifts that seek to overturn or radically change the culture, it can be small ideas that grow into big ones. That is a core principle of innovation at Google where famously employees are given time in their normal working week to come up with innovative ideas.

[124]Published 2010 – www.johnkay.com/books

Google's approach to innovation is, like the company itself, evolving but some of the company's core innovation principles were documented by Google Vice President Marissa Mayer. Her video *Nine Principles of Creativity Learned at Google*[125] makes interesting viewing and some of those principles speak directly to these notions of avoiding the grand plan and using intuition as part of the innovation process. Here are some edited highlights of what she says:

- Innovation, not instant perfection: There's a lot of instances where we've launched laughable products. At Google we make mistakes every time; every day thousands of things go wrong with Google but if you launch things and iterate really quickly, people forget about those mistakes and they have a lot of respect for how quickly you build the product up and make it better.
- Users, not money: We believe that if we focus on the users, the money will come. In a truly virtual business, if you're successful, you'll be working at something that's so necessary people will pay for it in subscription form or you'll have so many users that advertisers will pay to sponsor the site.
- A license to pursue your dreams: Since around 2000, we let engineers spend 20 percent of their time working on whatever they want, and we trust that they'll build interesting things. One of our researchers would go to 10 or 15 news sites each day looking for information and he thought, "Why don't I write a program to do this?" So he used a Web crawler to cluster articles and later emailed it around the company – that's how Google News came about – he didn't intend to build a product, but accidentally gave us the idea for one.
- Ideas come from everywhere: We have this great internal list where people post new ideas and everyone can go on and see them. It's like a voting pool where you can say how good or bad you think an idea is. Those comments lead to new ideas.

Obviously the Google formula can't work everywhere but there is no doubt it's a highly innovative and successful company from which many players could learn a lot – especially those communications and computing giants who find innovating hard because they are so wedded to their existing approaches.

I haven't failed – I've just found 10,000 ways that won't work![126]

Mayer's point about learning from mistakes is well made but it assumes that the organization that you are working in tolerates failure and encourages leaning from mistakes. Google's attitude to product launch risks ridicule but works on the principle of iterative learning and feedback loops when they say, 'this is work in progress, tell us what we can do and what you'd like to see'. You can't get a bigger lab than the outside world, nor a bigger sample of public opinion.

Sadly, many organizations don't operate that way and encourage people to play it safe, not take risks or challenge conventional wisdom. But imagine where mankind would be if we punished

[125]http://ecorner.stanford.edu/author/marissa_mayer
[126]Thomas Alva Edison

babies for falling over when they are trying to walk and or for getting the words wrong when trying to speak.

But somehow when many executives leave home in the morning, they leave that life experience behind and want instant perfection on every product development, every marketing campaign and every deal. Learning like their children do and they did themselves once, through making mistakes, just isn't tolerated in many companies and this attitude creates a culture of 'keep your head down' and 'do what you're told', rather than putting new ideas forward and taking risks.

Too many organizations – in business as well as in the public sector – have cultures and organizational beliefs that any failure is unacceptable: only serial success will do (especially in government – when did you last hear a politician admit that they screwed up?). That drives people to have to build and then maintain their reputation by claiming to reach every goal and never being seen to make mistakes; constantly covering up the smallest blemishes, blaming someone else or brushing problems under the carpet.

That search for ever and better success and never admitting or learning from failure is the main contributor to massive mistakes like Enron, the BP oil spill in the Gulf of Mexico, Lehman Brothers, News Corp's *News of the World* debacle, Royal Bank of Scotland, the Greek debt crisis and so on. The pattern is usually the same – the denials, the lies, the hubris, the falsification of data, the burying of problems, the finger-pointing as everyone tries to shift the blame onto someone else – until they become crises and disasters that can't be hidden any longer.

Even when the intolerance of failure doesn't reach the dizzy heights of some of those examples, it can still suck the lifeblood out of internal innovators and ultimately companies. Often senior executives, who made their names by introducing some critical change in the past, avoid further innovation because this time it might go wrong, tarnishing their reputation. They become frightened that the success of something new might put their achievements in the shade. Better to do nothing and keep your reputation intact, especially if retirement and a fat pension looms.

Whole cultures can adopt this line of thinking – a common proverb in Japan is "the nail that sticks up will soon be hammered flat" meaning: don't stick your head up or a mighty corporate Samurai sword might take it off. In Anglo-Saxon countries, its known as 'tall poppy syndrome': the thinking being that it's better not to be a tall poppy, they are always the ones to get their heads lopped off – don't go against the wishes and instructions of your line manager or the trends in corporate thinking, in the interests of hanging onto your job.

A corporate culture that punishes risk-taking and learning by mistakes is poisonous to innovation and since innovation is the key to success in the digital world, then companies that encourage that culture or at least tolerate it, are both stupid and doomed to failure. The digital economy, at least so far, seems to reward companies who are prepared to experiment, fail small scale, fail fast, learn from it and move on (Google, Facebook) and punish those who take the traditional corporatist approach (Netscape, MySpace and Yahoo).

Tim Harford, in his latest book: *Adapt: Why Success Always Starts with Failure*[127], examines this in some detail and explains with humor and clarity that the key to success is an ability to adapt, improvise and accept mistakes, while fear of failure paradoxically often leads to greater and more dangerous failures. His book is a sort of corporate *Origin of the Species* and will make uncomfortable reading for captains of complacent companies who think they know it all. Comparing companies and their habit of rising and falling to Darwinian selection, he shows how clusters of bankruptcies occur in a pattern that can be mapped to extinctions in the fossil record. As Darwin[128] said: "It is not the strongest of the species that survive, nor the most intelligent, but the one most responsive to change."

In the past century, 80 percent of the world's largest companies have disappeared – only General Electric and Shell are still around and since disruptive innovations bubble up in the marketplace by a process of trial and error, the more players there are in a market, the more a significant discontinuity occurs. The digital economy is likely to be the most fertile breeding ground for innovation in history and if you buy Harford's ideas, that spells even more danger for companies that don't know how to innovate.

Creating a low-fear environment so that risk can be taken to help spur innovation isn't just something that applies *inside* a company. Many small entrepreneurial suppliers could help large sclerotic companies to more rapidly introduce innovative products and services, but the fear-factor of punishment for failure often plays out in heavy-handed penalty clauses and restrictive covenants on patents in contracts, often made all the harsher because the big company fears that the small company might either go out of business or (somehow worse) become successful on their back.

Such entrepreneurial suppliers can make great partners, they're not the enemy, and the aim should be a win-win, because innovation is about the way we use and monetize these unrivalled assets to deliver value to customers fast. That means being much, much more receptive to new partners. Rather than seeing them as a commercial threat or invaders of our long-established systems and processes, we need to figure out how best to enable their ideas, please customers and ultimately make a profit for all parties.

For many companies, this is about not just thinking the unthinkable, but actually doing something about it – not just reading about it in books like Harford's, nodding wisely and going back to the 'real world' because the real world won't be there for much longer. Change or die out

---

[127]Tim Harford, *Adapt: Why Success Always Starts with Failure*, Little Brown, 2011. ISBN-13: 9781408701522
[128]Charles Darwin (1809-1882) English naturalist

is a basic tenet of natural selection: just look at other industries and see who made changes and survived and who left it too late and died out.

First-mover or fast-follower?

Much has been written on the advantages and disadvantages of being a first-mover in a market. The idea of first-mover advantage is similar to the old adage, 'the early bird gets the worm' – being the first company to sell a new product *may* provide long-lasting benefits or competitive advantages. First-mover advantage usually refers to the first significant company to move into a market, not merely the first company. As I said earlier, Amazon wasn't the first seller of books online, but it was the first significant company to make an entrance into the online book market.

The phrase 'first-mover advantage' was first popularized in a paper by a Stanford Business School professor, David Montgomery, and his co-author, Marvin Lieberman[129] and was much heralded in the lead-up to the dot-com boom in the 1990s, when the idea became unchallenged conventional wisdom in Silicon Valley.

There is now a growing backlash against it because although sometimes first-movers get rewarded with market dominance and higher-than-average profitability (say eBay or Facebook), being the first mover does not always provide advantages (like Netscape). This leaves the opportunity for other firms (like Google) to compete effectively and efficiently versus their earlier entrants. These companies then gain a 'second-mover advantage'.

Much of the problem with the idea of first-mover advantage is that it's hard to be clear about what it really means and as academics can't agree, it's hard to define any particular traits or moves to think about in positioning for the digital economy.

There are two stages to developing first-mover advantages. First, a company must have an opportunity to be first to market for something novel, either through skill or luck. Second, and perhaps the critical part, they must be able to capitalize on the benefits of being first. In Lieberman and Montgomery's original paper they described three benefits of being first:

- Technology leadership: Early entrants can lead other companies in their understanding and use of technology in ways that are hard for later entrants to copy, often due to a lack of big enough resources. In the digital world, this may occur at the enabling technology layer, for example with Intel, or Qualcomm, but for many players who can obtain appropriate technologies on the open market it is relatively easy for later entrants to overcome the lead held by the first-mover firm and even gain the advantage of later and better technology.

  An increasingly popular method of exploiting first-mover technology leadership is by acquiring patents for their technology and thus to try to prevent other companies from copying it and

[129]*First-mover advantages*: Marvin B. Lieberman, David B. Montgomery. Copyright © 1988 John Wiley & Sons, Ltd

then 'farming' that advantage through patent license fees. The digital economy is buzzing with a rising tide of patent law-suits on almost every conceivable aspect of the underpinning and enabling technology for the digital world. Even better than an exploitable patent, is if the first mover can establish their product as the industry standard, making it more difficult for followers to gain customer acceptance.

- **Control of resources:** The second type of first-mover advantage identified by Montgomery and Lieberman is the ability to control a vital resource that disadvantages later entrants. Facebook has done this effectively in controlling the supply of a vital resource – personal data – but other aspects like controlling the position on search engines or listings in app stores have become vital to success for many digital services.

- **Buyer switching costs.** This first-mover advantage comes if you can ensure that it is costly or inconvenient for a customer to switch to a new brand. Mobile phone companies exploited this mercilessly until number portability was forced on them by many regulators around the world. Other switching barriers may be more subtle – the pain and grief of moving your address book from device to device; re-learning a new user interface and so on. Facebook again has a huge advantage here – switch to another social network and none of your friends will be there.

Switching costs impinge on brand loyalty and the first company to offer a product of acceptable quality may earn brand loyalty. If you focus on it intently, like Amazon and Apple, uber-brand loyalty can be a significant barrier to switching to a competitor. If you skipped it, there's more on brand loyalty and developing a great customer experience in Chapter 8.

First-mover disadvantages...

Despite some real advantages of the three types of benefit described by Montgomery and Lieberman, there is good reason to be careful, as there may be first-mover disadvantages, or fast-follower advantages to be had. For example, the first entrant may spend heavily on growing a market (R&D, advertising, promotions, education and so on) only for later entrants to benefit from a ready-built and informed customer base. Fast followers may be able to learn from the mistakes made by the first movers and may even be started or staffed by émigrés from the first mover. If first movers become complacent, later entrants may punish them by taking advantage of market disillusionment and changing customer needs: the Motorola then Nokia then Apple and Samsung trail. As the digital economy gathers speed, we may well see digital first movers increasingly susceptible to second or later-mover success.

In their paper, *Pioneer advantage: Marketing logic or marketing legend?*, Peter Golder and Gerard Tellis[130] found some interesting facts that further confuse the picture over whether being a first mover or a later-stage player is the better strategy. In their analysis of 500 brands in 50 product categories, they found that fast followers have much greater long-term success; those in

---

[130]Golder, Peter N; Tellis, Gerard J *JMR, Journal of Marketing Research*; May 1993

their sample entered the market an average of 13 years later than the pioneers and almost half of the first movers failed.

What does it all mean? It means that sadly there are no magic bullets in the digital world, just like anywhere else. It all comes down to strategy, how you play the game and probably quite a bit of luck.

When you're finished changing, you're finished[131]

There's an old joke that goes, "How many psychologists does it take to change a light bulb?" The answer is, "None, it has to want to change itself." And any industry wanting to be a big player in the digital world has to want that too and must not only accept the need to change and embrace innovation but to actually do something about it to move ahead.

Here are a few tips based on the collective wisdom that I've purloined from many people, including those I've mentioned in this chapter:

- From little acorns... Don't dismiss small ideas: they can have very big, unforeseen results and remember that ideas can come from anywhere, so be receptive to all sources.

- Avoid the 'grand plan'... Don't base innovation project investments solely on the comfort of grand business plans, acres of market research and advice from big-name consulting firms, spending fortunes and months planning until you know you're on to a winner. Start small, try things out, especially internally where appropriate and with feedback from the outside world wherever possible. It's a great reality check, even if the responses are not flattering or what you expected.

- Move fast... Industrial-strength engineering and five nines' reliability is not always necessary and may be too slow in fast-moving markets where the emphasis is on acquiring users not profits.

- Customers 'know good when they see it'... Really focus on what your customers want even if they don't know it yet. Conventional product marketing wisdom of asking customers what they want and then building it breaks down in the digital world so do lots of market testing and market education as early as you can in the product or service development cycle. Listen to users – as often as you can and as many as you can.

- Experiment, adopt and adapt... It doesn't matter if you don't know exactly what you're doing, so long as you have the wits to spot a potentially good idea when you see it and have the courage to do something about it. Even if the market doesn't respond to it, if the idea has a kernel of something interesting, morph it into something that the market needs.

[131] Benjamin Franklin (1706-1790) American statesman, scientist and philosopher

- **Empower people...** Give people the power to make their own decisions, rather than escalating everything upward – it's too slow and too limiting and anyway, why would someone remote from the market have any better insight?

- **Use adversity positively...** Accept that creativity arises out of adversity – tough times do not automatically mean fewer options. Use constraints as a positive, not a negative stimulator of innovation.

- **Allow people to learn from mistakes...** Foster an environment that encourages and enables innovation and allows people to make mistakes provided that they can learn from them. This may mean setting up an incubator or subsidiary away from the potentially stifling influence of the parent organization.

- **Grow a culture that encourages experimentation...** A corporate culture that punishes failure and rewards only successes is likely to be low on experimentation and innovation. Accept that failure is part of the learning process, not a catastrophe, but fail quickly, learn well and move on. Often you don't need to kill something, just tweak it based on feedback from users.

- **Build partners...** Reliance on partnerships is inevitable, so learn how to manage them. Remember that small companies are usually highly innovative because they have to be to survive – use that energy rather than crushing it.

- **Consider open innovation...** Don't let ideas die on the shelf – if you have not got the resources to exploit ideas yourself, seek partners and innovate 'inside-out'.

Innovation case example: Mobile Payments – M-PESA, Kenya
This case study, about Safaricom's successful innovation of mobile payments services in Kenya, demonstrates a number of the key points that I outlined above.

First it's about innovation, not invention. Safaricom did not invent mobile payments – similar services had already been pioneered in other parts of the world – but they adapted and adopted ideas of others into a highly successful service positioned for the Kenyan market.

Second it shows that speed is important – moving before the competition (both direct and indirect) really understands what you are doing.

Third, it shows the value of building partnerships – in this case with the banks, who initially felt threatened but now successfully partner to the benefit of both parties.

Finally, this case shows the very real advantage of first-mover advantage: fortune favors the brave.

There are countless examples of new innovations but when you look at the communications service sector, they are surprisingly thin on the ground. Sure, there are plenty of brilliant technological innovations that make today's communications as ubiquitous, reliable and cost effective as they are but when it comes to services, it is somewhat arid territory. The two big innovations in the mobile sector – short message service (SMS) and pre-paid services were, in fact, less innovations and more accidents – SMS being a technological accident and pre-pay being an accounting accident.

But that can't be said about the concept of mobile payments, which have been evolving over the last decade. Like many innovations, its time has not yet fully come, but some form of marriage between the mobile and money will emerge. The prize is huge – Mastercard and Visa settle over $7 trillion a year and already handle over $500 billion orginating from mobiles. As with many of the opportunities in the digital world, success is not innovating something truly original, it's around doing it better than someone else and disrupting the existing market.

Some services take time to get all of the enablers in place before they can really take off at scale. Remember that today's cloud-based applications like Salesforce.com struggled to live up to their hype a decade or more ago when application service providers (ASPs) were going to sweep the board. The networks and enabling technologies just weren't fully baked back then, but they are now and cloud is booming.

One of the barriers to mass market success for mobile payments has been the absence of productive cooperation between key stakeholders in the ecosystem, mainly the financial >

institutions and the mobile network operators. There is a whiff of 'turf wars' underneath the smiles: each industry fearful of the other, debates over who 'owns' the customer; difficulties around branding; and an inability to arrive at a workable revenue sharing model.

Because of these issues, mobile payments success has been limited and many mobile payment initiatives are still in a pilot stage. There are, however, some notable exceptions that have been commercially launched on a large scale and include Paybox in Austria, G-Cash in the Philippines, NTT DoCoMo's Osaifu-Keitai in Japan and M-PESA in Kenya.

Safaricom's experience

The market for mobile communications in Africa has been booming in recent years and in 2011 it became the world's second largest mobile market. In Kenya, local operator Safaricom has also had staggering success with its mobile payments service M-PESA which it launched in March 2007 – and not only financially: it has brought major benefits to society in Kenya. Safaricom is a part-owned subsidiary of Vodafone, which actually owns the solution and provides it under license.

M-PESA was a ground-breaking innovation and by 2011, it had over 14 million subscribers and more than 28,000 agents across Kenya. Over a third of Kenya's gross domestic product passes through the system each year and despite initial objections, Kenya's banks have benefited greatly and are now making money from 'zero' deposit accounts, which wouldn't have been viable without M-PESA and enlightened regulation, as well as providing other wholesale services.

Part of M-PESA's success has been to provide the platform that enabled people to run innovative business models over it, from being able to buy a day's insurance for a herd of cattle going to market, to bars in Nairobi that will only accept payment by M-PESA because it saves the time and trouble inherent in handling cash and cuts the risk of robbery.

M-PESA is operator-centric, working through an application that sits on all Safaricom SIM cards. To put money on your phone, you walk into an authorized agent, hand over your money and then receive an SMS saying that the money has arrived on your phone. To send money to someone else, you go to the pay menu on the phone, look for the person in your phonebook, or add their details, send them the amount. If they have an M-PESA account, they are notified that they now have the money on their phone and if not, are directed to any M-PESA agent who will give them the money.

Arguably the biggest losers from M-PESA's success were bus drivers, who previously were often paid by city dwellers to take money back to their home villages each week. But other network providers lost out too – before M-PESA, Safaricom had around 45 percent market share and after it was about 70 percent. They benefited hugely from being highly innovative and gaining first-mover advantage to the detriment of competitors.

Although Kenya's banks initially demanded that the regulator should stop M-PESA from trading, when their bid failed, it spurred them on to think about what value they could gain from it and they now successfully partner with the service by providing a range of banking services and growing a mutually supporting ecosystem. In 2010, the Central Bank of Kenya issued new agent banking regulations allowing banks to engage a wide range of retail outlets for transaction handling (cash in and out) and product promotion (receiving account applications, though applications must be approved by bank staff). This paved the way for banks to start using M-PESA outlets as a channel.

M-PESA's value chain is straightforward; all revenues from providing the service go to Safaricom, from which it pays its agents, license fees to Vodafone and other operational expenses. Originally, Safaricom had one big bank account (although it now has a second), with the Commonwealth Bank of Kenya, through which all the transactions pass – the Bank provides a sort of wholesale service, from which it too makes money.

As Dave Birch, Director of Consult Hyperion, explains, "If you are a poor person in Kenya, what do you do if you have some money left over at the end of the day? If you hide it under the mattress, you could be robbed. If you could put it somewhere and earn a bit of interest, you'd be very happy and now you have M-KESHO, provided by the Equity Bank, running over M-PESA."

It's interesting that with all these schemes, banks are pursuing mobile payments on the wholesale side. Supporting these retail customers makes little sense, but in aggregate, there is a very attractive wholesale business emerging.[132]

---

[132]James Anderson, quoted in the TM Forum *Quick Insights* report, *Mobile money in action: Exploring the value chain*, written by Annie Turner, published December 2012, which is available from www.tmforum.org/QIMobMoney

10

CHANGE: EVOLUTION OR TRANSFORMATION?

Evolutionary approaches like 'Lean' work very well when products are evolving organically in stable markets, but the digital world is moving so fast that unless you take a dramatic approach to change, you risk being left behind – rather like being in the Oklahoma Land Grab with a patched-up buggy pulled by a lame horse as your competitors whizz past in newfangled automobiles.

Managing any change, but most especially the root and branch change demanded by the digital world, is a very challenging, complex process with many facets and problems. The odds of succeeding are stacked against you, so the more you can tap into the experience of others who have already trodden this path, the more chance you have of getting it right. Let's be clear, you and your company probably won't get a second chance at this. This chapter and the rest of this book focus on some tools and techniques for improving the odds of success.

What aspects of the business should be changed?

The stock answer to this question from a consultant is, of course, "it all depends" and is usually the preamble to the sound of a very large check being written before you get a clear answer! However, there is a lot of truth in this and the answer, naturally, depends on where you are starting from and where you want to get to next: the vision and lighthouse goals (see Chapter 6). These two parameters set the breadth and depth of the transformation program and the jargon for these two points is *as is* and *to be*. Don't spend much time analyzing the *as is* because it won't tell you much, the consultants will cost you a fortune and anyway, it will very quickly become *used to be*!

Players like Google and Facebook have built their companies around a digital economy model but more established players like communications, cable and satellite and media operators will find the journey more challenging and may need multiple change programs. This is because the most likely course of action for the many, vertically integrated communications companies will be to de-merge into multiple companies or at least autonomous divisions so they can focus sufficiently on each.

A maturity model is a useful tool in understanding the degree of change required. Such models look at the journey in a number of phases and across numerous factors. Since my background is communications and it's the market I know best, the example I've used in Figure 14, overleaf is a transformation maturity model for communications service providers and cable/multi-service operators (MSOs). I've based it loosely on the Six Sigma maturity model as an illustration that you can adapt to your needs.

The model takes a number of indicative factors of a communications or cable provider and looks at them in a spectrum of change, from an unreconstructed monopoly provider through the kind of attributes that will be required to prosper in the digital economy. A model like this is not static and as providers move from left to right, the left-hand end will become irrelevant and new definitions of a market leader will be needed.

This is only a rough guide, and most companies will not fall into nice neat buckets and anyway, the attributes will change considerably depending on the position in the Russian doll of providers that I outlined in Figure 10 on page 83.

Figure 14 – Transformation maturity model

External management					
Customer experience	Unresponsive	Reactive	Inconsistent	Consistent	Systematic, designed approach
Supplier management	Lowest bidder	Whole life cost focus	Strategic supplier approach	Mutual respect	Symbolic, shared risk / reward
Partner approach	Correspondent	Controlled, walled garden	Few strategic partnerships	Symbiotic, shared risk / reward	Go-market partner of choice
Business management					
Benchmarking	None	Low level KPIs	Enterprise-wide KPIs	Best in class, own industry	Best in class, multi-industry
Portfolio management	Unmanaged	Slow follower	Fast follower	Innovator	Innovation leader
Revenue management	Chaotic	Basic but repeatable	Defined, standardized	Managed and controlled	Continuous improvement
Vision and leadership					
Ability to evolve	Individual heroics	Basic project / process mgt.	Standardized planning	Impacts measured and controlled	Continuous feedback loop
Innovation	Weak / discouraged	Tolerated but not rewarded	Rewarded, failure not punished	Active encouragement	Systematic and effective
Culture	Monopoly / paternalistic	Arrogant	Competitive	Combative	Entrepreneurial
Leadership	Few visionaries	Departmental focus	Cross org buy-in	Visible, energetic top leaders	Ingrained in culture
Infrastructure management					
Agility	Sclerotic	Poor	Inconsistent	Good end-end	Systematic and highly responsive
Information	Fragmented, inconsistent, inaccurate	Fragmented, poorly accessible	Federated, complex access	Federated, good access	Common, accurate, highly available
Systems	Legacy / fragmented	Complex / bespoke	Customized COTS	Standardized COTS	Highly simplified, standardized
Processes	Legacy / fragmented	Fragmented by department	Some end-end rationalization	Rationalized end-end	Systematic optimization
Networks	Legacy / fragmented	Fragmented – per service	In-transition	Mostly up to date	Multi-service – all-IP
	Un-reconstructed	**Starting out**	**In progress**	**Transformed**	**Market leader**

This maturity model defines a very broad range of facets that may need to be considered for transformation, such as the physical infrastructure, systems and processes through cultural issues and the way customers and partners are handled. On the X-axis of the model is the maturity of the provider and on the Y-axis are the various aspects of the company. At the intersections are some descriptions that might be typical at that point in time.

Another way of looking at the issue is to consider an overall change program as a series of interlocking program elements which, while they need to be part of an holistic plan, can be separated to make it easier to understand from a process perspective. Figure 15 gives a model of some typical change programs and how they interact with each other.

Getting the right relationship between these elements is very important: they are highly interactive and impact each other seriously. The gears graphic is a good way to look at the issue – change programs must not be looked at or run in isolation. Due to the dynamic nature of the market, there will be a lot of iteration and an agile program methodology (see Chapter 12) may be an appropriate tool. However, before you even start, you need to have a good idea of where you are going.

Imagine how hard it would be to build a road if you didn't know where it was going to, how long it would be, what volume of vehicles it needed to carry, or how big those vehicles will be.

Figure 15 – Inter-locking change elements

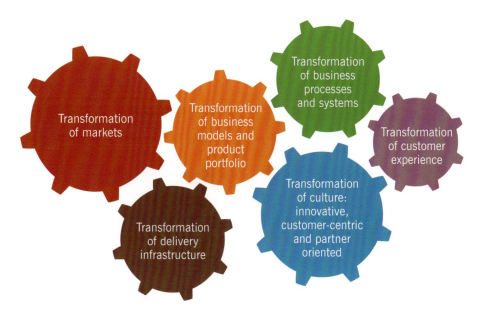

In technology-driven companies, there is a tendency to want to leap into transformation of the underlying infrastructure first – a natural driver because both communications and computing technologies have been constantly evolving technologically for decades.

This approach isn't necessarily wrong, since very often technology advances make products possible that could not be built before and in doing so change the market. So my 'gears' in Figure 15 can be driven from a number of directions but you can also see the potential for the machine to break down if there is not good alignment between the gears.

However, I'm not going to concentrate on the infrastructure issues in this book – there are acres of better advice on the merits of different data center designs or network architectures. What I want to concentrate on are the business issues: business models, product portfolio, business processes, business agility, customer experience levels and the cost base. Without a clear understanding of these aspects, infrastructure transformation is sterile and probably won't deliver its planned return on investment.

There is more cause and effect around these business issues although they are still very interactive. Almost certainly, delivering new services within new business models will force business processes to change, probably radically and since operating costs have to be as low as possible, a very high percentage of these business processes will have to be automated through advanced software systems.

Giant leaps or baby steps? Transformation or evolution?
One of the questions I am asked very frequently relates to the size of the steps in a change program. Due to the underlying fear of failure, most people persuade themselves that small, incremental steps are much more successful than radical leaps – there isn't a right or wrong answer, both have their uses in transforming a company and both are needed for players in the digital economy.

But it's a bit like catching a bus – if you have plenty of time, small, leisurely steps work just fine but, if time is short, you need to take big, rapid strides to get on the bus instead of running behind it. Most market disruptions become apparent to incumbents late in the day and big strides become the only option in many cases. The digital world is proving that point.

There are three main approaches. The first is evolutionary change through incremental improvements to existing business models, processes and systems. The business models and service portfolio don't change much, but the delivery process and infrastructure are evolved to take account of market shifts, such as price pressure.

The second is a radical 'big bang' transformation to accommodate new markets, business models or products that can't be easily or efficiently delivered using existing platforms. Third is a hybrid where new business models, business processes and systems are developed in a separate structure while existing services continue to be run on the current platform, optimized where this makes sense.

In the third, hybrid scenario, services that have a viable future are ported over to the new platform once it has been fully 'hardened' while 'sunset' services reaching the end of their life stay with the old platform, which is eventually turned off.

Each of these approaches has their strengths and weaknesses.

Evolution through incremental steps. Evolution through incremental and continuous change steps has been a very successful approach in many industries and is the basis of the 'Lean' approach. At its heart is the principle of *kaizen* – the Japanese concept of continuous and gradual improvement that lies at the heart of business concepts such as Total Quality Management, Quality Circles and so on. Japanese people distinguish between innovation (radical) and kaizen (continuous). Kaizen literally means *change* (kai) to become *good* (zen).

Kaizen is a very useful approach in improving the business efficiency and quality of a company's products and services where the underlying business model and service portfolio are not changing radically. This approach has been used extensively in manufacturing industry, for example among automobile makers. The kaizen or lean model was originally developed by Toyota and it served the company extremely well for a generation in moving from a small, obscure manufacturer of low-quality cars with poor labor relations to become the world's leading auto manufacturer.

In recent years, Toyota seems to have forgotten some of its own core principles with its highly publicized quality issues, but that does not invalidate the approach that has been used so successfully in a huge number of companies across a wide range of industries in recent decades.

When applied to a service industry, the lean focus needs to be on driving effectiveness of the core business processes that underpin service delivery, mainly improving momentum (agility, time-to-market, quality and cost management). Typically, when examining any process for effectiveness it turns out that 80 percent of the process problems will cluster in 20 percent of that process – a typical Pareto analysis.

The lean approach pragmatically steers effort onto eliminating those 20 percent hotspots or bottlenecks in the process. Once eliminated, the next 20 percent is worked on and so on in a continuous kaizen fashion. Nothing says that the approach to eliminating the bottleneck cannot be radical and highly innovative; indeed it must be because the 'easy wins' are usually garnered early in the cycle and later improvements must come through ingenuity.

The key message here is that becoming a lean provider is not something you do for a while and then magically arrive at a state of 'leanness' where you can stop and rest. 'Lean' is a comparative term – nothing stands still and most certainly the market will not, so the lean approach needs to become institutionalized and continuous – it never ends.

Evolutionary steps using a lean approach rigorously and continuously applied can be very effective at systematically driving out cost and time from a process while continually improving agility, customer experience and quality of the service. It's a discipline that all types of service provider should practice because customer expectations continually rise, the demands of 'more for less' are ever present and competition never goes away.

Innovative transformational leaps. Where the business is changing fundamentally, the evolutionary approach may not be enough and it may take too long and a more radical approach may be needed. Unfortunately, many companies tried and failed using 'clean sheet' approaches such as Business Process Re-engineering a decade or more ago. That doesn't mean the idea was wrong, what it usually means is that they failed to execute the program correctly and forgot many of the key success factors that I'll talk about in Chapter 11.

In many cases, the internal 'white cells' of resistance to new ideas becomes very apparent. The digital world is evolving so quickly that aspiring players may have little choice but to adopt a more radical transformational approach to move quickly enough to the kind of business models, cost point, agility and customer service level that the market demands. A continuous lean/ kaizen approach to processes and systems won't work fast enough because the business models and services are likely to change rapidly and substantially.

Business models are fundamental to the design of the operational model on which a company runs and if the business model is changing significantly, continuous improvement of processes that are becoming irrelevant doesn't get you very far. Worse still, it can ensure outmoded ways of doing things continue, even though there is the appearance of change. While the big appeal of continuous improvement is that it is relatively low risk and big leaps are generally seen as highly risky, it's a much bigger risk if your company goes out of business because it didn't move far enough and fast enough while there was time.

Let's put this in some practical terms. Providers, such as communications and cable operators, usually have a well-established set of processes and systems to deliver their core products and in many cases these have been established over a long period of time. There is very often a lot of room for improvement of these 'legacy' systems and processes since typically many were designed and installed in a period of high growth and high margin when nobody was too bothered about high levels of efficiency or customer-centricity. Almost certainly they were never designed for the kind of agility needed to deliver different business models and services.

Making radical changes using a low-risk, incremental approach doesn't work well because any new component needs to be compatible with the rest of the process flow and systems that it needs to connect to, which tends to preserve out-of-date work practices. Think of it as undertaking a heart transplant: you can take out the old heart and put in a new one that will beat faster and pump more blood, but the new heart has to connect perfectly to the rest of the body's organs, arteries nerves and so on.

So while you have made a theoretical improvement, the rest of the body continues to work in the way that it always did and since other organs may be impaired, the true benefit of the new heart cannot be fully realized – at best you stay alive but aren't going to be an Olympic champion. That's the same for a service provider – if you want to change the billing system or order management system you can put in a new one that might run on newer, faster technology, but it has to be integrated to all of the other systems and hence the existing process is preserved. That's not transformation – its patching up a leaky boat.

There's often a lot of pressure to take this approach: it appears to be lower risk but it's also easier on IT budgets since change can be spread over a period of time. Usually and most persuasively, the operational and human impact is reduced since, if the new system is customized to do what the old system did and preserve the process, there is minimal retraining and negotiation with unions regarding new work practices and so on.

The question is, did it get you anywhere? Have you really changed the way the business works to deliver new services, at lower costs, in a faster time to market and with a better customer experience? How can the new system on its own really support very different business models and services when the old process has been preserved? And are the savings real? New systems that have to be made to retrofit existing processes and old, custom-built software will almost certainly have to be specially developed or tailored for the purpose, bringing much higher, whole-life costs than standardized, commercial off-the-shelf systems.

I've been working with communications providers for a long time and until recently, the incremental improvement of legacy systems was conventional wisdom – it is relatively low risk, gives the impression of modernization and change, and can deliver some incremental improvement to a business. The big point here is that it only works when the market is changing gently and the business models and portfolio are similar to what went before.

This approach won't be able to keep up with the rate of change that the market is now demanding. It will be like being in the Oklahoma Land Grab in a patched-up buggy with a lame horse while competitors whizz past in newfangled automobiles.

The third way. So what's to be done? How can you move forward to capitalize on new markets and opportunities while you run a multibillion-dollar business at the same time, and run it more effectively, without taking undue risks? The answer lies in looking outside the digital service business at how other industries approach the problem.

Let's take automobile manufacturing again as an example where the lean approach of continuous improvement was pioneered and which will deliver incremental improvements in build quality and reductions in build costs on an existing production line with an evolutionary approach to car designs. But what if a competitor makes a big leap and you are at a serious disadvantage, in terms of either entering a new market or because you rapidly start to lose market share? Do you go back and re-program the robots? Or sit down with the unions and renegotiate age-old work practices? Or take a greenfield site and build a factory with brand-new processes using state-of-the-art robotics and a newly trained and eager workforce?

In reality, you may do some of both – that is, up your game as fast as possible on your existing facility and models while designing and building the new plant. Then you run them in parallel for a while to get the bugs out of the new systems on limited production runs, and then finally switch over production of new models entirely to the new plant while you phase out older versions. Volkswagen has even systematized this and extracts 'long tail' value from previous models under its Skoda brand, while its Audi unit pioneers the leading edge.

For a service provider, the same approach can be taken: you run a lean approach, continuously improving your business with existing products, but in parallel develop new business models and services supported by a 'clean build' systems and process platform. These new services are likely to be relatively small in volume early on and your existing systems take the load on core, high-volume services.

Just like the greenfield car plant, there will be a lot of bedding in of the new platform and ironing out problems, but these will not affect the majority of the business. As the new platform is established and refined, it can progressively be loaded with the older services that have a future life while those that are being phased out will stay on the old platform, which is progressively scaled down and eventually closed.

The three steps are illustrated in Figure 16: first there is designing the delivery platform and other needs of the markets that you want to occupy. This obviously needs to leverage existing competencies, processes and systems wherever possible, but the opportunity should be taken to introduce as much 'clean sheet' thinking and investment as possible.

Figure 16 – Three separate transformation focal points

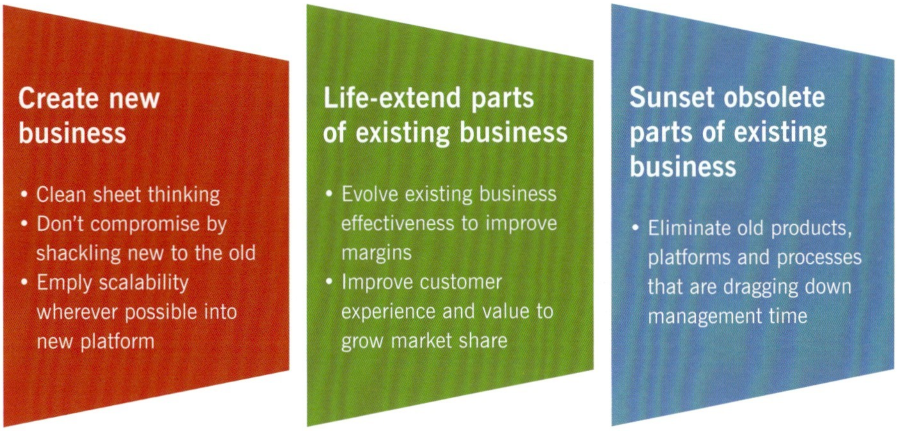

Create new business

- Clean sheet thinking
- Don't compromise by shackling new to the old
- Emply scalability wherever possible into new platform

Life-extend parts of existing business

- Evolve existing business effectiveness to improve margins
- Improve customer experience and value to grow market share

Sunset obsolete parts of existing business

- Eliminate old products, platforms and processes that are dragging down management time

You must avoid letting established ways of doing things reduce the effectiveness of new business areas because you probably won't get a second chance at it. Scaling the new platform can also be done cost effectively if it makes appropriate use of cloud-based service partners so that costs of operation scale with volumes.

The second phase (often in parallel with the first) is to life extend and evolve those products, processes and systems of those parts of the *current* business that will sustain into the foreseeable future and will benefit from improvements and optimization and can be 'cut-over' to the new business model and platform when appropriate. Finally there are those products and services, processes and systems that should soon be withdrawn from the market because they are making too poor a return and/or are diverting management time. Shut these down as quickly as is feasible, simplify your service and operational landscape, allowing management attention to be focused on the first two phases.

To help figure out which falls into one of the three areas, the company will need a good picture of its future target markets and product portfolio business models (or the 'to be' as the experts might say). In the journey into the digital world, that's difficult because there are a lot of grey areas where trial and error are needed to find out what works, but it needs to be 'good enough' to make some basic decisions.

I once served on the advisory board for a major service provider's transformation program where the mandate from product management was that the new operational platform must support every current service as well as all new (but not yet defined) services. That was a terrible abdication of responsibility – in other words "since I can't be bothered to think about this, I want you to over-complicate and over-engineer the investment so that anything I might ever want will be there"!

The result – engineering design teams struggled valiantly with such a mandate, the costs of supporting all existing services were huge because many were proprietary and to recreate them using standardized, commercial off-the-shelf components was impossible, so it had to be customized at vast expense. On deeper investigation, some of these products were either already almost obsolete – for example, 64 kbps private leased lines in an era when broadband services were already commonplace.

This may sound ridiculous, and in hindsight it clearly was, but unless the company in its entirety is fully behind a 'joined up' program it's the kind of nonsense that arises. Too many departments can shrug their shoulders and assume that change is somebody else's job so they can take it easy and carry on as before. It's why you can't transform a company just by throwing the problem to the IT people or some other function and let them get on with it.

Perhaps an even greater reason of having all of the major functions of the company lined up behind a single transformation program is the willingness of different departments to change. If business processes have been encapsulated in custom-built IT systems it's going to be very difficult to change ageing technology for more cost-effective, commercial off-the-shelf, systems. If the users are not willing to change their business processes – it simply can't be done.

I see this reluctance to change the way the business works over and over again because of the disruption, retraining and sometimes workforce resistance that it entails. So new systems are made to mimic old ones at significant cost, but far more damaging than that is that it preserves outmoded and arcane business processes that never change – there is the appearance of a modern infrastructure, but in reality the same old ways of doing things are preserved until the company falls off a cliff.

The actual cost of transforming versus the opportunity cost of *not* transforming

Ah, I can hear you say – doesn't that mean you end up with parallel systems and process platforms and doesn't that mean a lot of extra cost? Almost certainly yes, operational costs during that transformation period will probably be higher but they are likely to be small in comparison to the cost of lost opportunities and *not* being able to enter new markets fast enough.

The hybrid approach also offers a considerably lower risk path in case of delays or failure especially to 'cash cow' services. In any event, the costs of custom engineering new systems to fit in with old ones as part of an incremental approach are likely to be huge and fraught with unforeseen problems.

Typical integration and customization costs of new systems being retrofitted to a legacy environment are at least five times the cost of buying the base system. In addition, the whole life costs are considerably higher than this because systems need to be re-integrated with every software upgrade. So the extra costs of parallel operation need to be weighed against the benefits of entering new markets more quickly and not taking huge risks with existing revenue streams.

The new target platform does not need to be on the same scale initially because it will only be supporting a relatively small number of customers and services. As long as the contracts with suppliers have a payment model geared to scale designed into them, the level of duplicated cost can be managed.

You need to think about this holistically and be visionary enough to design agility and flexibility into the operational infrastructure to accommodate business evolution. You have to think about what the target processes and systems need to look like. You must be rigorous about building it in a way that can support both new and those existing services that will sustain and evolve into the future. And you have to ensure that you insulate customers and partners from your strategy, as far as possible; that is, change the inside without changing the outside too radically or too suddenly.

You can't stop improving the old platform because you still have to squeeze every ounce of margin out of it, but you can take a very structured approach to maximizing the 'bang for the buck' of where you make those investments in process and system optimization.

Building from scratch is far easier and much lower cost than trying to transform a legacy platform into a state-of-the-art position because of the customization and integration issues that I already mentioned. The need to make everything backwardly compatible anchors you to outmoded processes. You really need to do your homework and truly understand what the design goals of the new platform are in terms of target operational costs, business models, and products and services to be supported. And you have to be forward-looking too, so be able to flexibly support currently unknown requirements. To help with this, use appropriate standards, which should be deployed to integrate commercial off-the-shelf systems and a process model that will be compatible with that of your service partners.

11

INCREASING THE ODDS OF SUCCESS

Embarking on and successfully delivering a disruptive change program is always a gamble – when to move, where and how fast. But the best gamblers are experts at assessing the odds and stacking them in their favor. Here we look at ways of doing just that.

Identifying the need for change is relatively simple – many armchair pundits, including me, do it all the time. Chances are, you have had a conversation over the water cooler today where someone said "of course you know what's needed round here is…" and then espouse some radical change theory. *Delivering* change takes a lot more energy, guts, enthusiasm, leadership and luck to pull it off successfully.

In survey after survey, the success rates of major change programs and the ability of companies to evolve into new markets aren't good, with more failing than succeeding. That obviously makes senior executives nervous, especially when their company is still doing well, so they tend to put them off for as long as possible. They often leave it too late, making the problem even harder to solve.

In this and later chapters, I give some pointers as to how the success rate of major change programs can be increased and how to structure such programs. The first step in this is to understand the most common reasons that change programs fail in the first place.

Why do transformations fail more often than they succeed?
To understand why transformations have such a high failure rate, we need to look at a wide range of case studies to understand what is going wrong. A good insight can be obtained from research across a wide range of industries by consulting firm McKinsey[133] who found that it is relatively rare for transformation programs to succeed and put the average success rate at lower than 40 percent. Most importantly, it found that the application of some basic principles can greatly increase the odds of succeeding.

McKinsey was able to quantify the success rates of transformation programs depending on a number of criteria and showed that the failure rate of major change programs was highest when the company is in a defensive position and reacting to events, and lowest when an already successful company is proactively striving to do even better. While this seems to contradict the common wisdom that it should be easier to transform a company when its back is against the wall, this advantage is usually outweighed by the difficult circumstances that the company is in – management is often fighting fires daily to keep the business on track while trying to implement fundamental change.

Figure 17 (overleaf) shows this clearly:

High growth companies like Google, Amazon and Apple are transforming continuously from a position of strength and success – in terms of Figure 17 they can be regarded in the offensive/proactive quadrant.

More mature companies such as established communications and computer companies, with their embedded ways of doing things and often with their margins under pressure as

---

[133]Exhibit from *"Corporate transformation under pressure"* April 2009, McKinsey Quarterly, www.mckinseyquarterly.com

Figure 17 – Transformation success factors

Share of transformations described as extremely / very successful

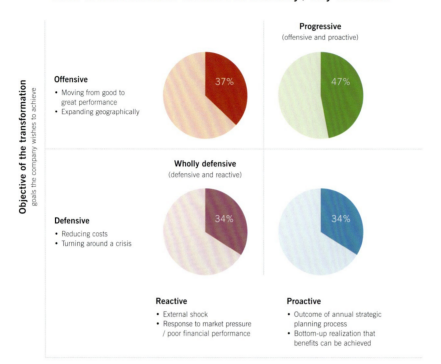

Exhibit from 'Corporate transformation under pressure' April 2009, McKinsey Quarterly, www.mckinseyquarterly.com.
Copyright McKinsey & Company. All rights reserved. Reprinted by permission.

markets saturate, could be considered in the defensive/reactive quadrant. This would seem to automatically give an advantage to newer entrants but it is worth digging deeper into the McKinsey research, which looks at the underlying reasons for success or failure.

It found that certain tactics promote more successful outcomes: the most important of which are setting clear aspirations and targets, exercising strong leadership from the top, creating an unambiguous structure for the transformation and maintaining energy and involvement throughout the organization. Companies which used all of these tactics more than doubled the success rate to more than 80 percent of the time.

So while established companies maybe starting from a defensive position have a much larger ship to turn around, it is possible to improve the odds of success considerably by the application of some fairly basic (but often missing) management disciplines.

Strong leadership is critical

As I travel around the world talking to senior executives about change, I'm often surprised at the lack of cohesion and joined up thinking. The CTO may talk about "transforming to an all IP network" while the CIO proudly explains the "transformation to a real-time billing platform", and the Chief Marketing Officer is preoccupied with "transforming customer experience". These are, of course, all valid moves, but they should not be run as disconnected or loosely-coupled activities and point to the biggest single factor for success in McKinsey's research: setting clear company-wide targets and driving them through with strong overall leadership from the top (we looked at the importance of clear goals and leadership in Chapter 6).

To some extent you can understand why CEOs are going to be reluctant to be open about the fact that their company has problems and needs to change urgently. Such a statement can often trigger nervousness among investors and cause the share price to slide: Stephen Elop's brutally honest message to the staff of Nokia on taking over the reins that they were "standing on a burning platform" and must "change behavior" triggered a flood of unflattering news reports and a dramatic fall in their share price: overall, Nokia lost $19 billion in market value in 2011. But, however unpleasant, his call to arms and clear decision-making has at least put in place an overdue transformation.

Although Elop came to Nokia from Microsoft, it's highly likely he would understand Nokia's business model well. That's not always the case for companies whose board members or the CEO may be very talented but have little background or real understanding of the market and their operations. Just look at the steep decline of Apple under John Sculley – whose previous experience was running PepsiCo. In the first instance, Apple's sales revenues went up impressively but then it lost all sense of direction on its products because he didn't have vision about where he wanted to go (see Chapter 4 for more on this).

Apple drifted and hit the rocks under leaders who apparently didn't understand the business or its market. That the company underwent such a spectacular transformation and renaissance when Jobs rejoined is a powerful testament to the impact an inspired leader can make.

I also mentioned the historic turnaround of IBM under Lou Gerstner. Although in 1990 IBM had its most profitable year ever, just three years later it was on its way to the largest loss in corporate history at that time and pundits were predicting its almost certain demise. The IBM board appointed Gerstner to preside over its strategy of continued dissolution into a confederation of autonomous business units. As he describes in his book *Who Says Elephants Can't Dance?,* he took IBM on a profound competitive and cultural transformation through a campaign to rebuild the leadership team and give the workforce a renewed sense of purpose. In the process, he defined a strategy for the computing giant and remade the ossified culture which, ironically, was the result of the company's terrific success over many years.

Steering transformations in the manner of Gerstner, Jobs and hopefully Elop requires a lot of talent plus a real understanding of the company where you are at the helm and the market in which you are playing. When the leader *doesn't* understand the company or market, they tend to compensate for it by surrounding themselves with advisors and committees to take decisions and filter ideas. Such an approach is a breeding ground for corporate politics, conservative decision-making and fudged compromises.

That's why the findings of the McKinsey survey are so important: they give us some clear insights into the factors that can at least double the chances of success. Full-on transformation, on the scale that the digital economy is demanding, means that all parts of a company – from the board and the executive team, right through to the operational parts of the organization – go through a fundamental rethink of organization, business models, core competencies, investment patterns, reward systems and the way each facet of the organization thinks.

Strong leadership is vital, but successful transformation cannot be driven top-down by edict – to really unlock changes to the way the business works, there must also be enthusiastic support from the individuals running the business who have a detailed knowledge of how to make it happen.

Equally it can't be a bottom-up driven initiative either. Over the years, I've met many people who clearly understand the need for change and are enthusiastic about it, but can't do anything about it because top management doesn't 'get it'. There are many reasons for this as I outlined earlier, not least of which is the fear of failure and being labeled as the person who took an ostensibly company successful company and drove it into the ground. Stock markets are often unhelpful in this regard because they want to see positive quarterly earnings statements and generally are unsympathetic about change programs designed to deliver medium to long-term benefits.

As I said in Chapter 5, I think financial analysts should be alert to the significance of their pronouncements and analytic approaches that cause companies who need to change to hang back 'just one more quarter' to squeeze a bit more milk from the cash cow. I also think that analysts should be asking some hard questions on behalf of the shareholders about the company's plans for transformation and should be negative about companies that aren't changing because it's unlikely that their way of doing business now will put them in a good position to reap the benefits of the digital economy.

Heroic mergers and acquisitions generally make the headlines, but the hard graft of rationalizing, simplifying, optimizing and innovating to get into a winning position is much more important and rather less common. The necessary changes aren't quick fixes, so much as having a clear vision of where the company needs to be and wherewithal to make those changes happen.

If it ain't broke, don't fix it

"If it ain't broke, don't fix it"[134] must be one of the most often quoted but ultimately wrong management maxims because it's all too easy for a board to put off risky and expensive change if, in the short term, business seems to be OK. That phrase must have been on the lips of many analysts, board members and senior executives at Lehman Brothers, Enron, Royal Bank of Scotland, Kodak and countless others… just before disaster struck.

The plain truth is that most people don't like change and find it hard to accept – especially if they can't see why it is needed. The U.S. automobile industry had at least 20 years to recognize that change was needed but couldn't bring itself to make it happen. We all remember the embarrassing spectacle of their CEOs flying in corporate jets to Washington at the height of the 2008 financial crash to ask the U.S. government for bail-outs so that they could finally get on with what they should have done years before.

As W. Edwards Deming[135] noted, "It's not necessary to change; survival is not mandatory": in other words, change or die. A root problem surrounding change is fear – fear of failure, of losing your status, of losing your job and your reputation. After all, if one of the aims of the transformation program is to automate what was previously done manually or rationalize product lines or move work to a managed services partner, people are going to be redeployed or maybe fired – and the survival instinct is a fundamental part of being human. For that reason, you have to balance the need for change with the message about how to execute it and why. The pace of that change and the success of that change will be evaluated through the prism of different mindsets.

Successful change programs have to deal with the soft, human issues that may be counter-intuitive, as well as the hard-nosed technology or business issues. Ignore them at your peril because unless the people who run the business are energized, motivated and incentivized to want to change, they generally don't.

Eight steps to heaven

In addition to the McKinsey work, there are a number of excellent sources of information regarding critical success factors for transformation that are useful additional reading. John Kotter's[136] approach has been widely implemented and successful in many types of industry

---

[134]Widely attributed to T. Bert Lance, the Director of the Office of Management and Budget in Jimmy Carter's 1977 administration
[135]William Edwards Deming: American statistician, professor, author, lecturer and consultant
[136]Dr. John Kotter is a Professor at the Harvard Business School; *Business Week* magazine rated him as "the #1 leadership guru" in America. Author of 17 books, his international bestseller *Leading Change*, Harvard Business Press, outlines a clear process for implementing successful transformation

Figure 18 – Kotter's transformation model

Step 1: Establish a sense of urgency
Identify market realities, crises and opportunities

Step 2: Create the guiding coalition
Assemble group with enough power to lead change effort and work as a team

Step 3: Develop a change vision
Build a clear vision to direct change and develop strategies to achieve it

Step 4: Communicate the vision for buy-in
Use every possible means to communicate the vision and strategy and lead by example

Step 5: Empower broad-based action
Remove obstacles to change, and encourage risk-taking and non-traditional ideas and actions

Step 6: Generate short-term wins
Create visible performance improvements and reward people involved in creating them

Step 7: Never let up
Build on early wins to change things that don't fit the vision

Step 8: Incorporate changes into the culture
Develop the means to ensure continued leadership development and succession

Source: www.change-management-consultant.com

and transformation scenarios and his eight-step transformation process is logical and simple to understand and the steps are shown in Figure 18:

Kotter's and other commentators' models follow a similar pattern of:

- analyzing the problem and building consensus around taking action;
- articulating a clear vision;
- getting buy-in from the people who will have to implement change;
- overcome problems and barriers;
- keep the energy flowing and people's enthusiasm up;
- reward those who generate success; and
- institutionalize the change so that it's permanent.

So far, so good and there are other models in regular use by consultants around the world that, although they may use different words and phrases, all essentially follow the same basic ideas. But which are the most important steps and what effect do they have on the likely success of transformation? Are all of the steps essential and how do they work together?

Figure 19 – Positive impacts of key tactics on transformation success

Transformation theme	Tactic	Did your company use this tactic?	Degree to which transformation was successful, %**
			■ Not at all ■ Somewhat ■ Very ■ Extremely
Aspirations	Establishing well-defined stretch targets	YES	2- / 42 / 46 / 10
		NO*	9 / 70 / 18 / -3 +167%
Leadership	Assuring strong CEO involvement	YES	3- / 48 / 40 / 9
		NO	9 / 67 / 21 / -3 +104%
Process	Organizing a clear structure for change	YES	2- / 47 / 41 / 10
		NO	7 / 62 / 27 / -4 +65%
Energy	Ensuring frontline ownership of change	YES	2- / 46 / 43 / 10
		NO	7 / 62 / 26 / -5 +71%
	Implementing equal mix of positive and negative messages	YES	2- / 52 / 38 / 7
		NO	7 / 60 / 27 / 6 +36%
	Launching large-scale, collaborative planning effort	YES	1- / 46 / 44 / 9
		NO	7 / 60 / 28 / -5 +61%

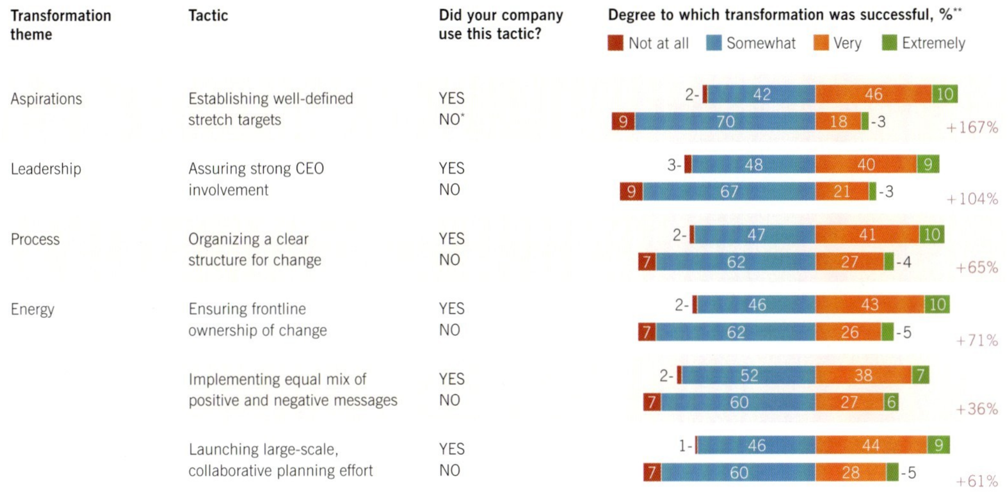

*In this and other cases, denotes any response other than yes (eg, stretch targets were set but they were not well defined).
**Figures may not sum to 100%, because of rounding.

If you don't know where you're going, any road will get you there

I quoted this earlier, and while it may be an old saying, it's still true in undertaking transformational change. The need for a vision and clear goals is the single most important factor if you're going to achieve your goals. In the McKinsey study, the researchers collated the responses from nearly 3,000 respondents in various industries and demonstrated a very strong correlation between transformation success and some common factors. Interviewees were questioned on the degree to which transformation was successful, measured against a number of factors most strongly correlated with success and the results are shown in Figure 19.

The company used yet another definition of key success factors, but again you can see that they follow Kotter's basic ideas. Not all of the tactics have equal impact and clear vision was the most important. Looking at the McKinsey survey results, you could rewrite the old adage as "if you don't know where you're going, you'll probably never get there"!

In addition to surveying the most important individual success factors, McKinsey went further and found that certain combinations of these tactics also have a big impact on transformational success. Companies not using any of the tactics had a less than 20 percent chance of succeeding while those using all of them together improved the odds to over 80 percent. These tactics were seen to be of value across many types of businesses, in many sectors and in various states of evolution. For players in the digital economy, and particularly those with large and difficult-to-transform processes and infrastructure, it is worth considering a number of relevant factors that build on these models and findings to arrive at a sound model and guide.

Transforming to what and when?

A critically important question to answer – and I refer to it a number of times in this book – is "what are you transforming to?" – in other words how radical and rapid should the transformation be and particularly "where do you want to be next?" For example, the phone business is a $1.5 trillion business worldwide and although margins are flattening it's still a very strong, huge cash cow business. Communications providers would be crazy not to continue extracting maximum value from their existing business as well as positioning themselves to exploit new opportunities in the digital economy.

On the other hand transforming to be the fastest, cheapest and best phone company in the world when the market for traditional voice and messaging as we know them today is likely to evaporate is about as smart as being the best manufacturer of steam locomotives in an age of electric trains! I don't mean to trivialize this and it's vitally important issue to resolve when setting out the overarching goals for the organization. Where a market, like communications, is changing and evolving, but is by no means dead, changing too quickly could be as dangerous as changing too slowly in terms of shareholder value. What's really difficult is to work out how much life is left in existing markets and business models and how and how long it will take for new markets to mature.

This is like working out how long you think you might live in order to plan your pension, it's hard and it's all too easy to convince yourself that life will continue as it is today because you can't see all the hidden factors in play. It's yet another of Rumsfeld's "unknown unknowns"! Even so, we can take some of the things we *do* know into account when developing a transformation plan. For example: we *do* know that the market models that have emerged in the digital economy are often very different from traditional models.

Transform for tomorrow, not today

One of the most important factors to take into account in transforming to the digital economy is that the business model you're working on is almost certain to change, so just improving the way the *current* business works is likely to fall short of the mark. It will undoubtedly help, but that will probably only in improving profitability as your core business fades into the sunset.

It's critical that the all-important activity of goal-setting defines the targets and requirements for the business *as it will become* rather than it is today. This is particularly tricky, since it involves quite a bit of crystal ball gazing and backing hunches. This is where guys like Steve Jobs, Jack Welch and Lou Gerstner excelled because they had a vision of what they wanted their companies to be. Companies led by good managers need armies of advisers and committees to figure out the future, generally play it safe and often do too little, too late.

And "play it safe, leadership by committee" people didn't win the Oklahoma Land Rush. They stayed in their comfort zone and never left home for fear of being trampled. Neither will they be winners in the rush to stake out territory in the digital world – those that do will be typified by companies with leaders who that are brave, bold and visionary *and* can also execute well.

Mastery of ecosystems is critical

One of the most important changes between traditional business and the digital economy is the increasing reliance on partners in the ecosystem (as we saw in Chapter 7) and success will be linked to mastering where you want to compete while building partnerships. As I said in Chapter 2, big corporations, especially communication players, have been used to controlling the entire product from end to end, via their own infrastructure; delivering the service in its entirety and 'owning' the end customer. As large and dominant players, they are used to 'calling the shots' in a negotiation. As someone who has sat on both sides of the table in such negotiations, I can say with certainty that they can also be rather arrogant.

Success in the digital economy is far more dependent on sustainable partnerships because the digital economy is much more complex: services are created from weaving together components from different service providers of many types and selling them though multiple channels to market. Technologists call this a service-oriented enterprise and it's not at all surprising that service orientation has become a very important design feature of modern software architectures.

Working in an ecosystem-based business model is more than just ensuring that digital goods can flow seamlessly along the chain. The standards that underpin the Internet largely take care of that aspect but the real challenge is in how the 'business wrapper' works.

By this I mean things like: how are customers' orders and contracts carried out when multiple parties are engaged in delivering the service? How is a great customer experience designed and delivered without getting into the usual finger-pointing of each component provider saying 'well my bit works', ignoring the customers' real problem? How does money move around the ecosystem where different parties may be allocated different portions of the revenue – for example, how do service level agreements and rebates work without manual intervention so that costs can be kept to a minimum?

An even bigger issue is determining who the customer is in a complex ecosystem. Google has billions of users but they don't pay a penny – the *customer,* that's to say the entity which pays the money, is the AdWords' advertiser. So customer experience management takes on a whole new dimension in a services-oriented business model in which multiple parties need to thrive for the whole thing to prosper. Management of the entire ecosystem is extremely important to the service retailer whose brand is on the line every minute of every day, but it is highly reliant on its ecosystem partners to maintain that brand's equity, which can so easily be damaged.

A great example of this is Amazon, which took the very bold step of opening up its online trading platform to third-party sellers – often to its online competitors. That must have caused some serious thinking by Jeff Bezos because from an end-customer's perspective, they're still doing business with Amazon although in reality they may be buying from a company that perhaps does not share Amazon's preoccupation with excellent customer experience. This potentially endangers the Amazon brand every time one of those partners falls short. Amazon was much too bright to trust its brand to luck; it built in, from the ground up, all sorts of levers to ensure that its trading partners deliver the kind of customer experience that Amazon always aspires to.

Being able to string together a number of online service components from different suppliers is a new art that few have done before. In the digital economy, people and companies – especially enterprises – want to use many applications and sources of information from many providers, but they also want a consistent overall service. So the key will be having companies at the user-end of the ecosystem delivering a consistent service and a great customer experience while working with many 'upstream' partners in a common and highly intelligent way. It's rather like the graceful swan gliding across the lake, but all the while its feet under the waterline are paddling furiously: ideally the end user enjoys a well-integrated, consistent service package and is ignorant of how hard that provider will have to work to achieve it.

Size matters

We can see the major players lining up to be that multiservice 'graceful swan'. Apple has a head start in providing a whole slew of digital goods and services through iTunes; Amazon is leveraging its position as a front-line retailer to start introducing a range of digital services as well as online goods; Facebook is beginning to offer a range of digital services; and Microsoft has Skype as a multi-million user platform on which to offer a greater range of services.

These players offer digital service providers and application developers an attractive and simple go-to-market route in the ecosystem. They offer a huge global customer base and common environment in which to work anywhere in the world. As we saw with the ill-fated Nokia store Ovi, in the fight against Google Play and iTunes, size matters. Having a large base of services and applications is key to the store provider winning customers and providing the easiest possible route to market for service providers and app developers – a perfect synergy.

As I've said several times, the lack of a cohesive and unified route to market is a big disadvantage for the communications providers and cable/multi-service operators, because their customer base is usually only in certain geographies. Collectively they may have billions of customers, but each operator only has a relatively small, geographic slice of that market. Small markets and having to do business with hundreds of partners in different territories is a serious handicap in the digital economy where service providers and app developers want to reach markets of billions of people with very low costs of delivery and minimal difficulties. Advertisers too want to reach targeted groups within large populations, not the customers of phone company A or B.

That this issue should not have been solved yet is surprising, since communications companies figured out how to deliver a completely seamless global service across a federated set of hundreds of different operators worldwide, long ago. Ten digits will typically get you to any individual on the planet with all of the billing being taken care of and everyone getting paid their share because of the foresight of having a small number of international standards covering signaling, settlements and so on.

These agreements were largely made at a time when operators were monopolies and did not compete against each other. However, what goes around, comes around and with common enemies, such as the Internet giants, there is definitely more appetite for collaboration between operators recently, but it pre-supposes they have a common view of what needs fixing.

To sum up: being able to visualize what the company wants to become as a part of the transformation process is crucial, otherwise you'll be simply producing 'a better mousetrap'. And of course visions have to be turned into practical reality.

12

MAKING IT HAPPEN

Although an inspired leader is essential, no single individual, no matter how good a leader they are, can transform an entire company: creating a clear vision; communicating it to employees, shareholders, customers and suppliers; driving numerous projects; overcoming obstacles; keeping up morale and energy; and changing an often deeply ingrained culture.

So they need to build a 'coalition of the willing' around them with the right people, motivation, skills and trust, who can actually deliver a successful transformation program.

So far I've concentrated on *why* companies should transform and some aspects of *what* to transform to. I've also laid out some key competencies that will be important and some critical success factors. But now it's time to get a bit more down to the *how* of transformation and change. Figure 20 tries to capture these, based on good information from McKinsey, Kotter and others.

We've covered a fair bit of the reality check: vision, goals and leadership plus some of the key attributes needed, such as customer-centricity, innovation and partnerships. This and subsequent chapters are more about making it happen and, of course, nothing will actually happen if you never start.

Figure 20 – Overall picture for transformation success

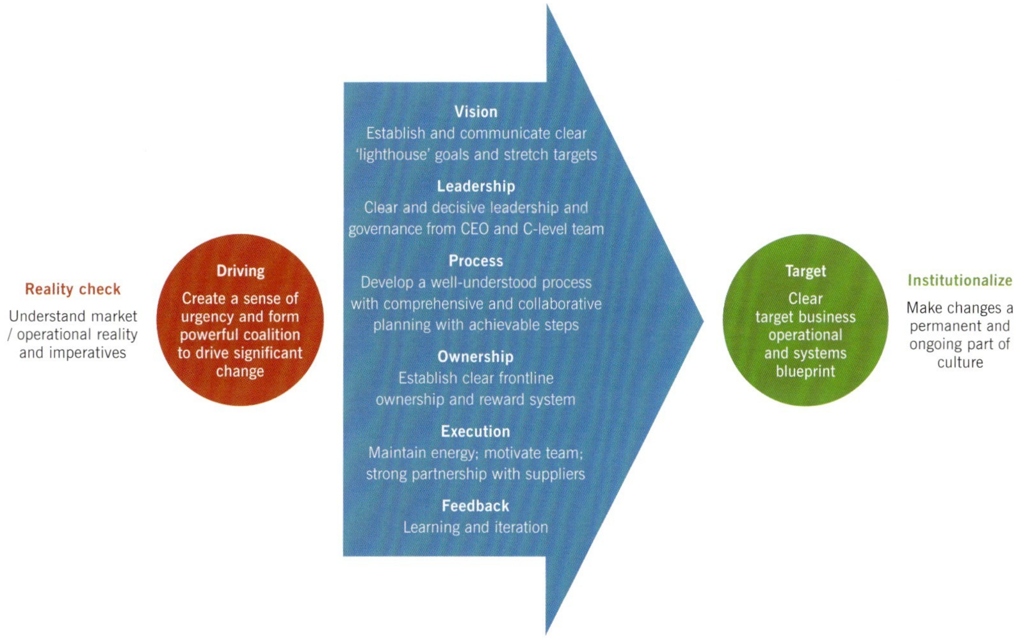

Reality check
Understand market / operational reality and imperatives

Driving
Create a sense of urgency and form powerful coalition to drive significant change

Vision
Establish and communicate clear 'lighthouse' goals and stretch targets

Leadership
Clear and decisive leadership and governance from CEO and C-level team

Process
Develop a well-understood process with comprehensive and collaborative planning with achievable steps

Ownership
Establish clear frontline ownership and reward system

Execution
Maintain energy; motivate team; strong partnership with suppliers

Feedback
Learning and iteration

Target
Clear target business operational and systems blueprint

Institutionalize
Make changes a permanent and ongoing part of culture

A journey starts with a single step

Lao-tzu's[137] statement, "A journey of a thousand miles starts with a single step" is very appropriate here because getting started is so hard that many companies never do it and nearly half of the companies that fail to make the changes that they need, make their mistakes at the very beginning. Recognizing that change is needed is intuitive – just watch a child at play and how they constantly modify and adapt the game. As adults, our daily business lives are constantly assaulted by information that tells us to change – hourly movements in the markets, mergers and acquisition news, new product announcements, competitor moves, thought-provoking blogs and so on, that prod our thoughts on the future.

[137]Lao-tzu, *The Way of Lao-tzu,* Chinese philosopher (604 BC-531 BC)

But turning those passing thoughts into concrete action is hard, and building a coalition of decision-makers and resource holders to turn those ideas into action is much, much harder. Even where a sense of urgency is commonly felt, it can be very difficult to reach consensus with all the key stakeholders on a common vision of what needs to be done – just ask the Greek government!

I once asked Matt Bross, when he was Chief Technology Officer at BT, how he had been able to get board-level approval for a $20 billion transformation program of its networks and systems and his typically wry reply of "near death experience helps" said a lot – the nearer a company gets to Doomsday the clearer becomes the action plan and the easier it is to create a sense of urgency and consensus. However, as we saw from the McKinsey work, the later in the cycle the decision to transform is taken the less successful the transformation program seems to be. You simply 'run out of runway' and your 'plane may never take off – or worse, you crash into a ditch.

So it's pretty obvious that transformation will be more successful if it's undertaken in good time while the company has the financial resources to carry it out properly and is not consumed with firefighting – that means gaining an early consensus on the need for change and creating a powerful coalition to drive change forward. I can't stress how important this is and how hard it is to drive people out of their comfort zones – maybe Matt was referring to his own personal near death experience given the amount of energy it must have taken from him to get top management and the board to sign off on a huge investment program. Not only was it big, but BT was the first major communications player to announce a shift to a fully transformed, all IP network and I'm certain he got the inevitable 'who else is doing this?' question and had to give the usually wrong answer in conservative companies of 'nobody – we're the first'.

One reason he may have succeeded may be in what John Kotter refers to as "aiming for the heart", in other words, convincing people must have passion and feeling in it, not just acres of analysis and solid business case rationale. Leaders inspire people to greatness and connect to their deep emotions: to bring an idea to life with energy and passion; engage the senses of the team by simple and imaginative messages that people want to aspire to – heart as well as head. Jobs knew this and while he was clearly a very difficult and unforgiving guy to work with, nobody could ever accuse him of lacking passion for what he wanted to change – and don't forget, he wanted to change the world, not just his company. Richard Branson of the Virgin group (one of whose airplanes I'm sitting on right now) would be another who can put passion into an idea and get people to back him. It's not just business leaders – try listening to the speeches of political leaders, from Aung San Suu Kyi to Kennedy, Martin Luther King to Nelson Mandela, and not feel motivated and uplifted by their passion.

So getting moving on the journey towards the digital world must have much more than just compelling business logic: it has to have inspirational leadership to motivate and inspire people to want to follow it, something dry and dusty committees can never do. This is why big-name analyst firms can't actually make a transformation happen from the sidelines. If it doesn't have sustained intuitive and emotional involvement from the leadership team, it almost certainly won't happen.

True leadership is that ability to get people to want to follow you. But to make things actually happen, leaders need a powerful coalition around them and must create one with enough passion, stamina, loyalty, energy and decision-making ability to drive through a major change program – perhaps lasting years. It can be exhausting and is one of the big differences between people who can lead and people who can manage. If you missed it, I described more about leadership and the qualities of leaders in Chapter 6 and I make no excuses for reiterating it here – those companies that do make it big in the digital world will be those who have outstanding leadership, otherwise nothing much will happen.

But no single individual, no matter how good a leader they are, can transform an entire company: creating a clear vision; communicating it to employees, shareholders, customers and suppliers; driving numerous projects; overcoming obstacles; keeping up morale and energy; and changing an often deeply ingrained culture. Although an inspired leader may be at the helm and in reality may even be a 'benevolent dictator' they also need to build a 'coalition of the willing'[138] around them: people with the right skills, motivation and energy to drive a successful transformation program. The coalition must share common objectives and must share a significant level of trust because things *will* go wrong – their judgment *will* be questioned and they *will* have doubts along the way, so trust between them is essential – it's the glue that makes the team function well. I've had the privilege of working with and sometimes leading coalitions with the right, people, motivation, skills and trust and they can move mountains. But I've also had the miserable misfortune of working with the opposite and they couldn't move a molehill!

By a coalition, I absolutely *don't* mean creating another committee – you've probably gathered by now that committees aren't my favorite cup of tea. There are exceptions of course but, all too often, committees are made up of representatives from every department, often consisting of people with too much time on their hands who are there to stop things happening rather than make something happen fast. They often make 'safe' decisions: in other words they maintain the status quo or something close to it, often with numerous reasons for inaction, which of course they document in copious minutes to prove their impeccable logic. They usually have the excitement and passion of watching paint dry and are usually driven by what they perceive is good for their career. Most people learn pretty quickly that large companies often don't reward risk-taking and so committees usually want to spend forever trying to get perfect information on which to make a decision.

Quoting Kotter again, the efforts of low-credibility committees are often "doomed from the start

[138]Although most associated with U.S. President George Bush, one of the first people to use the phrase was President Bill Clinton in June 1994

and, as a result, the company's competitive position gets weaker and the industry leader gets a little further ahead".

In a world changing in front of our very eyes, if you try to either conclusively prove that change is required by having perfect information, or you devolve decisions to a disinterested cross-company committee, you will undoubtedly have lost the Oklahoma Land Rush. The digital world is evolving rapidly but also haphazardly and will continue to take many unexpected twists and turns, so if you want to be a strong player, then almost by definition you have to make decisions rapidly and with much less certainty than in an established and stable market that you know well. So it's absolutely necessary to have a group of committed, passionate and inspired individuals who are prepared to stake their career on the outcome, rather than a faceless committee.

As a checklist of assembling such a group, Kotter defines four key qualities required to build an effective guiding coalition, shown in Figure 21:

Figure 21 – Kotter's factors for successful change coalitions

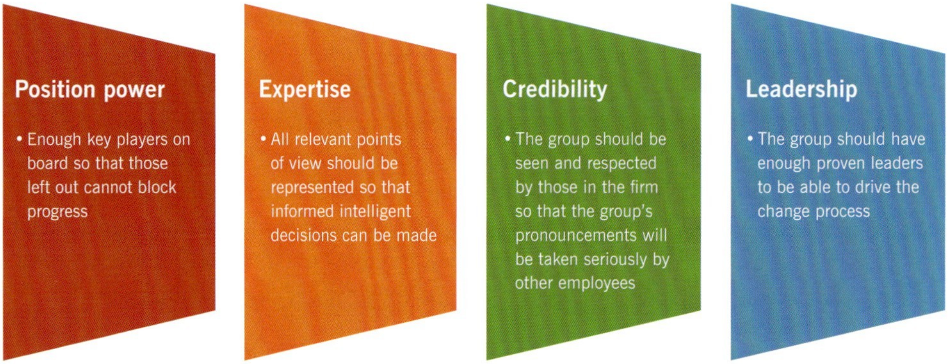

Position power

• Enough key players on board so that those left out cannot block progress

Expertise

• All relevant points of view should be represented so that informed intelligent decisions can be made

Credibility

• The group should be seen and respected by those in the firm so that the group's pronouncements will be taken seriously by other employees

Leadership

• The group should have enough proven leaders to be able to drive the change process

A guiding coalition with a rounded mix of talents is essential and assembling one is a big job that is vital if the transformation process is to succeed. It's also vital that the guiding coalition has a clear perspective on where the transformation is leading and recognizes the urgency of the situation. This combination of urgency to make change, a clear and common vision of what change is needed and an energetic and powerful group of people to drive and deliver the change is a vital component of the success of a transformation program – it cannot be left to others, it can't be put off, it can't be undertaken by just one part of the business and it certainly cannot be devolved.

Program governance and management
As programs gather momentum and move from the early heady days of a few pioneers with lots of ideas to the more mundane reality of actually delivering change, there's a strong need for a linkage

mechanism that ensures continual alignment between the business strategy, people right across the company and delivering real-world results. Known as program governance, it's there to help the transformation program deliver on its promises by providing oversight and control during its execution. It must also help managers assess the program's current state and adjust content and direction if necessary, especially in such a fast-moving and volatile area as the digital economy.

In Chapter 11 I reviewed a number of factors that can increase the odds for success in a major change program. Well executed program governance is a major contributor to success and the inverse is also true. Survey after survey supports this: 70 percent of change management projects do not meet objectives – *Forrester;* 75 percent of all e-Business projects fail to meet objectives – *Gartner;* 70 percent of CRM projects fail to meet objectives – *Butler Group*; IT's ability to deliver successful projects currently has its highest failure rate in over a decade – *Standish Group*.

Without effective governance to keep them heading in the right direction, transformation programs can soon end up with a 'headless chicken' scenario where everyone runs around energetically but aimlessly – and, ultimately, fruitlessly. So having good program governance and management and improving the odds for success are very important from a personal level right through to the corporate level.

As I was researching the area of program governance for this book, I was surprised at how many of the standard references seem to have started life in the U.K.'s Office of Government Commerce. At exactly the same time, I was reading about the same U.K. government facing up to scrapping a massive $20 billion IT program to computerize health records for all U.K. citizens, which failed largely because of poor governance – unclear and continually changing requirements, scope creep, too little interaction with and guidance from the supplier, too little of a shared partnership – too much 'us and them'. Sadly the usual way out is to blame the contractor – sometimes with justification, but often the fault lies just as much with the buyer or equally with both parties.

So, as they say, it's not just about *talking the talk*, it's about *walking the walk* as well – actually having some proactive governance and processes in place, not merely a token program office somewhere with lots of pretty wall charts and graphs – and I'm sure my share of the $20 billion of taxes bought plenty of those. It's very important that the people who are implementing change really know what they're doing: understanding the requirements, understanding the strengths and weaknesses of different suppliers and partners, and working very closely with them but ultimately always being in control. This is a 'smart buyer' approach but sadly, all too often, the buyer lacks the necessary skills. This problem isn't just confined to providers of digital services – major projects fail all too often because the requirements were unclear or unstable, too little governance was exercised during the implementation cycle and the supplier was not always up to the task.

Program governance is a bit like steering a large cruise ship: there are many parts that have to work well together in order to arrive safely at the distant port and for all of the passengers to have had a great time. The captain on the bridge has a vital command role but a chain of command, shared processes and decision making among hundreds of officers and crew make it actually happen. As we saw with the Costa Concordia disaster, get any one of those components wrong and you end up on the rocks.

Governance embraces multiple dimensions of people, partners, roles, structures and policies and is much more complex than the management of an individual project. As I've stressed repeatedly, programs related to the digital world are highly dynamic and must respond to constantly changing external events and drivers, so effective governance has to facilitate identifying, assessing and responding to such changes by adjusting program direction, components, features, cost or timelines. Without this, the program will be constantly reacting to events and struggling to catch up with changing conditions or, even worse, deliver a product that does not meet current business needs.

There are a number of ways of implementing a governance structure but it's essential that its roles cover all of the important management and oversight functions as well as the relationships between them. It must be clear on authority and decision-making, in that the program management and oversight is efficient and a clear process for decision making, especially regarding changes, is straightforward, simple and timely. Figure 22 gives a typical model for a typical governance structure – it's not meant to be prescriptive, so use this as a guide in developing your own structure:

Figure 22 – Typical program governance structure

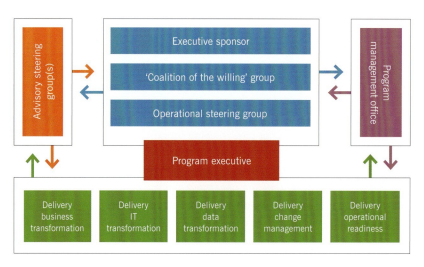

Usually the role of the executive sponsor will be the senior leader who is accountable for achieving the overall goals of the program. For a major transformation initiative that has significant impact across the organization, multiple executives from the 'coalition of the willing' would typically share this accountability, which may be supplemented by a steering group that looks frequently at detailed operational issues.

Steering groups are a forum in which the representatives can raise issues and adjust direction, resources or timing and can either work as a decision-making group acting by consensus, or as an advisory group to the executive sponsor and delivery teams. They should focus on enabling progress and maintaining momentum, and not become progress prevention committees. So, their role is to monitor program progress, understand issues and changes, provide advice and assessment of potential impact, make needed adjustments and give direction to the program director.

Any large transformation program will consist of multiple delivery projects spanning many disciplines, each with its own project manager. The program manager's role is to orchestrate and manage these projects via their respective project manager. Table 2[139] gives a comparison of the two roles:

Table 2 – Program director versus project manager roles

Program director	Project manager
Integrates efforts, continuously assesses and refines approaches and plans, ensures good communication	Plans, organizes, directs and controls the project effort
Directs managers to achieve defined outcomes aligned with business strategy	Manages for on-time delivery of specific products
Acts as the implementation arm of the program sponsor(s) and / or steering committee	Manages work within the project plan framework
Manages managers	Manages technical or operational staff

The support services behind the program director and the delivery projects is typically provided a Program Office, which provides support along administrative, financial, process and staff dimensions associated with successful program execution. A good program office is a goldmine of useful information and practical support to the program – bad ones are an overhead that suck up resources and deliver negative value, so ensure yours is the former, not the latter. Administrative support should include conformance tracking of plans, resources administration and physical and technical environment support as well as reviewing and tracking of financial expenditures, generation of required reports and financial documents. The program office should also administer policies, procedures and practices that provide an operational framework for program staff and

[139]For which I am indebted to Michael Handford of IBM

this should encompass issues such as time reporting, contracting for outside resources, expense control, training, communications about the program and internal reporting practices. This function may also deliver any other common services required across the program.

There are many standard tools and techniques to help define and support the governance of major transformation programs and the two most widely recognized and used frameworks are:

- PMBOK[140], which is the internationally recognized project management standard text from the Project Management Institute in the U.S. It provides the fundamentals of program management applicable to a wide range of projects. The Project Management Institute has grown to become a global advocate for the project management profession with more than 240,000 members in over 160 countries.
- PRINCE2[141], which was developed originally by the U.K.'s Office of Government Commerce and is widely recognized and used extensively to provide a method for managing projects within a clearly defined framework. It describes procedures to coordinate people and activities in a project, how to design and supervise the project and what to do if the project has to be adjusted if it does not develop as planned.

  It provides a common language for all participants in the program – the management roles and responsibilities involved in a project are fully described and are adaptable to suit the complexity of the project and skills of the organization. Each delivery project is specified with its key inputs and outputs and with specific goals and activities to be carried out – thus allowing for automatic control of any deviations from the plan. Divided into manageable stages, the method enables an efficient control of resources. On the basis of close monitoring, the program can be carried out in a controlled and organized way.

Whichever method or variant is used, Mary Whatman advises some good 'rules of thumb' to use:

- *Implement the right amount of governance*: The adage "too much is just as bad as too little" applies to the governance of transformation programs. Too much will impede the progress of the program while too little will allow programs to miss scope, quality, schedule and/or cost. Creating a governance structure that meets the size, complexity and risks of a given program is a critical element of success.
- *Engage the right type of leader:* for individual projects as well as the program director. I've said it so many times and it's not just about the person at the top – leadership needs to cascade down the organization. Often the best kind of leader is one who shares the characteristics of a benevolent dictator – an authoritarian leader who exercises power for the benefit of the whole program or project rather than for his or her self-interest. Consensus in transformations, especially when under time pressure, rarely works.

[140]www.itgovernance.co.U.K./pmbok.aspx
[141]www.prince2.com/what-is-prince2.asp

Figure 23 – PRINCE2 process model

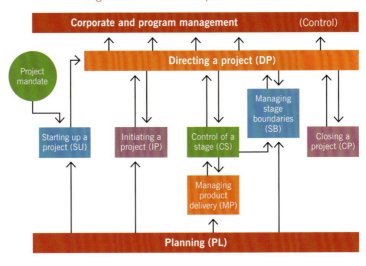

- *Delegate decision making properly*: A big part of the governance process is about taking decisions:
  - ensure that each part of the program structure is empowered to make decisions with a clearly defined scope;
  - define a process by which to make those decisions;
  - define a standard structure to document and communicate decisions; and
  - define a means by which to escalate (hopefully not many) decisions to the next level of authority.
- *Stakeholder involvement is critical but needs limits*: Understanding the needs and impacts of the key stakeholders is a critical factor in success as they mature along the transformation path with the project team but they must not be able to mislead, delay or interrupt the program progress without cause or reason.
- *Change management should be an element of governance but should not dominate it:* In the dynamic digital world, change is inherent throughout the process. Managing the change, the impact if done or not done is a process required at all levels of the governance structure.
- *Do not lose sight of the current business*: When a separate organization is used to implement the transformation program, the governance process must include a function that assesses program impacts on the current business. When transformation programs are undertaken with existing lines of business, it is very important to set clear priorities to ensure the right balance between 'business as usual' and ensuring that the transformation program is delivered on time, on budget, on quality, meeting or exceeding expectations.
- *Communication must be part of every team member's responsibility*: There is no substitute for the right amount of communication to educate and inform while minimizing the impact of the change and uncertainty.
- *Stopping a project* that isn't delivering on its objectives is as important as starting one.

Typically programs will adopt some form of a plan-design-build-operate approach, but while this is a well-proven technique, it stems from projects that have a clear start and finish cycle with clear requirements. Pioneering new ideas or services may not have this luxury and the cycle will need to build in a lot of iterations to ensure you don't end up building a new platform for business models and services that have fallen by the wayside. This is where the *Agile* project methodology can be very useful since it has the concept of iteration and progress in bursts built in – more of that and other delivery approaches later.

The program can be undertaken in-house, or all or part of it can be contracted to a specialist partner such as a major systems integration firm. Flick back to Chapter 7 for more on managing these types of partnership but also be aware of the need for caution in outsourcing program governance. While your company may lack the experience, skills and perhaps the vision to successfully manage a full transformation program, far too often the problem gets 'thrown over the wall' to a supplier who may also lack the necessary competencies or knowledge to do the job, but with the added problem of fuzzy requirements and minimal guidance and control.

So neither approach may be a great recipe for success. The right answer is usually a blending of the two managed by a strong governance structure where the customer steers the requirements and overall program but brings in specialist help where necessary or to address the need for interim resources during the transformation. Having an external 'coach' engaged from the beginning of the process is usually a good idea because they can help make a realistic assessment of the relative strengths and weaknesses of the team and can help advise on direction based on experience of undertaking similar programs with other providers.

This problem of not properly specifying or managing the contract is often exacerbated in situations where the company is in difficulties and has taken short-term cost reduction steps that have had the effect of stripping out vital operational and IT functions. In the main, the digital world is a highly cost-optimized, software-centric one and lack of internal skills to guide suppliers can be a significant cause of failure.

Program and project delivery processes and approaches

The plan-design-build-operate model offers a very basic set of steps in implementing a new operating platform for digital services. In reality, these need to be fleshed out considerably since this is a major program involving very considerable investment and resources. There are a substantial number of different delivery disciplines that can be deployed and each has relevant merits, advantages and disadvantages.

I don't intend this chapter to be a detailed program delivery methodology guidebook – there are plenty of those – but it is important that a common methodology is used because many parts of the company and many suppliers/contractors will be engaged in the program. Without a common program delivery methodology, significant confusion is likely to reign and the project risks will escalate.

Figure 24 – Typical plan-design-build-operate cycle

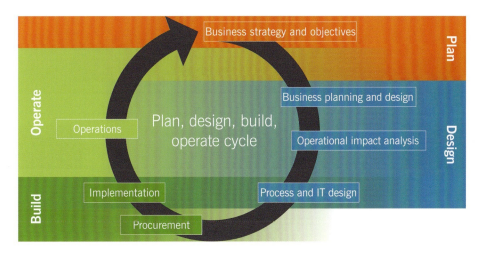

Major project delivery methodologies include the following:

Traditional 'Waterfall' approach

This is likely to be familiar to many people and identifies a sequence of steps that are laid out in a plan with the next series of tasks undertaken after formal completion of the previous. Waterfall development is fine for well-defined projects, but often fails in projects with a high degree of uncertainty and where requirements have not been finalized and can change – and it is likely that transformation in the digital world will require significant change of tack on many occasions.

Critical chain project management

The critical chain delivery methodology is a more sophisticated method of planning and managing projects that puts more emphasis on the project's physical and human resources while getting different professionals working together: the goal being to increase the success and completion rates of projects. Projects are planned and managed to ensure that the resources are ready when the critical chain tasks must start, subordinating all other resources to the critical chain. The critical chain methodology is closely related to the critical path method and is widely used in many forms of projects, including construction, aerospace and defense, software development, research projects, product development, engineering and plant maintenance.

These methods often use tools such as the Program (or Project) Evaluation and Review Technique (PERT), which is a statistical tool designed to analyze and represent the tasks involved in completing a given project. Figure 25 shows a typical PERT chart, although for a major transformation project it would be very much larger and orders of magnitude more complex.

Figure 25 – Example PERT chart

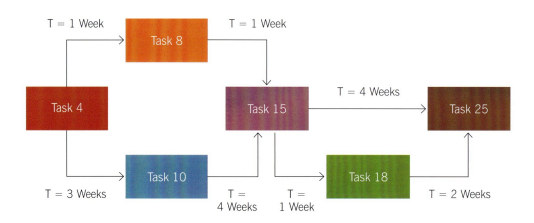

Event chain methodology

This is yet another delivery methodology that complements both the critical chain approach and the critical path methods. The event chain methodology is better suited when projects are in an uncertain environment because it factors in risks and uncertainties in order to better manage events and event chains that will affect project schedules. Event chain methodology is based on the following principles:

- **Probability of risk:** An activity or task in most real-life projects is not a continuous uniform process. Tasks are affected by external events, which can occur at some point in the middle of the task.
- **Event chains:** Events can cause other events, which will create event chains. These event chains can significantly affect the course of the project. Quantitative analysis is used to determine a cumulative effect of these event chains on the project schedule.
- **Critical events or event chains:** The single events or the event chains that have the most potential to affect the projects are the 'critical events' or 'critical chains of events.' These can be determined by the analysis.
- **Project tracking with events:** Even if a project is partially completed and data about the project duration, cost and events occurred is available, it is still possible to refine information about future potential events and helps to forecast future project performance.

Agile methodology

The Agile methodology is an approach typically used in software development and indeed that is where its roots lie. However, it is now becoming more popular as a delivery methodology[142] for other project types. It helps teams respond better to the unpredictability of a transformation project and takes a very different approach to the traditional 'Waterfall' methodology.

There are many specific Agile development methods but most promote development, teamwork, collaboration and process adaptability throughout the lifecycle of the project. They contrast sharply with Waterfall delivery approaches as they are very flexible, with projects seen as a series of relatively small tasks conceived and executed as the situation demands in an adaptive manner, rather than as a completely pre-planned process. Iterations are short timeframes (time boxes) that typically last from one to four weeks.

Each iteration involves a team working through a full development cycle and aims to deliver a working solution that can be demonstrated to stakeholders. Team composition in an Agile project is usually cross-functional and self-organizing without consideration for any existing corporate hierarchy or the corporate roles of team members. Team members normally take responsibility for tasks that deliver the functionality each cycle requires.

By focusing on the repetition of abbreviated work cycles as well as the functional product they yield, the Agile methodology could be described as *iterative* and *incremental*. While in the Waterfall approach, project teams only have one chance to get each aspect of a project right, Agile allows every aspect of development requirements (design and so on) to be continually revisited throughout the lifecycle. Typically project teams stop and re-evaluate the direction of a project every couple of weeks so there's time to steer it in another direction.

Adherents of the Agile *inspect-and-adapt* approach claim that it can greatly reduce project risks, costs and time to market. As a project team's work cycle is limited to two weeks, it gives the project sponsors repeated opportunities to adjust the project for success. In essence, the Agile methodology links better to changing business needs in dynamic situations where the market or requirements are changing quickly.

Agile methods emphasize face-to-face communication over written documents and work best when the team members are all in the same location. Most Agile teams work in a single open office (called a bullpen), which facilitates such communication. Team size is typically small (5-9 people) to simplify team communication and team collaboration. Larger development efforts may be delivered by multiple teams working toward a common goal or on different parts of an effort. This may require a coordination of priorities across teams. When a team works in different locations, it maintains daily contact through collaboration tools like videoconferencing, shared message boards, voice, email and so on.

[142]For example, see John C. Goodpasture's *Project Management the Agile Way: Making it Work in the Enterprise*, J.Ross Publishing, 2010 ISBN-13: 9781604270273

Agile methodologies are still controversial, with a number of factors preventing their widespread adoption. They were designed for small, fast-moving software projects and many people are unsure about their value in large-scale, complex projects.

Figure 26 – Agile approach

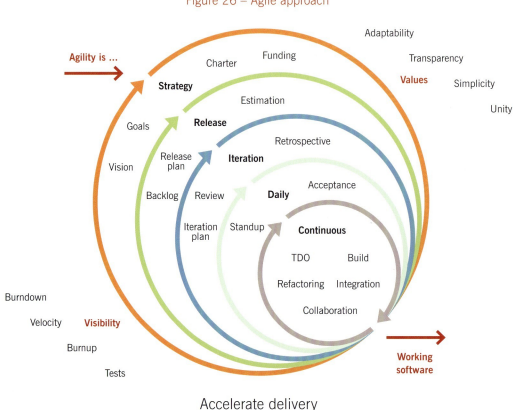

Accelerate delivery

Which is best – Agile versus traditional Waterfall approaches?

This is one of those 'when did you stop beating your wife' types of question – every answer gets you into hot water! But there's no doubt that Agile is becoming increasingly popular and allows for the kind of frequent changes that a transformation to the digital world might encounter. Agile has a number of advantages and is good when requirements are hazy or the business environment is uncertain. It's also lightweight, with lower overhead meaning project costs can be considerably less than using traditional methods.

Agile methods have definitely gained in popularity in recent years to overcome drawbacks of the traditional Waterfall method. In the same way that water flows down a waterfall and can't come back up, some see Waterfall as slow, inflexible, heavily regulated and regimented. On the other hand, Agile sprang from smaller, rapid deployment software projects rather than large-scale, multi-disciplinary projects of the type implied by a corporate transformation – and some would argue that the method doesn't suit large-scale, mission-critical programs. As a starting point for many transformation programs, a blending of the two methodologies is used, taking elements of each that suit the intended project culture and developing a customized and documented delivery approach that is evolved and managed through the project management office.

A good case study of 'enterprise' scale use of Agile is at British Telecom over the past few years. A good write-up on this can be found on the Agilistapm.com site[143].

Lean Six Sigma

As I outlined earlier, a 'clean-sheet' transformation to a new target structure and incremental transformation of an existing structure are not mutually exclusive. Even the clean-sheet approach will need incremental enhancement going forward to continuously optimize operating costs and service quality levels. So service providers, even brand-new entrants into the marketplace, need to understand how to build and how to improve their processes and systems wherever they are in their lifecycle.

When we wrote *The Lean Communications Provider*, I had been fortunate enough to spend some time at the Massachusetts Institute of Technology and had gained a good insight into Lean techniques. While I understood that 'Lean' was about more than just reducing process costs and indeed was heavily weighted to improving quality, the dictionary definition of the word itself reinforces the cost reduction emphasis: *thin, esp. healthily so; having no superfluous fat*. Indeed, much of the transformation that has taken place in communications and cable service providers in the intervening years since we wrote that book has been largely about downsizing and cost reduction. But get too thin and you don't perform very well – people die of anorexia nervosa. Lean is all about being the *right* weight with the *right* fitness level for the job in hand. Just as athletes continuously improve their fitness through their training regimes, companies need to be similarly fit to face the challenges ahead of them.

However, the Lean approach does have its limitations and so in recent years, practitioners have married two important corporate fitness regimes – Lean and Six Sigma – and not surprisingly it is usually called Lean Six Sigma or as Six Sigma Lean (presumably in Australia!). This integrated approach builds on the knowledge, methods and tools derived from decades of operational improvement research and implementation.

While Lean focuses on process optimization, Six Sigma has grown out of its original focus

[143]www.agilistapm.com/casestudy-british-telecom/

of measuring and eliminating defects to zoom in on meeting customer requirements and stakeholder expectations. So the Lean Six Sigma approach draws on the philosophies, principles and tools of both to aim at business effectiveness, not just cost-cutting and efficiency.

The aim of this combined approach is summed up in a nice quote from the IBM Institute for Business Value[144]: "The Lean Six Sigma approach drives organizations not just to do things better but to do better things." In the quest for transformed organizations in the digital world, this is exactly what is needed and proponents of Lean Six Sigma emphasize that it has moved far beyond being a methodology primarily for process improvement (such as refining existing processes to reduce costs, improve performance and provide better customer value) and can be used for driving innovation of operations services and business models.

Eliminate process hotspots

When using an evolutionary approach like Lean Six Sigma in an existing business area, the main idea is to focus on the 'hotspots' in a process that cause high levels of cost, excessive time delays or are the cause of a bad customer experience. These are relative terms since the approach is to look at your core business processes and systematically eliminate or at least significantly reduce the most obvious hotspots – and then repeat the process over and over again to progressively improve processes on a permanent basis.

So where do you start? Do you start at processes beginning with the letter A and work through to Z? Do you start at one end of the process and work systematically through to the other end? The problem with that is that you will not focus in on the biggest problems first and will not make the greatest gains in process improvement as quickly as you should.

The basis of the Six Sigma approach is to manage change through measurement and, by measuring factors such as time, costs and customer impact it allows you to identify the most important hotspots and focus maximum effort on those that need to be dealt with first. Once you have dealt with the biggest impediments to whatever you are trying to improve (such as agility, cost reduction, customer experience and so on), you can then move onto the next most important set of problems. This requires you to have a way of seeing those problems and a very important tool is to use benchmarks to help you identify them.

But how do you know which are the hotspots? The answer comes about through benchmarking key elements of your processes.

Benchmarking

There's an old saying about "not being able to see the forest for the trees" and this can be a problem with the concept of key performance indicators (KPIs). Many people will be familiar with these and their role as the backbone of measuring operational performance – thousands

[144]www-935.ibm.com/services/at/bcs/pdf/br-stragchan-driving-inno.pdf

of them are measured every day to drive behavior right across the spectrum of operational performance – from the number of rings before a customer query is answered; to the number of times a customer appointment is broken; to the jitter and delay characteristics of transmission systems. But the problem with them is that, from an overall business viewpoint, they can clutter that view because there are often too many of them, they are not focused on the business outcome and they're too detailed.

In general, KPIs are set on a departmental basis and used to drive performance and rewards for that part of the business. End-to-end measures, right across the business or focused on complete business process are less common. Even less usual is the comparison of the results to other peer group companies or to other industries. This is important because it is relative efficiency and effectiveness that is important to customers and shareholders. Their idea of good service or good returns constantly changes as market conditions change and they compare one supplier with another. KPIs set in isolation of what represents 'best of breed' may drive behavior towards a goal, which, even if met, does not satisfy customers or alternatively may drive the operators into uneconomic operations, resulting in reduced profitability.

Some external benchmarking does in places such as market analyst reports that compare statistics often taken from annual reports to shareholders. When assessing relative performance *between* companies, these statistics are at best unhelpful and at worst downright misleading. They suffer from the opposite problem to KPIs in that they are too *high* level. Business ratios taken at a gross level, such as revenue per employee, but which do not take account of the type of business that the service provider undertakes are fairly meaningless: for example comparing a mobile provider with a fixed broadband provider is not helpful, since they have very different cost bases and types of asset to manage.

There are a number of consulting firms who undertake benchmarking studies between various service providers and can help in understanding and analyzing where hotspots exist. The key point here is that you need appropriate measures for the task. As the basis of the transformation program you need sufficient detail to be able to focus the transformation activities on the most important areas, but not so much detail that you get lost in data. You also need a level of standardization on the metrics, both with other digital service providers so that you can make 'apples to apples' comparisons, but also ideally with technology providers who can generate the necessary data in the right format so that measures can be taken simply and easily.

TM Forum Business Benchmarking

A very pertinent independent source of standardized top-level business metrics and benchmarking data from a large number of digital service providers is provided by TM Forum (see Chapter 14) through its Business Benchmarking Program, which uses actual industry data provided for the industry and through partnerships with leading analysts and research firms. More than 150 communications service providers participate in the program to measure factors such as customer experience, operational efficiency, revenue and margin. Service providers either participate in various benchmarking surveys – the results of which participants get for free – or they contribute to studies on customer experience, mobile, broadband, billing and revenue management.

I'm grateful for and acknowledge the published work of Michael Hanford at IBM, Alan Calder at IT Governance Publishing and Mary Whatman, Parhelion GCA for some of their ideas regarding program governance.

13

GAINING OWNERSHIP AND EXECUTION

Remember school physics lessons, where you sprinkled iron filings on a piece of paper and they all lay in a random fashion? Then you put a magnet underneath the paper and the filings all instantly lined up around the magnetic field. Transformation to a common approach needs such a magnetic influence to align the whole company.

So far so good, but of course there are always many barriers to making change within any business, and running out of steam during the middle of a transformation process is disastrous. So this chapter will focus on getting the right people in the organization to own the changes that affect them; executing on the plan and making change irreversible.

When making any change, whether it is through evolutionary or radical transformation and whether the steps are large or small, the status quo has a formidable resilience and will preserve itself with vigor. I've already used the analogy of white cells in a human body that attack invading viruses and germs – organizations are just as good at rejecting invading ideas.

A significant amount of this resistance can be overcome by good communications with the people involved, explaining why the change is necessary, the benefits it will bring and making sure they understand what they need to do and when. However, there are some larger, structural barriers that need to be understood and dealt with if progress is to be made in reshaping the business for the digital world.

Many companies have historically been organized on a functional departmental basis: finance; procurement; human resources, network planning, network operations; service management; product management; customer service and so on. The 1990s saw a strong desire to increase accountability at the business and products level so these departments were often overlaid with business units, each having its own profit and loss responsibility. In reality, in a business with a large shared infrastructure like a communications player, it's difficult to assess true profitability of products and services since costs are often allocated on an arbitrary basis. Although they may be useful management indicators they are not necessarily of huge value in their own right.

While these 'silos' are very good at breaking down a monolithic organization into manageable parts, they drive significant fragmentation into the business processes that serve the customer. If each of these semi-independent units is responsible for only a part of the delivery of a service to a customer, ownership and responsibility of delivering a good customer experience can be very difficult and optimizing operational costs on an end to end basis, near impossible. The problem gets worse if multiple services are bundled to the same customer as this magnifies the fragmentation problem.

The situation also exists at group level in a multi-operating company conglomerate. Service operations in multiple countries may have common ownership but generally lack any kind of common operating model, metrics, technologies and so on because they have often been acquired from different initial owners.

Fragmentation is a very significant cause of being unable to offer a common set of services with consistent customer quality and at a consistently efficient operating mode at both a national or international level. It's certainly a big contributor to the inability of many companies to turn raw data from multiple systems in multiple departments into useful business information.

Poor customer service and high operating costs are not the only negative outcome of a silo-based, fragmented approach. Because the business processes get fractured, barriers exist at the 'borders' of each silo. These barriers are often in the form of different systems used by different departments, so that information cannot be easily shared, preventing easy exploitation of the significant treasure trove of customer information that most companies have about their markets and customers, weakening their marketing position. Crossing those boundaries significantly increases IT costs to provide complex integration and customization between dissimilar systems; reduces information flows to the lowest common denominator and significantly impairs agility. From an effective business operations point of view, fragmentation is a thoroughly bad thing.

Launching new services or making significant change to an existing one across these multiple 'fiefdoms' can be a nightmare for product managers because it requires the approval of all of the departments involved, each of whom have their own pressures and priorities, which are often not aligned to those of the product manager. The result is that the product launch moves at the pace of the slowest department and will have consumed dozens of meetings over many months.

Each department, particularly if they are profit and loss business units with their own priorities, budgets and objectives will tend to focus on what is best for their part of the business, not the business overall – that, after all, is the whole point of setting up autonomous business units in the first place. So they will evolve their own ways of working, invest in their own systems and prioritize those issues that help them meet their objectives to get their bonus at the end of the year. Business processes that cross these units often have no end-to-end ownership or optimization simply because the company is not organized that way. Steve Jobs saw this as dysfunctional and eliminated the problem by eliminating divisions.

Earlier, I talked about companies breaking up into one of three types of focused player – infrastructure providers, service providers and retailers. While these functions exist in many companies today they are not often organized with such clear lines of demarcation – indeed in most, the silos are organized around a line of business rather than functions. So a big implication of transformation is about optimizing the organizational shape that can facilitate the delivery of high-quality services at low levels of operating costs through high levels of process automation, information sharing and exploitation, but at the same time facilitate a clearer focus on one of more of these three key business functions.

Without re-aligning the shape of the organization to the business goals of the company you will be fighting an uphill and ultimately unwinnable battle if there are too many autonomous, silo-based units involved. So how can you overcome the disadvantages of a silo-based organization without massive and highly disruptive re-organization? A greenfield approach built in parallel to the existing organization is one approach and I covered this in Chapter 10. If this isn't possible and evolutionary change is being driven through an existing organization, *some* reorganization may be prudent but in the main, the major obstacles can be overcome with changes to reward systems, investment controls and the appointment of empowered teams who are responsible for the effective operation of business processes from end-end across departments. This inevitably produces matrix-type organizations and while these are common in many industries, they are often difficult to implement if the corporate culture is firmly wedded to a hierarchical structure where people are used to having direct control of their own resource base.

Many communications companies are run on a hierarchical rather than matrix structure and the reasons for this go back to the roots of the telecom industry – government owned and therefore civil service in structure, often with military connections. Many newer communication service providers as well resemble this classical 'top-down' command and control structure because most people in positions of authority in operators grew up in a quasi-government or monopoly structure.

So transforming at the organizational level is quite a challenge. Implementing a radical restructuring around functions and processes rather than product lines would be the best approach if you have a clean sheet of paper, but in most cases you don't and the price is likely to be a significant hit to operational effectiveness in the short term. Implementing an overlay structure that forms a matrix is less disruptive but may run counterculture for many of the people involved.

Common processes and IT can help

A significant approach that can help solve this problem of fragmentation is to prevent the problem from getting worse and embark on a transformational plan to move from a highly fragmented set of products, services, processes and systems that previously underpinned the organization to a much more common and integrated suite.

This means centralizing decisions over systems and process design and implementation and progressively reducing or removing divisional autonomy in 'doing their own thing'. This approach can also be used to normalize operations between operating companies in the same group. This is easy to say and quite hard to do because of the cultural barriers and the 'white cell defense' issue.

Without significant and highly visible support from the CEO, anyone appointed to the job of implementing common systems and processes across the organization will soon run into barriers. The situation is often made worse by seeing this as purely an IT issue and empowering the CIO to go off and make change without getting the full buy-in and support from various divisional managers who control the way the processes operate in their division. This usually ends up with a confrontation between what should change – should the systems be customized and bespoke to fit the particular operational quirks of that department or should the process be implemented in a common way end-to-end and standardized, commercial off-the-shelf systems be implemented?

Needless to say, the life of CIOs in such organizations is relatively short and to overcome this issue, more and more providers are appointing Chief Transformation Officers with a much broader scope to change processes and systems across the company.

Imagine if each department in a supermarket – meat, vegetables, drinks, household goods and so on – had their own autonomous approach, their own supply chains, their own floor space layout and shelving, separate cash registers, staff uniform and pricing policies. While it may be quaint and resemble a cluster of small independent shops, supermarkets run typically on single figure net profit margins and have to be run extremely efficiently with common processes and systems across all lines of business if they are to survive in a brutally competitive market. The same is true for service providers – the luxury of each business unit and department 'doing their own thing' might be fun for the individuals concerned but is no way to run a modern, high-quality service operation in markets where margins are thin and getting thinner.

I purloined the graphic in Figure 27 some years ago from Larry Goldman, who is now a leading analyst at Analysys Mason. Rather sadly, it is still a common reflection of the organization of many communications service providers. In recent years this has started to change,

Figure 27 – Departmental level processes and systems create fragmentation

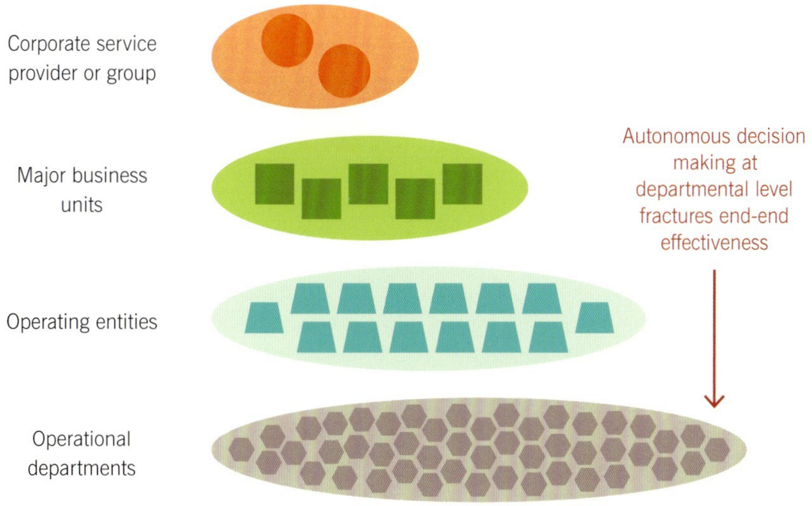

Corporate service provider or group

Major business units

Autonomous decision making at departmental level fractures end-end effectiveness

Operating entities

Operational departments

Source: Larry Goldman, Analysys Mason

with different providers making different rates of progress in moving to the highly optimized 'supermarket' model, but it is still very difficult to point to communications companies that you could describe as having solved the problem completely and being an example of best practice.

What can you do to remove the barriers?

A slow move towards a more effective operating model isn't going to bode well for companies who want to leverage opportunities in the digital economy. This is why I champion a greenfield or at least a hybrid approach to transformation. But, if it has to be evolutionary, one of the first things to do is to stop the problem getting any worse – there's an old proverb where I come from that says "when you are in a hole, stop digging". So one of the earliest actions to undertake is to recognize the problem and prevent the fragmentation of its core business processes and systems from getting any worse by neutralizing divisional authority to autonomously procure or customize new systems. From there the drive can begin to put the company on a path to progressively reduce process and systems fragmentation to as low a level as possible by step-by-step process and systems optimization and renewal.

There are several paths to being able to achieve this. In many cases it will be simpler to build a new process and systems infrastructure from scratch for the delivery of new services and progressively move existing services to that platform, rather than trying to rebuild out of date processes and systems on an evolutionary basis.

Whichever route is taken, some common controls are necessary:

- Consensus on direction. There has to be widespread agreement among senior executives on the need to transform systems and processes to a common, highly integrated and highly optimized approach – one division alone cannot achieve this.
- Empowerment. Somebody needs to be in overall charge of the transformation program even if this is on a matrix basis rather than a full structural reorganization. This is where Steve Jobs' concept of the benevolent dictator comes in.
- Incentives must drive transformation. The company's incentives and motivational rewards systems must be realigned to ensure that appropriate weight is given to transformation activities, otherwise people will carry on doing what they always have done.
- Common target. There needs to be a common target for the processes and systems that will be the engine of the new structure for the company to move towards, rather than allowing fragmentation to get progressively worse.

Get the right incentives and produce plenty of quick wins

Whatever laudable and lofty goals might be set for a transformation program, little will happen to make it a reality if the incentives and rewards that drive people's energies in one direction or another are not aligned with those goals.

If the aspirations of the company are to transform but the incentives are totally built around maintaining the status quo, guess what will happen? This is where the setting of lighthouse goals (see Chapter 6) is so important. It cannot be that only a small central group is charged with transformation and the rest of the company carries on with business-as-usual. If that happens, it is inevitable that the central transformation group will fail.

This sounds rather like a battle between good and evil, which of course it's not. Transformation to exciting and high-growth opportunities in the digital economy, rather than a slow but steady decline, are goals that if correctly explained, are highly motivational and should be shared by everybody. They do not necessarily have opposing goals when distilled to a high level, but they may disagree on priorities, timescales and implementation approaches.

I have been involved in a number of situations like this and the issue cannot be swept under the carpet: unless the targets and rewards systems are lined up, either the overall transformation program will stumble and be stillborn or else the short-term targets of the company could be negatively impacted. So management needs to find a way of ensuring that the whole company is incentivized to move in a common transforming direction, but also to ensure that the program delivers quick wins along the way that will ensure that the current business activities are supported.

Indeed, a continuous 'win' program supported by the right incentives for everyone who has to deliver them is an essential feature of a successful approach. Without evidence that the approach works, shareholders, executives and operational teams will become disenchanted and abandon the program. This is one of the key lessons from Toyota and other companies that have pioneered modern change approaches.

If the transformation program delivers bottom line benefits, they cannot just be aimed at remote shareholders and some of the benefit needs to be shared with the people who made it happen, if they are to be incentivized to go further and make more gains possible. They need to be steered to achieve the lighthouse goals for the company as well as the detailed key performance indicators for their particular part of that overarching goal.

Reward systems take many forms in different cultures and companies and it would not be sensible for me to give a detailed view of what these should be or how they should be implemented. Suffice to say, however, that without effective incentives in place to ensure that the company pulls in a common direction, the program will not succeed.

Returns for both employees and shareholders cannot be designed to deliver solely at the end of the program – any investment of time or money that does not show results fairly quickly is doomed to failure and a transformation program must be able to show continuous results.

Structured correctly, focusing energies and rewards on those steps that can produce important gains quickly will encourage everyone to want to go further and faster. It will win over the skeptics and it will outlast just one generation of senior management who were positive about the approach.

To reach its goals, a transformation program is a journey without a clear end but it is not a journey undertaken for its own sake. It is a journey designed to radically improve the company's position and be sustainable over a long period of time. A transformation program requires frequent successes to top up its 'credit' with its stakeholders. This must be built into the governance process – see Chapter 12.

Getting everyone on the same page

Transformation to a common, highly integrated and automated operational approach of processes and systems can't happen unless that program of investment is against an overall and agreed plan. This must be defined in considerable detail at the outset of the transformation program otherwise changes will be made and new technology acquired that actually makes the problem worse rather than causing progressive alignment.

Remember your school physics lessons, where iron filings were sprinkled on a piece of paper and all lay in a random fashion? Put a magnet underneath the paper and the filings all instantly lined up around the magnetic field. Transformation to a common approach needs such a magnetic influence to align all of the processes and systems into a highly efficient and effective whole.

There are three components to making this happen:

- Define common vision and goals: The vision of what a transformed approach would look like.
- Implement appropriate management tools: The management infrastructure, investment controls, disciplines, reward systems, management processes and tools to ensure that the company moves in that direction.
- Agree a common target: An agreed process and systems architecture, strategic suppliers and an agreed set of priorities of where to transform first.

At a working level, the vision needs to be interpreted into some tangible goals and actions. There needs to be a picture of how the company will work in its transformed guise and the phases that will need to occur to get there. It needs a detailed picture of how transformed processes should run end-to-end (usually starting with the customer and ending with the customer) and it needs to spell out how the systems and information that will implement these processes should be deployed.

These plans, even if clear and precise, will not make anything happen by themselves. Business-as-usual will dominate – and to make the vision come to life the direction needs to be endorsed and actively championed by senior executives in the company. They need to ensure that people are appointed with both the responsibility and authority to make sure that the architecture for the way the company will work comes to life. To do that, they need to have authority over new investment and the ability to make change within existing business processes and the way departments work.

Implementing this needs some careful thought and companies in different cultures may approach it in a slightly different way. Although the easiest way to achieve this is for a central group to have responsibility for defining the overall systems and process architecture and the authority to see that it is implemented, in practice, this can be fraught with problems. This is because the central group may have a perfect view of how the systems and processes should be implemented but are unaware of the practical day-day problems of each department. Pressing ahead with centrally driven change can thus impact current operational performance and grow resentment among current operational teams who will have to run the new system and processes.

This needs a careful balance. Is the operational department just dragging its feet or are its arguments valid? Are people just protecting their jobs or are they in a position of power? Does the central group really understand the business needs? This is where a matrix or 'dual key' approach can be useful – investment in systems and process re-alignments being made by a combination of the operational department and the central group responsible for overall process and systems optimization.

Where compromises are made these need to be carefully understood and documented. If the target process and systems architecture cannot be implemented, is it because the target is wrong or because the current operational need is so important it requires deviation from the target. Is it a temporary deviation and does a plan exist to get it back on track? Does everyone understand the whole life cost of that deviation, not just the short-term cost issues, but the costs of maintaining that variation in terms of systems maintenance and operational manpower?

Getting the balance right between the short-term needs of today's operations and the medium/long-term strategy of becoming transformed is the real art of management. That's when the program of removing the barriers is at its most important – ensuring that the incentives and rewards system ensures movement toward transformed operations rather than encouraging the status quo.

So now's a good time to tackle some of the technology aspects and look at a target platform for business processes and business systems.

14

REDUCING RISK THROUGH COLLABORATION – A PROVEN BLUEPRINT

Put simply, unless you get to grips with your service operations platform and transform it to being highly integrated, automated and flexible, you will fail in the digital economy. You won't have the business agility or offer sufficiently good customer experience at a cost that enables you to compete. Taking a custom engineered approach to doing this will potentially be a fatally slow, risky and expensive route.

Much of the focus of this book has been on the market and strategic positioning of different players in the digital ecosystem, looking at how to maximize the opportunities and minimize exposure to the many threats that are emerging so rapidly. Nevertheless, unless you have a well-oiled machine that can deliver services in your chosen market sector, at a price customers are prepared to pay and at an operating cost that enables you to make sustainable profits, you're still going to fail. Added to that, the well-oiled machine must be flexible enough to respond to a highly volatile market.

Senior executives ignore what happens down in the 'engine room' at their peril. You can have great marketing, innovative product ideas and good access to capital, but you will not survive long in the digital world if you can't get your products to market in a timely way, deliver a great customer experience, fix problems simply and easily when they occur and collect revenue efficiently and accurately.

The business of getting your service creation and delivery machine into that 'Swiss watch' state of precision and smooth running doesn't happen by accident and it is the absolute core of what a successful service provider has to do. Many entrants into the digital world will come from a physical product background with little idea of what it takes to deliver good quality services, on a massive scale, without operating costs killing their business.

This is where today's communications service providers have a great advantage, but they also are in grave danger of diluting it through bad habits formed in the years of high profits and these habits must be swept away. They include, as we have discussed in previous chapters, the fragmentation of business processes and systems across different departments with little end-to-end optimization.

This is compounded by their tendency to cling to out-of-date processes and work practices, such as building highly customized systems that are expensive to build and even more costly to maintain and update. Worst of all, senior managements have shown what is arguably almost criminally low interest in service operations until the margins started to fall.

In this chapter we examine what makes the best architecture for the sort of operational platform that communications service providers need to survive, never mind thrive.

Being standard or being different?

I'll start with laying to rest one of the biggest myths I frequently come across and that is the notion that designing your own customized operational infrastructure delivers significant differential advantage. It can certainly deliver massive differential *disadvantage* if it's inflexible, costs a fortune and delivers a poor experience to your customers. Probably the best way to ensure that disadvantage occurs is if you let your architects, designers and developers convince you that they can build a better platform than anyone else. They probably can, given enough time and money, but likely as not, you can't afford the cost of this or the time delays it will inject into your transformation process. And you definitely can't afford to take that risk, especially when the gains are likely to be minimal and the prospects for miserable failure are huge.

The argument that "we can't collaborate because we need to be different" is simply not true. Would your house be warmer and your heating costs lower than the people next door because you had your own special diameter copper tube installed or your own purpose-built radiators? Or would you be better off programming the heating controller in a smarter way? That's the difference between customization of a unique solution with all of its attendant costs, risks and delays, and the intelligent configuration of a standard approach.

So it's much more sensible to look closely at where significant differential advantage can be obtained and focus your resources into that small number of highly targeted areas while sourcing the majority of your operational capability on the open market, using established suppliers and orchestrating them to deliver you an operational infrastructure based on proven standards.

Commercial off-the-shelf systems have a number of big advantages – they already exist and you don't have the time and risk of building them; the suppliers get economies of scale in building once and selling many times, so it should be a lot cheaper and, if they follow open standards, the costs of integrating multiple systems together into automated process chains is reduced by orders of magnitude.

An analogy always helps. Airlines are a good one because they operate on tight margins, have big infrastructure and have become good at differentiating themselves without building their own airplanes, airports, runways, baggage handling systems et al. They use standardized aircraft to gain the economic advantages of buying and, most importantly, operating them. Airlines customize the aircraft in relatively minor ways, such as livery, upholstery colors, seat layouts and the positioning of galleys. To this they add other differentiators, such as rewards programs, on-time landings, the way customers are treated at check in/bag drops, in-flight entertainment, executive lounges and so on.

Whichever market segment you want to serve in the digital economy, you need to think very carefully about the balance between standardization and differentiation. This should not be a purely technology-driven decision: developers in general believe they can design something better than you can buy on the open market for a fraction of the price. They may be right – we'd all rather drive a hand-built Rolls-Royce than a mass-produced Chevrolet. The question is, can we afford to buy it, wait for it to be built, then run it? Figure 28 gives some ideas as to what should be standardized and where differentiation should focus.

Figure 28 – Standardization and differentiation

- Infrastructure
- IT and support systems
- Data architecture
- Integration architecture
- 99% of business processes

- Brand and market image
- Service innovation, quality features and packaging
- Customer experience
- Systems configuration
- Creative use of data analytics

Opting for a standardized process and systems architecture that can be configured to provide appropriate differentiation has a lot of advantages. As I said, it considerably reduces the risks, costs and timescales – all essential requirements if you are not going to be left behind in the digital world.

Second, you can use this architecture as the basis of competitive procurement for systems, their associated processes and professional services contracts: a standardized approach allows you to maximize your choice of suppliers and minimize the price you will pay. Systems costs are not just the initial purchase price, in fact that's merely a down payment – whole life costs, particularly for customized software, processes and custom integrations can multiply software license fees by many times.

Finally, your ability to recruit designers and architects who are already familiar with a standardized architecture is considerably improved, plus your training and bedding in costs will be much lower because staff are not dealing with a unique, homegrown approach.

Driving towards 'lights out' operations

Improving productivity by reducing manual intervention, cost and errors in routine business processes has consistently been the operational goal of many businesses. Most of the market for business computing has been driven by meeting this need. Process automation and integration, if done correctly, has long been recognized as a highly effective way of improving service to customers while reducing costs. In a digital, and especially an M2M, world the idea of managing countless billions of devices that involves some form of manual intervention is ludicrous from both a cost and practical standpoint.

The established approach to this is usually based on 'hard-wiring' systems together in a chain using complex, customized integration techniques, but this is only really effective when the business model and service products are stable and rarely change. This is not the case and hasn't been for some time: the market is moving fast and the ability to accommodate changes of new or variations of services and new business models, rapidly, has become ever more important. Hard-wired, inflexible systems are an ever bigger obstacle because they require major rewrites of applications and complete re-integration and re-testing exercises, all of which are slow and expensive, and result in major business inflexibility.

To sum up, three main things need to happen to communications providers' operational processes and systems to be competitive in the digital economy:

- **Automation:** driving high levels of process automation using a sophisticated integration technique to provide operational flexibility designed to accommodate change instead of a simple but rigid 'hardwiring' approach.
- **Simplification:** reducing the number of 'moving parts', that is, deploy the minimum number of systems by moving to common systems that support multiple services rather than building a service delivery chain for each individual product or service.
- **Standardization:** fragmentation of processes, information and systems leads to a lack of business agility, higher operating costs and lower customer experience levels. Imagine trying to build a house from different sized and shaped bricks.

Achieving these goals needs strong, clear governance over the processes and systems used end-end in the enterprise. If multiple partners are involved in the delivery of a service, clear guidelines between them are essential, as we established in Chapter 7. At the heart of this governance should be a common architecture to ensure that all parts of the company are on the same page regarding the business models and processes that are to be used to create and deliver services.

It should also enshrine a uniform approach to the structure of information that flows around those processes; a consistent set of business applications that are used to automate the processes and information; and a standard approach to how the whole is glued together. 'Benign dictatorship' is often cited as a good model – centralize the governance then control new investments to ensure that different parts of the company or companies within a group move towards this common goal, accommodating different needs only when they are truly needed.

Fragmentation is a constant problem and good governance isn't something you do once, it has to be ongoing. Systems architecture can suffer from numerous hands tackling bits of it in different ways and at different times. Without strong governance, even the best design becomes a fragmented and costly mess. In a dynamic market, successive mergers, acquisitions and divestitures typically create a mishmash of approaches; while successive management reorganizations and different divisions doing their own thing regarding processes and systems soon generates chaos. Add to all that indifferent top management, which often doesn't look into the engine room and soon you just cannot compete.

In Chapter 10, we discussed the options for moving towards this all-important common architecture on an evolutionary basis if there is enough time or through a hybrid approach of building a new operational platform running alongside the legacy one, initially to carry new services but to be progressively loaded with the older services that have a future. Services that are in the process of becoming obsolete stay on the old systems, which are eventually turned off.

Whether the plan is on a slow, fast or hybrid basis, having a clear target to aim for that covers all aspects of the operational platform is essential. It should cover the process architecture, the information architecture, the systems architecture and systems integration. It must have enough detail to be used as the basis of technology procurement, for outsourcing or using managed services for some operators and as a framework for software development.

Which target?

Developing the common architecture from scratch is a very large task, probably running into hundreds of man years of scarce and expensive highly skilled effort.

An alternative approach is to contract a supplier to provide all of the underpinning process and systems engineering using their own architecture. This would be a viable solution but it has two major flaws. Firstly, you would obviously be locked into and dependent upon that supplier and so unable to take advantage of competitive supply and pricing. Secondly, it's not clear that many suppliers offer a sufficiently broad and fully integrated range of technology and expertise to cover the entire service operations landscape.

I believe that the best option is to follow the industry-agreed standardized architecture for service operations. It's interesting that the first two companies to be liberalized in the 1980s, BT and AT&T, were the companies that founded a specialist organization to focus on building such a set of standards for network and service operations. The organization that John Miller (then at AT&T) and I (then at BT) founded is today the TM Forum, a not-for-profit organization, owned by its members, which now total almost 1,000 companies across 200 countries. They include over 230 service providers whose customers collectively account for 90 percent of the world's communications' end customers and 90 percent of the systems and software used to run those services.

Indeed, one of the biggest attributes of TM Forum and the work produced by its dedicated, expert members is that is helps mitigate risk – no small matter when, as we have discussed, so many transformation programs fail, and badly. As Erik Hoving, Chief Strategy, Innovation & Technology Officer, KPN Group, said to me once: "Service providers never make small mistakes; you measure them in millions of dollars, so anything you can do to minimize them is worth a lot."

Collaboration is the key

The heart of the Forum is the Collaboration Community, which now has more than 50,000 individuals participating. By unlocking the power of 'crowd-sourcing', you are tapping into the wisdom and experience of large numbers of professionals who you would not otherwise have known existed.

There's an old African proverb that says: "If you want to travel fast, go alone, but if you want to travel safely, go with some friends." Transformation to the digital world actually needs both – the market is moving faster than many of the players that supply the market and without speed they'll be left behind. Yet if they screw up their transformation, by doing too much on their own, they'll be left out in the cold.

The Forum strives to provide both. It's true that any time that you need agreement from a lot of people, it takes more time than if you just have yourself to consult. There is no doubt that the *creation* of approaches through collaborative effort is slower than doing your own thing.

On the other hand, a big benefit of collaboration is that the ideas are exposed to many viewpoints and so rigorously road-tested and that, ultimately, makes the ideas better. The really big pay-off comes when you *implement* that idea or standard created, because you really do get both speed and safety – at least the way the Forum has done it – because the creators and other users of the standards are available in a few clicks to help guide and support that implementation.

While in the early days, collaboration was in the shape of face-to-face meetings with paper documents and flip charts, the Community these days runs almost exclusively online, borrowing from social networking tools and techniques such as wikis, blogs and so on to help people communicate. However, there are two Action Weeks – at the moment one in Europe in winter and one in the U.S. in summer – when many Community groups come together to cement progress and plan future activities.

Over a period of time, through the Collaboration Community, the Forum has built up a comprehensive set of industry standards and best practices designed to enable highly effective service operations for all types of online and digital services. They are collectively known as Frameworx – I'll explain what the main elements are, what they do, how they help and how they work together later in this chapter. This is a huge body of work and is available to Forum members free of charge, supported by a wide range of services such as technical and design support, advice, training, career certification, procurement support and advice and a conformance certification program to ensure that commercial products meet the specifications contained within Frameworx.

As I outlined above, using Frameworx as the basis of your target operational approach has some major benefits: following a path which others have already trodden is always lower risk than trying something for the first time, also you can start immediately. Commercial off-the-shelf products conforming to these standards are available in the market, as are growing numbers of trained architects, designers and software engineers who are familiar with them.

The Community provides a fair and legally safe environment for all types of digital service providers, software suppliers and systems integrators to collaborate on resolving pressing industry issues, and define industry standards and best practices. I say 'legally safe' because any time you get companies, often fierce competitors, agreeing anything there is always the potential risk of anti-trust problems arising and increasingly issues such as the licensing of intellectual property, (patents, copyrights and so on) to deal with. So the Forum aims to provide a fair environment where such issues are managed and contained.

Not being locked in to a specific supplier or technology means you can source from the best supplier offering the best deal and the availability of conformance certification and procurement support take cost, risk and time out of the buying process. Finally, as Frameworx is collaboratively developed by the industry in online communities, there are tens of thousands of people around the world who can be drawn on for advice or guidance to help you with implementation, and Frameworx is endlessly extended and refined to meet members' needs.

The Community helps companies of all sizes become part of the process to decide on the standards they should work on together to enable the flexibility and speed they need to underpin future growth. Led by service providers and attracting participation from hundreds of industry suppliers, the Collaboration Community spans numerous industry sectors, including fixed and mobile communications, cable and multi-service operators, cloud service providers, content providers, defense organizations and enterprise users.

Altogether, the advantages of industry collaboration become very substantial compared to the time, cost and risk of doing it yourself and having to customize all of your systems. The Community is also supported by a comprehensive document library, program management, source code management, scheduling and so on, plus dedicated support by the Forum's highly qualified professionals to help with program management.

Another unique aspect of the Forum's collaborative approach is the Catalyst program. It is TM Forum's rapid prototyping environment where suppliers and systems integrators work together for between three and six months to create solutions for critical industry operational and systems challenges. The great advantage is that these projects accelerate development and validate the Forum's standards and best practices. They culminate in live demonstrations at the twice-yearly TM Forum *Management World* events.

Each Catalyst project draws on Forum standards, expands those standards or explores new areas for standardization, working to enable more rapid implementation of solution to improve effectiveness and efficiency. The findings of each Catalyst project are contributed to the Forum's Collaboration Community as extensions to existing best practices and standards, or as the groundwork to launch new Collaboration projects. The results are often translated into commercially valuable products.

Frameworx – developed by industry for industry
Frameworx is the only standardized service creation and operations blueprint for digital services and has gained considerable traction in communications, cable, cloud services and government and defense markets. It focuses on those generic business functions that any type of digital service will require, such as service creation, authentication and security, service level monitoring, order management, problem management and charging and settlements. It includes revenue assurance, enterprise risk and fraud management.

Frameworx provides a common, service oriented process framework, which was originally conceived for communications services, but its application is much wider because very few processes are specific to communications providers: most are generic business functions like order management processes, problem management processes, billing and payment processes and so on that are applicable to any digital service provider.

Figure 29 – Services are like Lego™ bricks

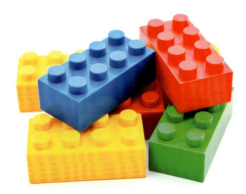

Service oriented Lego™ bricks
As I've said a number of times, the digital world is moving towards an ecosystem of cloud-based service partners. While each may provide a capability in its own right, by combining the individual service components from multiple providers together, and provided they meet some basic standards, the combinations can be used to create an almost infinite number of solutions to meet individual or enterprise needs.

The technology approach that allows the delivery of capabilities as a set of services has dominated software design in recent years and is known as a Service Oriented Architecture or SOA for short. It's a way to design systems that builds in flexibility or, put another way, it is a set of principles and methodologies for designing and developing software in the form of interoperable services. These services are well-defined business functions that are built as reusable software components. The simplest way to imagine these components is like Lego™ bricks that have a standard way of plugging together, but can be used in a multitude of different ways and come in a variety of shapes and sizes.

In reality, the elements in an SOA are a lot smarter than Lego bricks because they contain intelligence that allows other SOA services to recognize the capabilities that each offers. They can negotiate with each other. For example, different providers may collaborate in the ecosystem to provide services to a customer but they use different technology to implement them. In the past this would have demanded a complicated integration between the systems, usually on a 'hard-wired' and inflexible basis.

If both use an SOA-based approach at the points of touch between the systems, they can expose information to each other across a well-understood and well-defined interface to access them. This greatly increases agility and markedly reduces integration costs.

For the non-technologists among you, SOA terminology does sometimes get confusing when used in the context of digital service providers. They use similar terms but with somewhat different meanings: SOA defines reusable functions as *services* (*or business services*) and the application that exposes this capability as a *service provider.* Other terms such as *broker* – a piece of software that brings an application and a service together – are similarly confusing when used by non-technical people trying to understand how to automate business processes.

The systems within a digital service provider are very rarely built on exactly the same technologies. The problem is much greater when integrating between service providers and across widely disparate applications in web-based or cloud-based environments, implemented on multiple platforms. SOA is therefore an ideal approach for use as the 'glue' between processes and systems, both inside and between service providers in the ecosystem, since the interface is described in terms of protocols and functionality, not a fixed technology.

Frameworx is built on a service-oriented design and uses standard, reusable, generic blocks that can be assembled in unique ways to gain the advantages of standardization while still allowing customization and enabling differentiation and competition at the service level. This is very important since different service providers may wish to compete on different aspects of their business.

Standardization should not get in the way of differentiation but, as I've said, you don't have to customize everything to be different. In particular, differentiation should not be achieved through customizing software (and incurring big additional lifetime costs) but through configuration of standardized software packages. The rule is to only be different where being different produces tangible benefits. In most cases, being different on the basics just produces more cost; things take longer and you can't benefit from enhancements made by others.

Frameworx platforms – a strategic concept in managing IT evolution

IT development is typically focused around specific projects and often constrained by needs of particular parts of the business. This usually ends up creating a complex, fragmented and ineffective architecture. This significantly increases IT costs and compromises the effectiveness of the end-to-end business processes that run across those systems.

While an SOA offers the vision of a well-structured, lean and agile approach efficiently supporting the business, getting there in evolutionary steps is a complex, multi-year program. I described the problem of system by system evolution in Chapter 10 and a good way of visualizing the problem is like picking up a slice of pizza with lots of stringy bits of cheese still connecting the slice to the pizza: each string represents an interface to another system.

Some of these interfaces will be well understood and documented, knowledge of others may reside only in the organizational memory and are generally the cause of serious cost and delay for each round of development and systems integration testing.

A simplified architecture minimizes the impact of changes like this and Service Oriented Architectures provide a mechanism to do this called *Domains*. This concept is fully supported within Frameworx (but termed a *Platform*, as the Domain term previously in use within the Frameworx Information Framework).

In simple terms a platform is a 'black box' into which you put all your systems, processes and people who perform a specific business function. For example, customer management functions and systems could be such a platform. The platform allows all the complexity of customer management to be 'hidden' from the rest of the business by simply defining a set of services that the platform offers to other systems. These services (called Business Services in Frameworx and described more fully later in this chapter), define the functions performed by the platform, the service level agreements underpinning them and also organizational policy constraints.

A digital service provider can use the platform concept to aggregate its existing systems into a defined set of platforms based on its current business model. As it evolves, it would typically look first at what Business Services are required to support its new business model and how they should be combined into new platform definitions. This method provides clear baseline and target architectures, which are the basis of IT transformation planning.

As each company's transformation journey is likely to start and end at different places, it's not possible to tightly standardize platform definitions into a 'one size fits all' approach, so Frameworx defines a reference set of 15 platforms and associated Business Services as a starting point for developing a Frameworx-based SOA.

This seemingly simple concept has two profound implications. First, the focal point becomes the touch points, or Business Services, between platforms, so consolidates many functions into a platform view. This dramatically reduces the number of 'bits of stringy cheese' interfaces and also allows those services to be rapidly connected together to create new end-to-end business processes as business needs change.

The second big benefit is that since these processes may run across separate providers, a platform (being a self-contained 'black box') can be placed anywhere in the service ecosystem. This is a big help in facilitating business decisions over using partners to provide specific capabilities as required to support changing business goals.

Later in this chapter I'll talk about this area of standardized 'trading interfaces' between ecosystem partners being a major growth area for Frameworx.

Frameworx in more detail

The Frameworx suite consists of four major components (shown in Figure 30, overleaf) plus a large number of supporting services to aid understanding and implementation. The four major component frameworks are:

- *The Business Process Framework (sometimes known by its former name eTOM)* – a comprehensive standardized process architecture for both business and functional processes.
- *The Information Framework (sometimes known by its former name SID)* – a common reference model for enterprise information that digital service providers, software providers, and integrators use to describe management information.
- *The Application Framework (sometimes known by its former name TAM)* – which provides a common language between digital service providers and their suppliers to describe systems and their functions, as well as a common way of grouping them.
- *The Integration Framework* – which delivers a service oriented integration approach with standardized interfaces and support tools.

Although the four frameworks can be used independently, the real power comes when they are used together. This is very important in achieving high levels of automation of business processes while maximizing agility and supporting changes:

- a clear 'map' of the business processes being automated (the Business Process Framework);
- a common way of describing information implemented on all systems so that information can be utilized seamlessly between the systems (the Information Framework);
- a well understood set of the functions provided by the business systems that handle those transactions (the Application Framework);
- an integration approach that allows for simple and flexible interconnection (through the Integration Framework).

Figure 30 – Frameworx

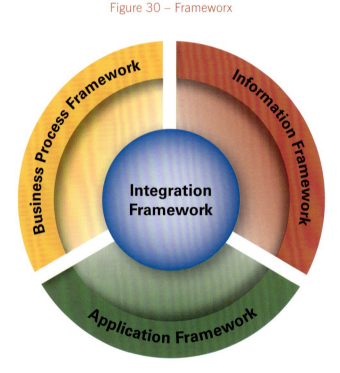

The Business Process Framework

The Business Process Framework is the heart of Frameworx because without a clear and comprehensive view of the end-end business processes running either inside a service provider or between them in an ecosystem, it's simply not possible to drive towards maximizing business effectiveness – in other words achieving high levels of business agility and a great customer experience with the least possible operating cost. A consistent view across an entire process chain – which increasingly spans multiple companies, is critical to prospering in the digital services market. Unfortunately, many large organizations often only have a high-level, limited view of this and cannot drill down to the detail that really matters.

The Business Process Framework is an industry-agreed, comprehensive and multi-layered view of all of the key business processes that a digital service provider needs to run their business. It provides a guide to best practice and as a target process template for use either within or between service providers in the ecosystem. It's supported by a range of off-the-shelf tools and comes in machine readable as well as document-based formats.

In addition, as digital services become ever more software centric, the core service creation and delivery processes need to be well integrated with IT management processes, so thanks to close collaboration between TM Forum and another organization, the itSMF, the Business Process Framework and the major IT process standard called ITIL can be used in close combination. The Business Process Framework simplifies and assures consistent, enterprise-wide ITIL implementation by providing an out-of-the-box business set of processes and flows.

Frameworx is also aligned with the architectural standards of yet another body called The Open Group, whose TOGAF[145] architectural framework is widely adopted. This means it is able to deliver business agility through component re-use, essential in today's fast changing market.

The Information Framework

Just as it's difficult to develop highly effective processes without a clear 'map' of how they work and interact, it's also impossible to automate business processes and get the right information to the right people or system at the right time without consistent use of data right across the enterprise. Without a common information approach, information is locked up into isolated islands of data making it very difficult to get a comprehensive view of what is happening. This hampers customer self-service, holds up marketing and product management activities, and damages the customer's experience.

It also makes the organization rigid because any change means major re-engineering of information flows. With a common data approach, the organization can be much more agile and able to cope with rapid change; information is available to the right people at the right time and in the right format. In comparison, piecemeal integrations between dissimilar systems usually results in the lowest common denominator level of information.

The Information Framework provides a solution to this – a definition for information that flows throughout the enterprise and between business partners. Supported by off-the-shelf tools and published in machine readable formats, the Information Framework provides a common information model that reduces complexity and allows the definition of standardized integration points. There is a strong link between this Framework and its sister Business Process Framework. It describes the types of information present in a service provider's business and is particularly useful for bridging between players in the ecosystem.

---

[145]TOGAF is a detailed method and set of supporting resources for developing an Enterprise Architecture and is developed and endorsed by the membership of The Open Group

Information is usually transferred between various systems and applications using a technology called an enterprise data bus. Although it is tempting to think that a common data bus is all that is needed to share information between systems, this is a bit like saying all you need for the whole world to communicate is a telephone system. What happens when one person is speaking in Mandarin and the other in Swahili? You need some form of translation.

Many data buses do this well but even if the language can be translated, the *meaning* of what is being said may not work. There's an old saying that even if a lion could speak you would still not understand what he was saying because his view of the world would be so different to yours. Imagine a quantum physicist and a musician trying to have a conversation about their relative expertise where they both use the same words but mean entirely different things by them.

So to share information between applications along an automated process chain (which while pretty smart are still a lot more stupid than physicists and musicians), you need a telephone system (the communication bus), a translator (protocol mediation) and common ground for understanding of information to be meaningful. This latter function is the key value that the Information Framework provides.

So the Information Framework provides the next important piece of the puzzle to get high levels of automation of business processes through tight but flexible integration between systems.

The Application Framework
There are typically hundreds (or even thousands) of software applications and IT systems required to run a digital service provider's business. Historically, the communications service providers who pioneered automation of service delivery, custom-built these systems themselves (or had software custom-built for them) and usually ended up with a wide variety of systems with no common definition of functions or even terminology. As the market started to move towards standardized and commercial off-the-shelf systems, the lack of any common framework for defining the functions and definitions of common systems led to time-consuming and often confusing discussions between users and suppliers.

Before this framework was developed, I was working as a consultant to both communications service providers and suppliers and after sitting through too many interminable discussions about how a provider's systems did what they did (they all do much the same thing but you would never have known it because they packaged the functions in many different ways and called them all different names), I developed my own systems framework giving a 'baseline' definition of typical operational systems and clustering systems logically using the ITU hierarchical model called TMN, which I also had a strong involvement in developing.

This became the basis of a document called the Telecom Applications Map (or *TAM* by which it is still sometimes referred) and has evolved with a lot of help from many people and companies into the current Application Framework. This provides a standard classification structure for operational applications and it has been widely adopted as the lingua franca of the operations systems world. A common approach and definition means that systems procurement is much more straightforward as both buyers and sellers can actually communicate using the same classification approach and terminology.

So the Application Framework provides a way of grouping process functions and associated information into recognizable applications. It provides a common language and identification system between buyer and supplier for all application areas.

The Integration Framework

The Integration Framework defines how the processes and information behind these systems can be automated by defining standardized SOA-based interfaces called *Business Services*. These are specifications for pieces of functionality useful in the design and implementation of complex software. Software developers implement Business Services and make those services available through any popular software technology (examples include Corba, Java, XML and Web Services) and increasingly via cloud services.

The Integration Framework aims to include:

- A library of Business Services and interfaces.
- Service Oriented Enterprise development guidance and guidelines for the development of additional Business Services.
- Software tools that speed up the production of standard interfaces along with reference implementations and conformance testing capability.

All of the main Frameworks have direct links to each other and the Integration Framework uses these to produce SOA Business Services, which are its mainstay. To recap, a Business Service is a standard package of reusable capability that carries out some part of a business process using a software application. In effect it 'hides' the underlying complexity of implementation aspects of a system by exposing the information that another system may need to use in a common format. A Business Service may represent a capability either at a high level (for example a business transaction between two corporations), at a low level (the functionality supported by a particular aspect of a software program) or anywhere in between.

The Integration Framework provides a template against which new Business Services can be created. The Business Service specification is a detailed definition of what the Business Service provides and which can be implemented as a real piece of software, created using a standard toolset, programming language and so on.

Figure 31 – Frameworx Business Services

Standard SOA Business Services and interfaces expose application functions with standardized process and information:

- Multiple implementations can be 'hidden' behind a common standard.
- Systems can be upgraded, removed or replaced much more easily.
- Multiple sourcing from suppliers.
- Function can be transparently and flexibly in-source or outsourced.

Process

Frameworx
Business
Service

Information

Technology

People

In the past, interfaces were developed in isolation and tended to incorporate fixed ideas about the information model and business process it was serving. Like many other standards organizations, the Forum has developed a number of these types of interface. They can be very valuable, but have the disadvantage of often being restrictive when it comes to incorporating features and functions outside the scope of the standard. There may be many reasons why these extensions are needed – specific legislation or work practices within the service provider or exposure of special features from a supplier's technology or system.

The Integration Framework aims to overcome this lack of extensibility by linking the other Frameworks; it uses software tooling that can directly generate interface software code. This is known as a *model-driven approach* and while it is still in its early stages it is already showing that such tools can radically reduce the time taken to develop new interfaces and improve their quality as they generate documentation and test kits at the same time as producing the interface.

Frameworx implementation support
As you can tell from the descriptions above, Frameworx is a comprehensive and rich set of standards and guidelines, so inevitably they are complex. This is why the Forum provides a lot of support services to help companies implement them, shown in Figure 32 and followed by a brief description of each of the support services.

Frameworx Guide Books, industry best practices and case studies – The online *Frameworx Document Library* contains a comprehensive set of guidebooks, best practices and case studies from service providers around the world, providing a 'how to' reference guide to implementing Frameworx. The guidebooks cover each of the component Frameworks in detail, and extend into important areas such as Revenue Management and Service Level Agreement (SLA)

Management. Of particular interest to implementers should be the *TM Forum Case Study Handbook,* published annually, which is packed with success stories from companies around the world who have implemented Frameworx and/or exploited the Forum's other collateral and activities and successfully applied it to a range of business issues.

Figure 32 – Frameworx implementation support services

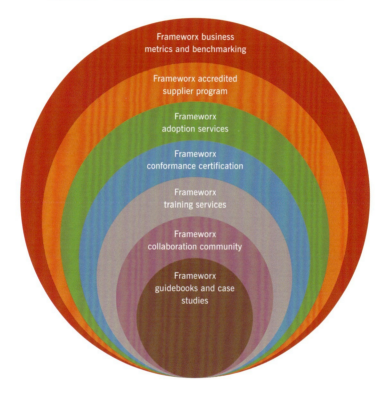

Frameworx online community and help desks – The Collaboration Community provides a sophisticated online set of collaborative workspaces, wikis, blogs, document management and so on for over 50,000 industry professionals from around the globe, who share their experiences and expertise in using Frameworx for a wide variety of business projects. Members can communicate directly with industry colleagues and work with Forum experts and support staff.

Frameworx Training and Certification – This is a comprehensive, worldwide training and certification program to help people understand how to use Frameworx and become certified in that expertise. There are now thousands of certified individuals around the world and the certification program enables technical staff to demonstrate their knowledge of Frameworx, enhancing their career prospects and providing a growing worldwide pool of expertise.

There are several types of training, ranging from Executive Transformation Courses to Technical Training and Certification, and Best Practice Courses. The Forum arranges closed sessions for a specific company at its premises, organizes open enrolment courses around the world and increasingly the courses are available online. Attendees learn how to implement and fully utilize Frameworx standards and best practices and students can also obtain Knowledge and Career Certification, giving further validation to their experience and knowledge.

Frameworx Conformance Certification – These conformance assessments enable suppliers and service providers to independently verify a product or solution's conformance to the Frameworx Business Process and Information Frameworks through an independent and thorough analysis of a supplier's self-assessment. The Forum's assessors score adherence to each Framework on a sliding scale and then publish an online report detailing the product or solution's level of conformance.

Solutions that meet the conformance assessment standards are awarded a TM Forum Certified Conformance Mark that can be used to publicize a solution's conformance to Frameworx. In addition, conformant products and solutions and their assessment scores are publicized on TM Forum's web site.

Conformance certification is sometimes viewed by suppliers as an overhead, but in fact it can substantially reduce the cost and time taken to respond to requests for proposal by providing a standard, industry-agreed assessment of conformance. If the Frameworx Procurement Templates (which fully align with the conformance certification reports) are used by the buyer as the basis of their request for proposal, it's much easier to understand customer requirements because they provide a clear mapping of product features to service provider's business needs.

This significantly simplifies what is usually a complex and expensive process of the supplier understanding the customer's requirements and the customer understanding what the supplier has for sale. Suppliers only have to undergo conformance certification once per software release and the results can be leveraged in multiple bids, considerably reducing sales costs.

Conformance certification also reduces the risks associated with complex integration projects by providing the detailed information required to develop an integration roadmap. It can simplify the complexity of integrating products acquired through merger and acquisition activity – from both a technical and product portfolio perspective.

Finally, conformance certification also covers systems that implement the Business Metrics Automation program, by which systems suppliers make available Frameworx business metrics in a common and easily available format.

Frameworx Implementation Certification – this support service is for service providers who want to verify how their current or planned internal business processes and information architecture meet Frameworx standards. It is a version of the conformance assessment program specially tailored to this need and provides an independent assessment to validate and improve the efficiency of their organization, comparing adherence to the Frameworx Business Process and Information Framework standards on a sliding scale. Implementations that meet the rigorous certification standards are awarded the TM Forum Frameworx Conformance Mark.

Combined with TM Forum Benchmarking, these *Implementation Conformance Assessments* provide a clear view of how enterprise-wide operations compare to industry leaders, and where to direct future investment for maximum effect. Having your own operational architecture certified for conformance also helps reduce circular arguments with suppliers who may try to convince the buyer that an expensive custom approach is necessary.

Frameworx Advisory Services – Frameworx Advisory Services are custom programs offering practical advice on implementation of Frameworx, and Business Benchmarking for specific projects. These short-term engagements ensure that members can rapidly gain the advantages offered by Frameworx in any transformation program.

Frameworx Supplier Accreditation – This is a new program being introduced by the Forum and is based around the trained people and the competencies in Frameworx that a supplier has attained. In some ways it is analogous to product conformance certification in that it provides a way for the buyer to gain some independent verification that a systems integrator or solution supplier is actually competent in Frameworx-based design and deployment.

Accreditation is based on the number and type of developers and software engineers that have completed and passed certification examinations in various aspects and levels of Frameworx.

Frameworx Business Benchmarking – As I outlined in Chapter 12, successful transformation requires a good basis of decision-support information to measure both the current performance of the business (particularly to spot areas that are under-performing and need attention most urgently) and also to measure the improvement once changes have been made. Knowing how the provider's key operational areas compare to peers and comparators in industry can be a vitally important guide to transformation investment.

It's easy to get lost in key performance indicators (KPIs) and benchmarks. While detailed KPIs are usually necessary to help pinpoint bottlenecks and 'hotspots' in a process, too many metrics at the outset of a process transformation program will result in a position known where I come from as 'not being able to see the wood for the trees', that is, blinded by too much detail. If senior executives are to drive a program of change, they must be able to clearly see where the initial problems are and where the low hanging fruit of 'quick wins' might be.

TM Forum's Business Metrics and Benchmarking Program provides high quality, objective, standard business performance data to support optimizing operations and business transformation and is an ideal approach for any service provider embarking on either an incremental or radical transformation program. Unrivalled in its detail, scale, the program is free of charge to participating service provider members of the Forum.

Developed by service providers, for service providers and used by more than 170 service providers from over 65 countries, the Business Metrics and Benchmarking Program defines and gathers quantitative metrics ranging from tactical to business performance data and conducts qualitative surveys on topics of service provider interest. As the metrics are industry standard, they allows cross-industry comparison year-on-year, enabling the plotting of trends in order to make informed business decisions. The key value of adopting a Forum-based approach is that TM Forum Business Metrics are mapped to Frameworx (specifically the Business Process Framework) and provide a way to measure success based on an holistic, balanced scorecard.

The Forum's Business Benchmarking program focuses on a relatively small number of business and customer-focused metrics to form a balanced scorecard and, in particular, it concentrates on those operational processes that most impact revenue, cost and customer experience. It has now developed a maturity model to help digital service providers understand where they stand in comparison to other industry players. Service providers contribute data anonymously into the Forum's secure database and receive personalized reports and assessments of performance against other participants.

To simplify collecting metrics data, a number of service providers and their suppliers have collaborated to automate the collection of benchmarking information. TM Forum's Business Metrics Automation program works with software suppliers and consultants to incorporate TM Forum's standardized Business Metrics into products and solutions, allowing service providers to automatically upload metric data into the TM Forum Business Benchmark Database rather than collating and entering that data manually. This ensures consistent, accurate and apples-to-apples comparisons for both benchmarking studies and internal dashboards by procuring products with TM Forum Business Metrics built in.

Business Intelligence and other original research reports – The Forum has its own industry research and publications arm that produces regular *Insights Research* reports providing impartial intelligence, analysis and advice on the opportunities and challenges for the digital services market. They are all free to everyone within member companies, and available online: the larger ones are also available in print and distributed at our events throughout the year.

The Forum also publishes the *Business IQ* publication twice a year, which has become an essential, practical guide to business transformation for service providers. Each one provides analysis and business intelligence drawn from the Forum's Business Benchmarking program, often in conjunction with commercial industry analysis firms. It includes a mix of case studies, best practice in action, comparisons of progress with other industries, and expert opinion.

The reports are available for purchase by non-members and each includes information about relevant TM Forum activities and standards, including information about how to get involved.

An open digital ecosystem needs open standards – Frameworx evolution

Frameworx has a good pedigree: its origins are in the communications industry that pioneered virtual or cloud-based service concepts where you don't need to know or care what is inside a service – you just need to know what it can do for you, how much it costs and how to drive it, not how it works. But some people *do* need to look inside the cloud and see how it all works because they have the responsibility to deliver high-quality services, at low cost, that work first time, every time and can be changed simply and easily – Frameworx was designed and evolved by such people.

As the digital world advances, the number and types of service and service provider are 'mushrooming' and in order for them to work together in an open ecosystem, each needs to work with the other and that means having standards. Many of these standards exist already and the basic connectivity and interoperability standards such as IP and HTML5 are key building blocks. Frameworx focuses on *operational* standards that are the basics of any business: without them operating costs, agility and the customer experience are negatively affected. This is because of the problems of negotiating and integrating multiple component services that exists in the ecosystem to deliver a service to users at the right time, right price, right quality and at a cost point where everyone in the ecosystem can make a healthy margin.

For example, without some common, inter-provider standards for operational issues, how would you automate routine operational issues such as order handling and problem resolution across the ecosystem? How would you manage contractually-binding service level agreements when multiple players are involved if they all measure different things? How would you manage charging and settlements so that everyone in the ecosystem gets what they are owed and that can be properly audited and checked? How would you ensure that you are billing for everything at the right rate, how would you manage the product lifecycle from new product concept to eventual withdrawal across an ecosystem? How would you tackle risk management and fraud? How would you handle authentication, security and so on?

All types of digital services need agile, low-cost operations and all need to be able to work together if their services are going to be capable of being 'mashed' or federated together into overall solutions without a lot of cost, pain and grief.

If Frameworx didn't exist, the digital world would have to invent it as soon as the operational problems reached critical mass and people were losing money. Fortunately, a lot of what is needed is already addressed by Frameworx, but many emergent players don't yet fully realize either the extent of operational problems they will have or how to solve them, especially in consumer markets where many applications are free and if there are problems, customers are forgiving. As the digital world evolves and more and more enterprises use it to run their business, the sophistication and expectations of its users will rise. If we want to see the emergence of an open digital economy with true any-to-any-to-any flexibility and freedom, we will absolutely need that common set of inter-provider trading standards.

The alternative is to see a set of closed worlds emerge where one dominant player sets the standards, decides the rules and who's in and who's not in that closed world. As I said in Chapter 2, there are already thousands of proprietary interfaces in the digital world and multiplying at several a day (they rose from 4,000 in October 2011 to 5,000 and rising in the space of five months).

We've already seen fun and games where Apple has sought to exclude some Google services from iTunes – that's not a healthy, open ecosystem and as the world gets dependent on digital services, only an open market model will allow customers maximum freedom of choice and drive prices down to the lowest level. Open markets work – despite economic woes in some parts of the world, we are all immensely richer for having seen barriers to trade fall in recent decades and we must not let new proprietary barriers be erected to open trading in the digital world by anyone, especially by individual corporations. So we need to ensure that the digital world is based on an open digital economy, not a series of proprietary worlds dominated by a few big players.

Frameworx has evolved to underpin the world's largest communications businesses, who internally have faced and will continue to grapple with many of the same challenges that the digital world is rapidly heading towards. The digital world will involve an ever greater level of complexity, and to address this, Frameworx is already evolving to fully support the digital ecosystem but needs to go further – here are some of the areas of evolution that Frameworx needs to address:

Become service agnostic. While Frameworx supports many of the operational functions of any digital service provider, it was developed from a communications standpoint using that industry's terminology, concepts and examples. That can be off-putting to many developers and providers who come from a different background and may not see the relevance if it is couched in traditional communications industry language rather than service agnostic terminology. So one dimension where Frameworx is evolving is to become more generic and service agnostic.

More out-of-the-box tools. Today, Frameworx gives a great, in-depth set of tools and support to cope with legacy integration and evolution of the operational base, but as I've said repeatedly, the digital economy is moving so fast that much more rapid implementation approaches need to be applied. Frameworx has some good 'out of the box' tools and designs for rapid start-up or transformational change, and these must evolve much further, particularly in the Integration Framework and library of business services/interfaces and to expand the concept of TM Forum's Quick Start packs, which help users apply Frameworx to specific business issues.

Increased service aggregation support. As well as delivering a blueprint for operations *inside* a service provider, as I said above, Frameworx is needed to fully address the growing need for standardization and process automation *between* providers and underpin the service aggregation thrusts of many providers. So we need to see a rapid evolution of appropriate standards for integrating and managing sets of different types of digital services, which can be managed in a common way as well on-boarding new services into service catalogs used to store the appropriate high level detail of services, often sourced from third parties. This business-to-business need is growing rapidly to be the 'oil on the wheels' of the digital economy that takes out friction at the points of touch for business operations issues.

I call these *'trading interfaces'* because that's what they are – they enable business operations between players and by this I mean the operational interfaces that enable the whole service lifecycle end-to-end, such as embracing new customers, service level monitoring and problem resolution. Trading interfaces also facilitate service lifecycle management information to allow on-boarding of new services by another provider, including service descriptions and automated catalog management. This includes: charging, billing and settlements management; fraud, authentication and security standards; order management; customer relationship management; and so on.

Unless highly automated, these types of issues will severely hamper the development of an open digital economy because the costs of handling operational issues – like solving a customer service issue where multiple players are involved – is high. In addition, the customer experience of being passed from provider to provider (or more likely ignored by them) is horrible.

An important step in achieving this is the recently added Frameworx *Service Management Interface,* which provides the capability for provisioning, performance measures, service assurance reports and usage measurement for charging for any 'black box' digital service, even when the components of that service are spread through the ecosystem.

This interface greatly simplifies the operational headaches and costs of a service aggregator because it allows you to know what the service can do, what it costs, how to drive it and so on without needing to know the details of how the service actually works. Any digital service and any operational management system that has implemented the *Service Management Interface* can carry out these fundamental management functions. This will have a big impact on driving an open ecosystem for digital services and will no doubt grow in sophistication in subsequent releases.

This is positive, but digital service providers must get behind Frameworx and drive its evolution aggressively to expand its Integration Framework and provide an expanded and comprehensive set of inter-provider (SOA-based) standardized trading interfaces covering the whole lifecycle as I described above.

In addition, Frameworx is adapting to changing business models as well, which have interesting characteristics such as very short life-cycles and may need to be launched in hours and have a life of only a few days. Similarly, the ecosystem is not a static value chain and gets very dynamic in an *'any service, any place, any time'* world, where the head and tail of the chain might flip continually and need to be thought of much more as a matrix. A good example of this type of service is defined by the UltraViolet Alliance[146] – this takes a 'TV anywhere' approach that lets you view content on many types of device (smart TV, phone, tablet and so on) and through many types of service provider. Knowledge of your content purchases is held in a digital locker, so issues such as authentication, security and fraud management become much more important in an open ecosystem than if the data is being passed around inside a single provider. A newer program, based on UltraViolet, is Project Phenix, a project aiming to give consumers an easier and faster way to organize, store and share their digital content.

M2M support. If we thought that managing services that are used by human beings requires very low costs of operation and high levels of automation, then we 'ain't seen nothing yet' as the M2M world explodes. With billions or even trillions of low-cost connected devices and operational service revenues a mere fraction of those for supporting services on smartphones and tablets, operational issues will have to be ultra-standardized, ultra-slick and ultra-low cost. I'm not talking about huge sophistication, but the basics of setting up the device, authenticating it, seeing it is working properly, resetting it if it isn't, and extracting performance or charging data from it. Factors like these offer zero competitive advantage if done differently between supplier – it just adds costs and headaches for the provider of the service.

The deployment of connected devices in bulk presents another problem that needs to be managed. For example, take an automobile manufacturer using connected M2M devices to provide a vehicle monitoring service, which wants to source them, in bulk, to be fitted in cars at different plants around the world. It could be monitored by different M2M service providers – whether outsourced to a specialist or through their vehicle dealership networks.

The devices could end up anywhere in the world and be used in conjunction with a variety of

---

[146]www.uvvu.com/what-is-uv.php

digital services from a variety of suppliers. In this many-to-many-to-many scenario, customizing support because of a lack of operational standards will quickly become too expensive for the manufacturer, the service provider and ultimately the user. Standardization is the only way to resolve it – I don't mean standardize what the *service* does – simply how the service and the device are operated.

While early M2M deployments were able to withstand the cost proprietary approaches, as volumes build and devices get smaller and cheaper, standardization not just at the connectivity level but at the operational level as well will become essential.

Frameworx evolution. So the main thrust of where I expect to see Frameworx evolve is to simplify service operations within the digital ecosystem by providing operational standards (obviously in conjunction with many other standards groups as today), particularly at the points of touch *between* services and *between* services and connected devices. Figure 33 shows this graphically.

Figure 33 – Frameworx evolution

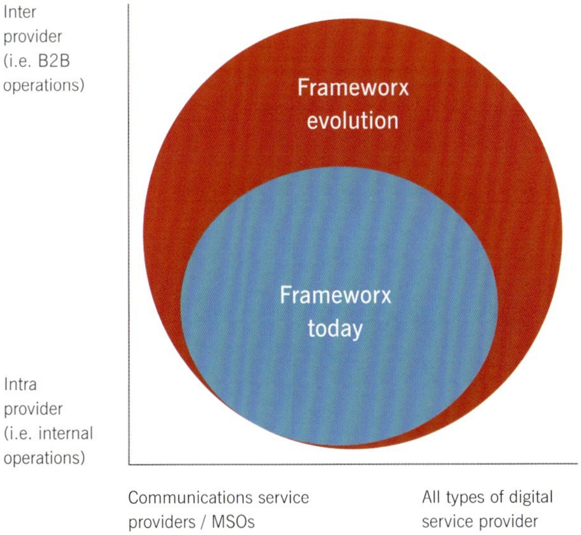

It's important to remember Frameworx isn't developed by a bunch of gurus sitting in a darkened room somewhere. It's driven and expanded by the people who need and use those standards: business people, architects, designers and developers across an increasingly wide set of industry sectors. The governance model, intellectual property rights procedures, access and collaboration model used to develop and enhance Frameworx will continue to expand with its user base.

The introduction of new ways of collaborating and an expansion of industry segments involved in Frameworx evolution means we've seen the number and type of person and company grow enormously in recent years. For example, the defense, enterprise and cable sectors, which initially were *users* of Frameworx, have now become significant *contributors* to its ongoing development, governance and evolution. To address the management complexity digital services bring, service providers of all kinds need to embrace the successful multi-industry collaboration Frameworx has been born out of and must remain appropriately open.

So in summary, Frameworx offers a rich set of standards designed for delivering a low-cost, highly agile service and customer operations. Born in the communications industry, it's moved a long way towards cloud and other virtual digital services and must accelerate this movement and grow its capabilities to help enable the evolution of a fully open digital ecosystem.

That's essential if we are to avoid seeing the digital world fragment into a series of closed ecosystems dancing to the tune of a few dominant players or perhaps worse, the whole digital economy gumming up with unacceptable operating costs. That will happen if every service provider takes their own approach and creates high trading 'friction' levels that lead to massive operational overheads and costs, poor agility and low levels of customer service. That would be a major failing on all of our parts.

15

...AND FINALLY

The problem with most management books is that they have about 10 pages of good ideas but another couple of hundred of padding, so you tend to browse through them rather than actually reading it cover to cover as you would a novel. I wanted to write a book that was genuinely useful and helpful and hopefully I've packed in a bit more useful information than that. If you've arrived at this chapter by having read your way through the whole thing, well done – I hope it's been worthwhile.

This wasn't quite the tome that I originally set out to write. I intended to write a book about how to manage successful transformations but it became more and more obvious in writing it that many people weren't too clear on the *why* and *when* aspects of such change. Several things began to come into clearer focus the more I talked, read and thought about the future and at the end of researching and writing this on and off over the past year, I feel like I've had a bit of a revelation (for those that don't know me, that's called English under-statement!), which wasn't exactly what I was expecting.

Whether it was happening anyway or I just began to see it more clearly, I do think we are at or near to a tipping point between the world of computing and communications that we've understood for a long time and a new digital world where the biggest change isn't so much the technology, it's the rules of the game. These are changing very fast and much faster than many people have appreciated – complacency is still pretty widespread. So the book has become more of a rallying cry and a call that radical action is needed and soon. Big, existing industries like communications are like a giant tanker, they can't turn quickly, so the sooner they start to appreciate the degree of turn, the more chance they have in ending up where they want to be before being overtaken by events.

That led me to think a lot more about what is needed to avoid the problems and capitalize on the opportunities of the digital world – not just the mechanical, programmatic issues that I had been intending to write about but more of the soft underbelly of change – the need for leadership, new competencies, great communication and speed. Sure, you need good processes, architectures and physical stuff but when you are entering a new world, if you don't have the right leadership, vision and core competencies, all of the program governance in the universe isn't going to help you succeed.

So my second revelation was to try to rescue the word *transformation* from its devaluation by a thousand marketing brochures to once again mean tangible, radical change rather than a fancy word for business-as-usual incremental change. *Transformation* to the digital economy isn't a small incremental nudge on the tiller, it's fundamental and very far reaching and needs to be undertaken now if the field isn't to be littered with casualties. The scale and scope of the digital world outlined in the first four chapters of this book are immense and difficult to grasp because they are unprecedented – a bit like trying to imagine light years. It has mind-boggling economic, social, demographic, political and technological implications.

The third revelation was just how inspirational some of the new players in the digital market really are. I've never been one to swoon at this month's darling of Wall Street but it's hard to deny the outstanding success of any company that has gone from having 60 days' cash left in the bank to become the world's most valuable company in just under a decade. The 'old' world has much to learn from new entrants – they haven't just been a bunch of kids who got lucky – they are reinventing the world and can teach us a lot. The world is changing – we are changing it and it is changing us. We need to move it and move with it. The challenges involved in doing that are huge too, but necessity has always been the mother of invention, and our industry has never lacked ingenuity and adaptability.

When talking about threats, it's of course easy to forget just how huge, profitable, strong and tenacious the communications industry is – it accounts for some 3 percent of global GDP and has been around for well over 100 years. Such size and stability are very comforting but I think that apparent safety is illusory. It's similar to people camping and feeling safe and secure in a tent when it's just wafer thin material separating them and the elements outside. It's the same with markets – the comfort level of history and the distance between success and failure is wafer thin: even the biggest and most powerful can be brought back to earth with a terrific bump if they are not constantly vigilant and innovative. Put another way, if you aren't scared, you don't understand the situation.

As I've stressed throughout, the digital world provides plenty of opportunities and threats to *every* business sector, although my focus has largely been on the computing and communications industries I've spent my working life in – which also happen to be some of the main pillars of the digital economy. As I said at the beginning, it's deeply ironic that these industries, which gave birth to and sustain the digital world, appear to be amongst the most vulnerable to it.

There is still time to accomplish much and retain a sustainably profitable business in whichever stratum or strata of the digital world you want to play in. But the five core competencies outlined in chapters 6 to 9 are not optional, so start putting them in place as soon as you can, then look at the various methodologies and routes examined in the remaining chapters and figure out which are useful to you and which to discard – they are plenty of others too, of course, and I hope the examples given have inspired you to seek them out and try them for size.

Writing this book has also helped shape ideas about the next stage of evolution of the Forum and its role in the digital world. It's been through a number of reincarnations in the two and a bit decades from the original organization we set up, but it has continuously grown because it has stayed continuously relevant. Now, through the collaborative efforts, dedication and resourcefulness of nearly 1,000 member companies in 200 countries, we need to focus on how we can facilitate emergence of a fully open digital economy and foster partnerships and innovation that enable the delivery of new digital services and business models in many combinations. The Forum has already started on this journey and I look forward to seeing the fruits of our combined progress.

And, really finally...

I come to the end of my little book. I hope that it has stimulated at least a few people to go out and grab some turf in the digital world. I know for certain that it won't turn out quite like my predictions, because it's not possible to foresee all events and their often unintended consequences – who would have thought social networks would boost boring old TV viewing? The most obvious outcome of people spending hours online socializing would be that this reduced the time available for watching TV and indeed this was the case initially, particularly among people under 30. Now it turns out that people are 25 percent more willing to pay for TV programs if their mates from their favorite social networks are watching too, so they can share the experience.

At best we can only project what we know now and in reality, things we never even considered pop out along the way to change that. It's that man Rumsfeld again, with his unknown unknowns.

Ah well, at least he contributed one useful thing to mankind.